Political Purpose in Trade Unions

Political Purpose in Trade Unions

by Irving Richter

London · George Allen & Unwin Ltd
Ruskin House   Museum Street

ISBN 0 04 331056 7

Printed in Great Britain
in 10 point Times Roman type
by Unwin Brothers Limited
Old Woking Surrey England

To my wife Jeanne

Preface

As this study in recent history is being written, the Heath Conservative Government is implementing its Industrial Relations Act of 1971 which has changed the legal basis of collective bargaining in Britain. Drawing on the Taft-Hartley Act of 1947 and other American legislation, the Government and the courts of Britain are attempting to turn around the 'voluntarist' system that has prevailed for many years and to force the national unions to accept legal responsibility for their members' industrial actions.

In resisting the Act and its present implementation the national unions are demonstrating a far greater level of genuine political action than that described in the text for the focal period 1947–66. Indeed, as early as 1967, the leaders of the Trades Union Congress, sensing that the Labour Government's incomes policies were threatening their traditional system of bargaining, were already beginning to shift away from what I termed the political passivity and spurious political activity that had characterized their behaviour since 1947. And by 1969 the TUC had moved its heavy guns for very effective action against Labour's own Industrial Relations Bill.

These recent events in Britain only reinforce the empirical evidence collected in 1964–66, and the general conclusions drawn by me from that evidence and from the American analysis concerning the basic purposes of trade union political action. Yet the behavioural pattern of the British unions was so significantly changed after 1966 that I felt it would be useful to write an epilogue, based largely on a two-month study trip to England during the summer of 1971, and this appears as the final chapter.

I could not have completed this study without the help of many people in Britain and the United States in gathering material and in the interpretation and writing. To start my investigation I was given a valuable week-long apprenticeship by the Yorkshire Miners' Association (the regional organization of the National Union of Mineworkers) and their sponsored Member of Parliament, Mr Roy Mason (Barnsley).

I chose as a model for this study the Amalgamated Engineering Union (changed in 1971 to the Amalgamated Union of Engineering Workers). I wish to acknowledge the heavy burden of work this created for that Union over a period of several years—including numerous letters and reports mailed since I returned to the States. I am grateful to all the officers and staff at London headquarters and various District offices, and to all the seventeen Engineer-MPs for their generous aid and warm hospitality.

In addition to the Miners and the Engineers there were many other unions, including the Trades Union Congress staff; the Labour Party staff; the Members of the Trade Union Group of the Parliamentary Labour Party; the staff of the Library of the House of Commons, and other libraries—all were unfailingly courteous and helpful.

For making available facilities and staff, and for their own direct guidance on numerous problems, I wish especially to thank Mr Jim Conway and Mr Hugh Scanlon, General Secretary and President respectively of the AEU; Sir Harry Nicholas, now Secretary of the Labour Party and formerly Acting General Secretary of the Transport and General Workers' Union (T & GWU); Mr Victor Feather, General Secretary of the Trades Union Congress; and Mr Clive Jenkins, General Secretary of the Association of Scientific and Managerial Staffs (formerly ASSET).

I had had long experience with American unions before understanding the American phase of this study. Not unexpectedly, however, the research for new material was complicated, mainly by the legal uncertainty that surrounds trade union political contributions, and by the internal dissension within the AFL-CIO during the period. Although I am sure they would prefer to remain nameless I received valuable aid from many individuals in the Detroit and Washington offices of the United Auto Workers, formerly AFL-CIO-affiliated and now independent; from the staff of the Building and Construction Trades Department, and the Committee on Political Education (COPE), AFL-CIO; from numerous friends and colleagues in other unions and in government.

Apart from those who aided in the gathering of material, a number of academic colleagues with expertise in several social science disciplines were generous in aiding in the interpretation and writing. Professors John T. Dunlop (Harvard) and Philip Taft (University of Chicago), the eminent labour economists and practitioners, while disagreeing with some of my conclusions, were enormously helpful in a number of extended conference and in correspondence.

Professors Philip Abrams (University of Durham), Raymond Loveridge and J. David Edelstein (University of Syracuse) each made useful suggestions based on their expertise in industrial sociology.

Drs William and Miriam Haskett (Federal City College) made numerous suggestions on writing style and were helpful in correcting some historical references. Dr R. L. Robertson (Mount Holyoke College) read an early draft and our many talks were useful for my economic formulations.

Mr John J. Mendelson, MP, and Mr Leslie Huckfield, MP, each a university lecturer in political science and economics helped me grasp British politics, and especially Labour Party trade union relations.

I owe to Dr H. G. Vatter (Portland State University), a writer in economic history and theory, and a life-long friend, a special debt for his steady encouragement, for his comments on the changing role of the State in the management of the mixed economies, and for many editorial suggestions.

The aid from Dr H. A. Turner, Burton Professor of Industrial Relations (Cambridge) is of a different order. I benefited more than I can say from his unique knowledge of British industry and unions and comparative industrial relations.

Of course any errors of fact and judgement in this book I claim as my own.

Washington, D.C.
July 1972

Contents

11

Tables

Charts

Chapter I

Introduction

When the conditions of social life are such that the individual may
be excluded through no unfitness of his own for co-operation . . . we
are brought face to face with the conditions of primitive ages. And
if you force him back upon the elemental instincts, one of two
things will happen. Either, if the individual is weak through physical
deterioration or incapacity to combine with his fellow outcasts, he will
be crushed and killed by society and putrify about its holy places;
or, if he has indomitable life and vigour, he will revert to the
argument of elemental forces: he will turn and explode society. . . .
[Are we prepared to] supersede institutions now immoral, because
useless and mischievous, by institutions which shall re-establish the
elementary conditions of social existence and the possibility of the
corresponding morality . . . namely, the opportunity for each
individual to earn his living?[1]

Origins

In this exhortation the Fabian writer, Sidney Olivier, was writing,
not, as one might easily suppose, about blacks in the United States
in the 1970s, but about the mass of unorganized workers in Great
Britain—in 1888. By that time, the New Model craft unions of
Britain had been protecting the skilled craftsmen in national 'amalgamated societies' for over thirty years. Similar institutions had
grown up in North America. The mass of workers in the Anglo-
American world, however, were excluded from the protective walls
built by these closed unions. The many unskilled and the cyclically
unemployed had no assistance, moreover, from the State for the
opportunity 'to earn his living'.

Living in a context of general worker insecurity, the nineteenth-
century artisans sought through the achievement of a monopoly on
the supply side of the factor market the creation of a sellers' market
for their skilled labour. For this purpose the leaders could see no
advantage in organizing the workmen with lesser skills. Thus closed
or 'exclusive' craft unionism stabilized itself in Great Britain and
the United States (with mining the most notable exception in each
case) as a means of benefiting a segment of the skilled—'the labour
aristocracy'—without pretext of being a 'do-good' institution.

[1] 'Moral' in *Fabian Essays* (London, Allen and Unwin, 1962), p. 157.

With the eventual organization of basic industries, and the possible interruption of production in them by strikes and lock-outs, the State, in the context of the contemporary 'mixed' capitalistic economy, has become increasingly concerned about the 'public interest' in industrial relations. Thus, quite apart from the unions' own complex and often conflicting set of preferences, their present economic importance has demanded that they be placed, along with employer groups, at the centre of political life. It is a truism that the unions have become great national institutions in Britain and in the United States, comparable in size and status to the other two actors in the industrial relations system—the State and corporate management. In every country, as Dunlop has noted, the three actors perform their roles within certain power contexts.[1] In the modern Anglo-American environment many an ordinary worker elected to national trade union office is apt to learn, usually on the eve of, or during, a national strike, that the institution he heads is affected with a public interest in industrial peace and is therefore a part of the 'Establishment'. His own leadership has become important not merely to his fellow-workers but to the State and the nation as well.

Unions are, willy-nilly, involved in politics; when they take their own institutional approaches to the political process they are engaged in 'political action', not necessarily or merely in the narrow sense of party politics, but in the deep sense of participation in the larger body politic.

Central Thesis

Trade union political action in the period under review, 1945–67, took many forms, and operated at many levels: from lending a sound truck to a local Labour Party or paying for tickets to a borough councillor's testimonial, to the elaborate ballet of political manoeuvres that first delayed James R. Hoffa's incarceration in, and then brought his release from, prison. But neither of these incidents can yield any general principles. For such purposes it will be more profitable to examine in some detail the political interests and activities of a carefully selected and representative number of British unions and related political institutions. In addition, a brief comparative reference is made in the present study to two polar types of American unions and to their relative impact on that labour movement.

In the evolving mixed economies of these two countries, the strategic political decisions affecting trade unions are made at the

[1] John T. Dunlop, *Industrial Relations Systems* (New York, Holt, 1958), *passim.*

16

national level. Welfare legislation, trade union regulation, incomes policies, tax policy, etc.—all are parliamentary concerns in Britain. In the United States, since the early 1930s, they have been mainly the concerns of the federal government, Accordingly, the unions in both countries generally concentrate whatever energies and resources they choose to devote to political action on national elections, on national legislative bodies, and on the national executive agencies. Although local politics remains important for the unions, especially in the federal system of the States,[1] the present analysis emphasizes trade union political behaviour and purpose as seen from a national perspective, first and mainly, in Britain and second, in the United States.

The central thesis of this study of the British model may be stated in two related propositions. First, contrary to the widespread impression that the unions were engaged during the period in furthering far-reaching socio-political objectives, it is contended here that the union leadership altogether abjured political action in a substantive, or programmatic, sense. The leaders felt they could continue to conduct traditional pure and simple unionism success-fully without significant involvement in national economic and political policy formation. Second, although they maintained the historic alliance with the Labour Party and indeed, beginning in the early 1950s, greatly expanded that commitment at the Parliamentary Party level, they did *not* rely on it either for their conventional bargaining function or for broad social policy purposes.

Their main motivations in the political arena during the period were: (*a*) to retain the alliance as a sort of insurance policy to protect the bargaining system; (*b*) to enhance their own bureaucratic image and security as leaders *vis-à-vis* the memberships; (*c*) to help assure the continuance of a Labour Party leadership that would not intrude into the traditional bargaining system.

A brief reference to the relevant aspects of the historical setting in the period will illuminate the meaning of the above thesis and the functional relationships between its components:

(1) The British Trades Union Congress-affiliated unions had for many years enjoyed full legality and general acceptance by em-ployers. A high proportion of the eligible labour force was organized —both in the economy as a whole and on a sectoral level. There was no significant challenge to their legal status during the period. Moreover, under conditions of peace, there was near full employ-ment. The combination of these two features—full legality and high

---

[1] Cf. Philip Taft in *Labor Politics American Style: The California State Federation of Labor* (Cambridge, Harvard University Press, 1968).

employment—provided the essential basis for reliance on the historical weapon of market bargaining. In the short run that emphasis could pay off despite the fact that, in the long run, the emerging mixed economy was making such an emphasis obsolete. The new era of mixed capitalism under both Labour and Tory Governments was, ever more insistently, calling for real participation by labour in all facets of national economic planning—not merely to implement policies initiated by corporate spokesmen and the Government, but to protect the shares and other vital interests of the labour force.

(2) Unlike the trend to centralization of structure in the major industrial unions of the United States,[1] the British movement during the period showed a general decentralization of economic functions—reinforced by full employment and the widespread acceptance of payments-by-results wage payments.[2] Many national leaders, however, resisted this *de facto* shift of economic power to the work-place, since at that lower level the workers were largely ignoring their national affiliations and following instead unofficial movements led by shop stewards. And, at the top, the same national leaders resisted giving added authority to the TUC for co-ordinated bargaining or for formulation of economic policies. Writing in 1962 on trade union 'morphology' in the post-war years, Turner discerned this trend. 'In each case—at top and at bottom—the key to the situation', he wrote, 'is the reluctance of powerful union leaderships either to accept greater central guidance or to expose themselves to greater rank-and-file pressure.'[3]

(3) Despite its nationalization measures, the Labour Government of 1945–51 made no serious attempt to introduce socialism. It embraced, as did the Swedish Social Democrats, '. . . an interventionist economic policy and a large sector for government services alongside of complete private domination in the field of industry [except steel] and agriculture'.[4] The British trade unions rejected manpower planning proposed by Labour, while they continued to pay lip

---

[1] Cf. George W. Brooks, 'The Case for Decentralized Bargaining', in Richard A. Lester (ed.), *Labor: Readings on Major Issues* (New York, Random House, 1965), pp. 426 ff.

[2] Cf. E. H. Phelps Brown, 'Guidelines for Growth and for Incomes in the United Kingdom: Some Possible Lessons for the United States', in George P. Schultz and Robert Z. Aliber (eds), *Guidelines, Informal Controls, and the Marketplace* (Chicago, University of Chicago Press, 1966), p. 161.

[3] H. A. Turner, *Trade Union Growth, Structure and Policy* (London, Allen and Unwin, 1962), p. 352.

[4] Assar Lindbeck, 'Theories on Problems in Swedish Economic Policy in the Post-War Period', *American Economic Review*, Supplement, Vol. 57 (June 1968), No. 3, Part 2, p. 79.

service to the notion of planning in general during these six years. (4) During the 1960s the trade union movement paid lip service to the incomes policies initiated by Tory and Labour Governments, but its structure and philosophy remained an obstacle to implementation of such policies. On the other hand, the unions did not see any need for advancing their own policy initiatives. The employment-legality parameters provided a generally favourable atmosphere for collective bargaining without new political initiatives.

(5) The predominant trade union leaders took organizational steps within the Labour Party to limit rather than to advance political action in a conventional sense. They did so because they wanted to be certain that the Labour Party would not choose a leader who would initiate policies that might endanger existing national bargaining patterns either by such radical innovations as 'seizing the commanding heights' or by Labour encouragement of work-place bargaining.[1] The relevance of these features of the historical setting will be made clear as the analysis proceeds.

Theory

Existing general theories on the subject of trade union political action provide little help either for analysis of the present situation or for predictions. Apart from Marx and Lenin, the two leading theorists who have projected models of trade union political action had initially become eminent in the analysis of trade union origins: the Webbs in Britain, and the Commons group in the United States. Although Lenin dealt with trade union political action,[2] his abstract and revolutionary orientation had the blue-collar proletariat as its exclusive empirical reference, and the context was early twentieth century *laissez-faire* capitalism.

Commons has written of his group's search in 'libraries, cellars and attics for original sources' on origins.[3] Having found such

---

[1] A key figure in their strategy, then Mr (now Lord) George Brown in fact stated: 'But Aneurin's [Bevan] feeling that Gaitskell had been rather foisted on the Party had substance in another sense. Hugh . . . owed his support to the backing he was given by the old hard core of the great unions . . . . Gaitskell was not elected to the National Executive of the Labour Party by the vote of the constituency parties, of the rank and file members. He was projected forward by Arthur Deakin and his colleagues, using the block vote of the unions to put him on the National Executive as Treasurer' (*In My Way* (London, Gollancz, 1971), p. 80).

[2] V. I. Lenin, *What Is To Be Done?* (1902), reprinted in *A Handbook of Marxism* (New York, International, 1935), Chap. 24.

[3] Commons and Associates, *History of Labour in the United States* (New York, Macmillan, 1921), Vol. 1, Preface, ix.

sources, competent scholars could arrive at reasonable conclusions. Today there is general acceptance of the Webbs' and the Commons group's main conclusions on the origins of trade unions. The analysis of political action, especially in the late twentieth century context, however, involves a far more complex set of phenomena. Unlike the research for trade union origins, where the *process* involved is a completed one, in dealing with the unions' political activity one confronts a continuing and inter-acting set of processes: the decisions by corporate policy-makers; the decisions by economic policy-makers; the legislative and executive acts of national governments directly affecting the unions and management, and the relations of labour's political action to existing party politics. Interacting with all these factors is the process of constant change in the structures of the unions themselves, which affects both their economic and political functions.

The Webbs' theory on trade unions in politics, first published in 1897, grew out of years of close study of the older unions, but was clearly influenced by the emergence of the new unions in 1889. Apparently because they saw a corps of socialists leading the new unions, the Webbs envisaged, and clearly hoped, that the socialistic 'Doctrine of Legal Enactment' would take the place of the 'Supply and Demand Doctrine', or market bargaining. The Webbs were persuaded not only that the poorer sections of the labour force would fare better under 'Legal Enactment' of wages, but that strikes, which they viewed as a form of warfare, would become unnecessary. The Webbs worked with and respected the older leaders, whose 'strong, self-reliant and pugnacious spirit' had brought them to the top in associations that were formed by 'people [who] discover that they can do better for themselves by uniting to fight someone else than by opposing each other'. But these very qualities, and the narrow objectives of the early unions, the Webbs observed, led most union leaders to become 'Conservative', in a social sense, even if they were willing, when necessary, to lead strikes. Having achieved a degree of control over their own trades, these 'Conservatives' maintained 'a strong presumption in favour of the *status quo*', 'distrusted innovation', and had a liking for 'distinct social classes'. They favoured a sort of feudal stability, 'based on each man being secured and contented in his station of life'.[1]

In reaction to the older craft union 'Conservatives', the Webbs were persuaded that not only the new unionists but 'collectivist' statesmen as well were already then beginning to recognize the 'need for a conscious and deliberate organization of society . . . based on

[1] Sidney and Beatrice Webb, *Industrial Democracy* (London, Longman, 1902 edn), pp. 596–9 and *passim*.

the scientifically ascertained needs of each section of citizens', instead of reliance on traditional collective bargaining.[1] However, the method of 'Supply and Demand' bargaining as developed in the era of *laissez-faire* remains to this day the most important single means of wage determination as well as the focus of trade union activity.

Marx, like the Webbs, was frustrated in his efforts to achieve social transformation through collaboration with the British craft unions.[2] Lenin, taking up the vision of a proletariat destined to rule under a socialist order, came to the conclusion at the turn of the century that the will to power had to be insinuated into the labour movement by a revolutionary party. Lenin polemicized against those Social Democrats who contented themselves with 'economism' or 'merely trade union work'. 'All that it achieved', Lenin had written, 'was that the vendors of labour power learned to sell their "commodity" on better terms, and to fight the purchasers of labour power over a purely commercial deal.'[3]

In his famous *Theory* (1928), Selig Perlman, a protégé of Commons and still the most famous theoretician on modern trade union political action, sought to clarify the 'misunderstanding' of the Webbs and other 'efficiency' intellectuals, and to rebut the Marxist-Leninists. He was able to note that thirty years after *Industrial Democracy* the British craft unions, having temporarily relinquished during World War I their market controls, quickly had fully reinstated those same controls at the close of the war. For Perlman this demonstrated that there was no significant departure from what he regarded as the essence of unionism in capitalist society—job control or 'pure and simple' unionism. Indeed Perlman, in this instance, saw a general retreat by 'mature' unions from reliance on political action, which was largely a 'mirage' foisted on manual workers by 'intellectuals'.

Perlman's insights into the economic functioning of unions—in Britain and the United States—have enduring value for the analysis of trade unionism under *laissez-faire* conditions. The British unions, throughout their long history, Perlman observed, have rarely moved seriously and in a sustained way towards reliance on political tech-

[1] Sidney and Beatrice Webb, *Industrial Democracy*, Preface, pp. liii, lv.
[2] See Chap II.
[3] Lenin, op. cit., Chap. 24. As noted in Chap. II, below, Lenin also argued with British and American union militants in the early 1920s that they should become active within the Labour Party as well as form their own Communist Parties to utilize parliamentary channels as part of the struggle to achieve the revolution. For Lenin, political action, like trade unionism in general, was only a school in which the proletariat prepared itself for revolutionary political action in a radical party organization.

niques. Ever since the 1860s, when they first won legality, 'the whole clockwork in the mechanism' of political action 'seemed to run down'. Successive threats to that legal status invariably aroused real political action, but attempts of socialists to expand the scope of such action to embrace revolutionary goals have met with evasion and frustration on the part of the dominant leadership. He concluded:

> The Unions as a whole will finance the Labour Party with its socialistic programme and socialistic leadership, and more than half the membership will vote for its socialistic candidate. . . . But the heart of British unionism is still in these jealously revered organizations that stand guard over the collective economic opportunity of each group—the jobs and the working conditions that go with the jobs.

This central concern for job protection has on occasion led the unions to show 'periods of enthusiasm for politics, succeeding, and being succeeded, in turn, by periods of aggressive economic action even bordering upon revolutionary syndicalism'.[1]

One question to be examined in this study is the extent to which Perlman's model is still appropriate in the British case. The empirical evidence will be interpreted to suggest that as late as the 1950s and 1960s pure and simple unionism remained the prevailing philosophy, although it is the present writer's conviction that this was the dying gasp of a theory that is now obsolete in a managed, mixed capitalist economy.

As is well known, running along with the business unionism current in British unions there has always been a strong socialist stream—beginning in the early nineteenth century, gathering force in the late 1880s, and reaching a climax in the Labour Party's adoption of its socialist platform in 1918. On the other hand, as one looks back at the British unions' true political action in the present century, it is clear that the movement resisted such political action on any sustained basis and resorted to it only when necessary either to ward off, or remedy, legal interference with the established bargaining system, or in reaction to a severe crisis situation.

Even at the founding of the Labour Party in 1900–1906 the unions showed no interest in political activity extending beyond the restoration of trade union legality. In the crises of the two great wars, the unions, like business, temporarily accepted planning. After the end of World War I, the trade union leadership resisted implementation of the 1918 socialist platform. As Perlman observed, it succeeded in reverting to the pre-war market bargaining system. Similarly, after

[1] Selig Perlman, *A Theory of the Labor Movement* (New York, Macmillan, 1928), Chap. 4.

World War II, it will be seen that the unions showed an anti-planning bias as soon as it became evident that such planning was to be dependent on continuing war-time manpower controls and rearrangement of traditional wage differentials. All of the above leadership responses may be viewed as consistent with Perlman's general model of normal non-crisis functioning of Anglo-American trade unions.

How does one reconcile the TUC leaders' support for the nationalization measures taken by Labour in 1945–47 with this tendency? The reconciliation resides in the fact that these actions, conventionally and perhaps naively viewed as 'socialistic', were seen *by both Labour and Tory* politicians 'not as marking the beginning of [the economic system's] wholesale transformation [but] designed to achieve the sole purpose of improving the efficiency of a capitalist economy. . . '.[1] How does this experience jibe with Perlman's model? It doesn't, in the sense that he equated nationalization with socialism, but nationalization in Britain did not interfere with traditional collective bargaining in the predominantly capitalist economy. There is no conflict, then, with his model. Indeed, when further nationalization proposals were made from the Left, the trade unions fiercely resisted precisely because they viewed such initiatives as directly and indirectly threatening the bargaining system, and entered massively into the political arena for the purpose of stopping this left-wing strategy.

The trend of history suggsets that the mixed economy will continue to evolve, even in peacetime, towards some form of national planning with a modicum of nationalization in the advanced capitalist countries. This will inevitably include intervention by the State into the industrial relations system—as part of the planning. As the politicizing of industrial relations proceeds—under government initiative—Perlman's model will become completely anachronistic. In the latter part of the 1960s, the British unions took some first real steps in the direction of such a transition, but in the period under review they remained essentially at the *laissez-faire* stage.

The Model

In what follows we will be using the method of comparative analysis, with the inquiry focused on a variety of national unions in Britain that are affiliated with both the TUC and the Labour Party. While it is by no means typical of present day affiliates, the empirical model we have chosen for extended analysis, the Amalgamated Engineering Union (AEU—as it was called at the time of this study) permits one

[1] Ralph Miliband, *Parliamentary Socialism* (London, Merlin edn, 1964), p. 288.

Chart I   Structure of the Amalgamate

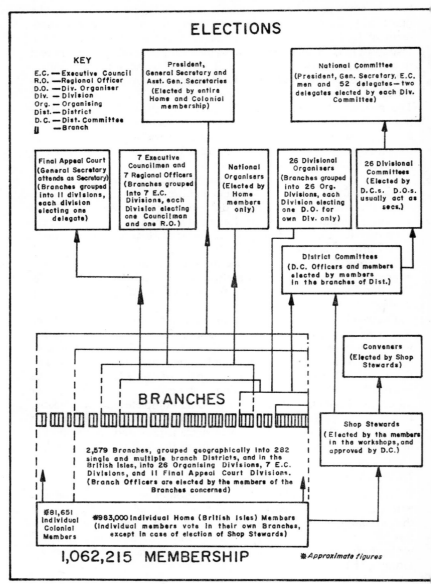

ELECTIONS

KEY

E.C. — Executive Council
R.O. — Regional Officer
D.O. — Div. Organiser
Div. — Division
Org. — Organising
Dist. — District
D.C. — Dist. Committee
Ⓤ — Branch

President,
General Secretary and
Asst. Gen. Secretaries
(Elected by entire
Home and Colonial
membership)

National Committee
(President, Gen. Secretary, E.C.
men and 52 delegates—two
delegates elected by each Div.
Committee)

Final Appeal Court
(General Secretary
attends as Secretary)
(Branches grouped
into II divisions,
each division
electing one
delegate)

**7 Executive
Councilmen and
7 Regional Officers**
(Branches grouped
into 7 E.C.
Divisions, each
Division electing
one Councilman
and one R.O.)

**National
Organisers**
(Elected by
Home
members
only)

**26 Divisional
Organisers**
(Branches grouped
into 26 Org.
Divisions, each
Division electing
one D.O. for
own Div. only)

**26 Divisional
Committees**
(Elected by
D.C.s. D.O.s.
usually act as
secs.)

District Committees
(D.C. Officers and members
elected by members
in the branches of Dist.)

Conveners
(Elected by Shop
Stewards)

BRANCHES

2,579 Branches, grouped geographically into 282
single and multiple branch Districts, and in the
British Isles, into 26 Organising Divisions, 7 E.C.
Divisions, and II Final Appeal Court Divisions.
(Branch Officers are elected by the members of the
Branches concerned)

Shop Stewards
(Elected by the members
in the workshops, and
approved by D.C.)

✱81,651
Individual
Colonial
Members

✱983,000 Individual Home (British Isles) Members
(Individual members vote in their own Branches,
except in case of election of Shop Stewards)

1,062,215 MEMBERSHIP

✱ Approximate figures

Source: **AEU, '1811–1961, One Hundred and Fifty Years' Progress—Ov**

Engineering Union (AEU)

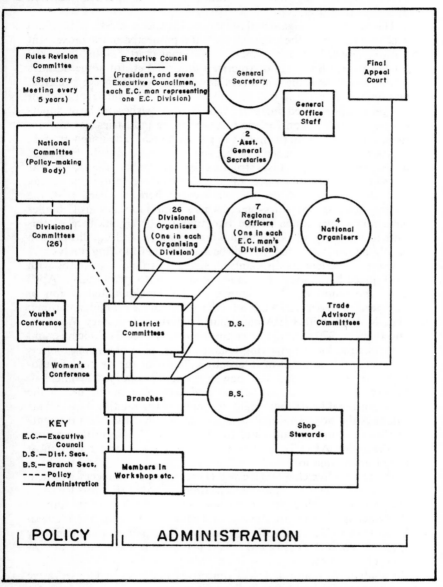

Rules Revision
Committees
(Statutory
Meeting every
5 years)

National
Committee
(Policy-making
Body)

Divisional
Committees
(26)

Youths'
Conference

Women's
Conference

Executive Council

(President, and seven
Executive Councilmen,
each E.C. man representing
one E.C. Division)

General
Secretary

General
Office
Staff

2
Asst.
General
Secretaries

Final
Appeal
Court

26
Divisional
Organisers
(One in each
Organising
Division)

7
Regional
Officers
(One in each
E.C. man's
Division)

4
National
Organisers

District
Committees

D.S.

Trade
Advisory
Committees

Branches

B.S.

Shop
Stewards

Members in
Workshops etc.

KEY

E.C.—Executive
Council
D.S.—Dist. Secs.
B.S.—Branch Secs.
- - - —Policy
———Administration

POLICY | ADMINISTRATION

a Million Members', London, 1961, printed booklet, pages unnumbered.

to view present day union attitudes from the perspective of a rich historical tradition.

The original Amalgamated Society of Engineers (ASE, 1851–1920) was long known as the 'New Model', and pioneered in the movement for strongly led, strongly financed national craft unions—a model for both early British and American unions. Yet, for some decades in the recent past the Engineers have been acquiring the principal features of a general union, and it might be said, from recent mergers and planned mergers, that it now wishes to be a super-industrial trade union for the metal-working industries. Its history, then, encompasses all the major stages of British trade union growth.

After many years of struggle between the centre and the branches, it reached a compromise structure in 1920 when the AEU was formed, with the balance of decision-making authority tilting towards the centre. Since then, however, there has been a strong shifting towards the work-place, where joint shop stewards' bodies have taken over much of the bargaining. The significance of this shift in the locus of decision-making on wages and conditions can hardly be overestimated, as will be seen in the following analysis.

Even as the leadership painfully struggles to come to terms with work-place bargaining, the union continues to grow. Since April 1970, the union has been known as the Amalgamated Union of Engineering Workers (AUEW)—the result of new amalgamations: first, in 1967, with the Amalgamated Union of Foundry Workers, and then in 1970 with the Draughtsmen's & Allied Technicians, and the Construction Engineering Union. At the time of writing there is a considerable amount of internal conflict over the degree of auto-nomy to be accorded the new sections—Foundry, Technical & Supervisory, and Constructional—and even over the nature of the organizational chart that might best convey the relationships. Chart I depicts the organizational structure as of 1966; the main elements of this structure remain valid for at least the Engineering Section, as the older AEU is now termed within the broader and most recent amalgamation.

In the next five chapters we will (1) review the Engineers' political history, particularly in more recent times, relating that history to its changing bargaining philosophy and structure; (2) trace its Labour Party activities prior to, during, and immediately after the General Election of 1945; (3) describe and analyse its expanded parliamentary sponsorship in the 1950s and 1960s; (4) measure the trend in alloca-tion of manpower and financial resources for political action; (5) analyse its major political objectives under both Conservative and Labour Governments in the post-war years.

Political purpose is of course not ascertainable through any single sector of activity. While our discussion of the model will provide a view of the interactions of the AEU with the Labour Party and the Trades Union Congress over an extended time period, Chapters VII and VIII are designed to provide new light on the political purpose of the broader labour movement, through a close examination of the hitherto neglected Trade Union Group of the Parliamentary Labour Party. That group contains all MPs sponsored by affiliates of the Labour Party in the TUC.

In the final two British chapters, in order to enrich the empirical foundation of the central thesis, we consider two additional examples of national trade union political action: the Transport & General Workers' Union (T & GWU), which is Britain's largest, as well as its most successful example of general unionism; and the Association of Supervisory Staffs, Executives and Technicians (ASSET—since known as the Association of Scientific, Technical and Managerial Staffs, or ASTMS), at the time of writing the fastest-growing of all white collar trade unions, and apparently seeking to become a general-type union for non-manual workers.

The American union analysis is presented here in a single chapter largely for purposes of contrast. There were of course important differences in national setting, in structure, and in political affiliations. Attitudes towards political activity by different types of U.S. unions varied during the period. There was not a single unified central labour federation comparable in scope and authority to the TUC until 1955, when the older predominantly skilled workers' American Federation of Labor (AFL) merged with the newer Congress of Industrial Organizations (CIO). The new, merged AFL-CIO and its chief spokesman, President George Meany, have since assumed increasing authority and responsibility as 'the voice of organized labor' on a widening range of issues.

The American movement has always fought for legislation directly affecting the job conditions of its members. It has also always fought for legality. During the period under study, the unions in the AFL-CIO had few points of agreement on political goals. But in contrast to Britain they did perceive their respective systems of collective bargaining as seriously threatened by first, legal restriction, and second, high unemployment. Largely because of the more insecure power context in which they operated, the unions supported an increasingly active role for the centre, as well as expanding electoral and legislative activities for their own sectional interests.

To trace the political purpose of the AFL-CIO, the empirical reference will focus on two polar types: the Building and Construction Trades Department, the leading group of national craft unions whose local unions were the models for Perlman's theory; and the former CIO affiliate, the United Auto Workers, known throughout the world as a model of modern industrial unionism.

While there is much continuity as well as discontinuity they part from the Perlman model in three important respects: (1) by accepting (and in the case of the open, industrial unions, campaigning for) the socialization of friendly benefits; (2) by accepting or welcoming a federal role in industrial relations; and (3) by exhibiting a general tendency—though one not shared by the crafts—towards partisan politics. But the acid test for Perlman's model is whether the political activity they did engage in would have been done under *laissez-faire*.

Chapter II

The Amalgamated Engineering Union: Its Historic Relationship to Trade Union Political Action

Because of its long history as the 'New Model' union, its present bargaining for all grades of workers in the engineering sector, and its continuing representation of skilled workmen in virtually every sector of the economy, the Amalgamated Engineering Union (AEU) may well be, as it often claims, 'the most important' in Britain. In any event it is today in membership close behind the number one union, the Transport and General Workers (T & GWU), having well over one million members and growing steadily. It forms the keystone in the Confederation of Shipbuilding and Engineering Unions (CSEU), whose procedural agreement with the Engineering Employers' Federation (EEF) covers some 3·5 million workers in about thirty unions—the largest collective bargaining agreement in the British industrial relations system.[1] The AEU's internal structure was shown in Chart I; its organizational ties to the industrial and political wings of the Labour movement are shown in Chart II.

There is an understandable tendency among all Labour Party affiliates to point with pride to early manifestations of socialism in their own organizations. The present day Engineering Union is no exception. Indeed, because of its long pre-eminence as a national union, predating the Labour Party's formation, it managed to have and boasts of its direct association with Karl Marx himself, as well as with the major early socialist movements and leaders. But the Engineers arrived rather late at an acceptance of political action as a continuing and permanent union activity. The purpose of the present historical chapter is to review some of the factors in the Engineers' historic resistance to political action, and to set the

---

[1] Workers in the 'engineering industry' are engaged in the manufacture, installation, maintenance and repair of goods mainly metal, and the fabrication of articles of plastic manufacture. It includes work as diverse as machine tool manufacturing, construction engineering, founding and forging, aircraft and vehicle manufacture, and the making of instruments and electronic equipment. Ministry of Labour, *Handbook of Industrial Relations* (London, HMSO, 1961), p. 27. The CSEU-EEF agreement is now (1972) suspended.

background for their relatively recent serious involvement with the Labour Party.

Chart II. Affiliations of the Amalgamated Engineering Union (AEU) to the Labour Party, the Trades Union Congress (TUC), and the Confederation of Shipbuilding and Engineering Unions (CSEU)

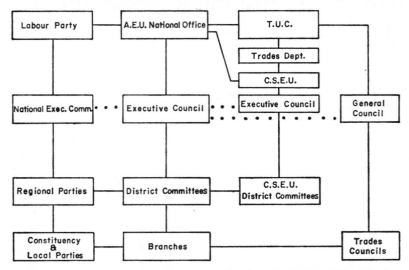

Dotted lines indicate that representation (on the NEC of the Party, the Executive Council of the CSEU, and the General Council of the TUC) is subject to annual elections.
Data Source: **AEU Rules.**

Early History: 1799–1867

The millwrights, steam engine-makers, blacksmiths and other skilled craftsmen whose societies eventually formed the national Amalgamated Society of Engineers, first banded together in local clubs for 'friendly benefits', i.e. for private mutual help in meeting the problems of sickness, accident and death. Through these clubs they provided grants for members 'on travel' in search of jobs, and soon began a system of mutual aid for out-of-work benefits. Trade union functions, in other words, began in benefit programmes.

However, some of the elements of a broader trade unionism were present among these craftsmen as early as 1799, when their masters complained that the new Combination Acts, designed to restrain combinations of workmen, 'had no effect at all among engineers

30

and millwrights'.[1] The independence of these craftsmen followed from the fact that their skills were scarce and thus in high demand and that, through the mechanism of their societies, they could control entry into the trade. These advantages helped to shape what became a typically monopolistic attitude of the societies towards themselves, towards the labour market, towards other crafts and towards the mass of the unskilled (and, as yet, unorganized).

The artisans' faith in their own exclusive market power precluded a *general* interest in political action. Indeed the predecessor of the Engineers' Society, the 'Old Mechanics' Society, had censured its General Secretary for becoming involved in an 1842 Chartist demonstration. There followed a rule that members could not claim benefit for being out of work due to 'any Political or Popular Movement'.

The national Chartist demonstrations may have helped persuade the authors of the *Communist Manifesto* that 'the ever expanding union of the workers . . . helped on by the improved means of communication [would] centralize the numerous local struggles . . . into one national struggle between classes'.[2] However, the national Amalgamated Society of Engineers (ASE), created in 1851 out of the 'Old Mechanics', rejected independent political action precisely because its leaders believed this would run counter to their main strategy of achieving a monopoly on the supply side, or creating a seller's market for their labour.

Built up from below—from the workplace and localities rather than from a national centre—the national ASE was noted for its internal democracy for many years. Yet, the very same narrow economic goals which brought the skilled men together kept them from extending their organization to workers in general, millions of whom were living at or below subsistence levels.

Turner, in his analysis of British craft 'closed unionism' attributes the indifference of these societies to other workers to three main factors: (1) they wanted no new claims on their large funds; (2) they feared a narrowing of the wage differentials between themselves and the ordinary labourers; and (3) they feared also that their monopoly of the better paid work might be threatened. Moreover, as industrial techniques developed, the craft societies manifested a '. . . certain obviously anti-social quality. The exclusive unions

[1] James Bavington Jefferys, *The Story of the Engineers* (London, Lawrence and Wishart for the AEU, 1945), pp. 9–12. While arguing with some of its interpretations, I am indebted to this official history for much of the historical background in the present discussion.

[2] Karl Marx and Friedrich Engels, *The Communist Manifesto*, reprinted in Emile Burns (ed.), *Handbook of Marxism* (New York, International Publishers, 1935), pp. 33–6.

relied upon a monopoly of certain jobs: but jobs were changing, so they were compelled to attempt to extend their monopoly to match. Thus much of the new, better class work that technical innovation created was withheld from the lower paid workers.' To maintain their privileged position in the labour market the Engineers, he notes, barred systematic overtime, refused piecework methods of pay, kept 'illegal' men from working the new machines, and limited membership to legally apprenticed workmen.[1] In these respects the historical continuity with the early craft guilds is all too apparent.

The Fight for Legality

It is noteworthy by way of contrast that in the mining and textile industries, where there was much less severe competition between the artisans and the unskilled sectors of the labour force, there was already in the 1860s significant union participation in parliamentary politics. The Amalgamated Trades formed their own informal pressure group, however, even before the Trades Union Congress was organized in 1868, when they perceived that there was a threat to the legal status of trade unionism. It is commonly known that William Allan, General Secretary of the ASE, was one of five leaders of the Conference of Amalgamated Trades (later called the 'Junta' by the Webbs) who lobbied to win appointment of friendly members of the Royal Commission of Inquiry in 1867. The 'Junta' then planned their testimony to: (1) assure that trade unionism would have protection of the law for purposes of protecting their funds but that (2) the law would not mean either liability on their part for damages or (3) that the State would supervise their negotiations with the employers.[2]

The entry into politics by the Engineers was, however, limited and exceptional. Allan had joined the National Reform League in 1865. When in 1869 he became Treasurer of the Labour Representation League there were protests from the branches and the Executive Council reaffirmed the Rule that 'the Society would not allow either political or religious matters to be introduced or discussed at any of its meetings'. However, it is significant that the Society raised no objection to Allan's continuing his association with the League's parliamentary agitation to establish the legality of trade unions, which issued in the Trade Union Act of 1871 and 1875.

The formulation of the ASE's fundamental purpose before the Royal Commission in 1867 was a classic expression of 'free market'

[1] H. A. Turner, op. cit., Chaps 2–4.
[2] Henry Pelling, *A History of British Trade Unionism* (Harmondsworth, Penguin, 1967) Chap. 14; cf. E. J. Hobsbawn, *Industry and Empire* (Harmondsworth, Penguin, 1969), pp. 125–6.

bargaining—and it was not alien to the philosophy which the Engineers' brief to the Royal (Donovan) Commission on Trade Unions and Employers' Associations would proclaim a century later: 'Both the owners of industry and labour were following the principle of buying in the cheapest and selling in the dearest market. . . . It is in their interest to get the labour done by as low a rate as possible and it is ours to get as high a rate of wages as possible and you can never reconcile these two things.'[1]

The validity of this model for the ASE's own members and for other craftsmen was so pronounced a feature of trade unionism that the Webbs observed that as of 1901: 'Scarcely a trade exists which did not, between 1852 and 1875, either attempt to imitate the whole constitution of the Amalgamated Engineers or incorporate one or other of its characteristic features.'[2]

Karl Marx and the First International

Even in its fleeting direct association with Karl Marx and the International Workingmen's Association (the first International) in 1871, the ASE's purpose was consistent with its closed philosophy, and its Supply and Demand Doctrine: to prevent the employers from importing blacklegs during the historic (and at first unofficial) Newcastle Nine-Hour Day Strike in that year, and to persuade those already at work on the struck jobs to return.

The International had been founded in London in 1864 for the purpose of assisting the rise of both industrial and political working-class movements. Although it had won some British union co-operation, the ASE's rejection of solicitations to join seemed to express the general attitude of craft societies, namely, 'that the best thing the foreigners could do would be to organize themselves into trade societies similar to ours and endeavour to get their wages up to the same rate as ours and then we could begin to discuss questions with them'.[3]

In their analysis of the International's associations with British labour, Collins and Abramsky use the Newcastle strike to illustrate craft union resistance to Marx's overtures. The minutes of the General Council of the International disclose that Marx, on being told by an ASE delegation of the Engineers' problem, commented that the unions were in the habit of coming to the General Council only when they were in trouble and otherwise ignoring its existence. According to the minutes, the ASE representatives replied that their

---

[1] Testimony to 1867 Royal Commission, quoted in Jefferys, op. cit., p. 77.
[2] Sidney and Beatrice Webb, *History of Trade Unionism* (London, Longman, 1902 edn), pp. 205–36.
[3] Jefferys, op. cit., pp. 88–9.

C

Society 'has the subject of affiliation under discussion' and could see the advantages of belonging to 'such a powerful and homogeneous association'. It is unnecessary to stress the irony of this last comment, since the ASE had already spurned the entire concept. At any rate, the ASE never fulfilled its implied promise.[1] Its outlook was still that of a closed craft union.

New Unionism'

The Engineering unionists as well as other workers were profoundly affected by the depression of the 1880s, the revival of socialism, and the subsequent growth of 'new unionism'. Tom Mann, an early member of the Marxist Social Democratic Federation (SDF), began his phenomenal career in the British labour movement by attacking the ASE (his own union) as well as other amalgamated societies for continuing to rely on their own out-of-work benefits and a 'closed' policy. 'None of the important societies', he wrote in a pamphlet in 1886, 'have any policy other than of endeavouring to keep wages from falling.'[2]

Mann, John Burns, and George Barnes, all ASE members who marched in the great SDF demonstrations on behalf of the unemployed in London in 1885–87, were leaders in organizing the 'New Unions' of unskilled workers and the Independent Labour Party (ILP) in 1892–3. These men are now in the Engineers' pantheon. Mann's bust adorns the Executive Council chamber at Peckham Road headquarters, and—as will be seen—his writings and ideas remain a pervasive influence, but in his actions on behalf of broadening the union movement and reforming the ASE, he acted initially as a socialist. The full-time leadership of the ASE as well as the membership resisted these trends because they saw the danger that outside political associations would mean a fundamental change in their 'closed' philosophy.

With the election of George Barnes, an associate of Mann's and a socialist, as General Secretary in 1896, the ASE entered into a strikingly new phase of political activity. Barnes had quit the SDF as too doctrinaire but had campaigned as an ILP member—and was identified with a militant industrial posture.[3] Apart from his own preferences, the ASE was now being pushed towards parliamentary activity by the employers' strategies, by the courts, as well as by the union movement in general.

[1] Henry Collins and Chimen Abramsky, *Karl Marx and the British Labour Movement* (London, Macmillan, 1965), pp. 219–20.

[2] Pelling, op. cit., p. 93.

[3] The Rt Hon. George N. Barnes, *From Workshop to War Cabinet* (London, Herbert Jenkins, 1924), pp. 42–6.

With increasingly severe international competition, the employers were by no means reconciled to dealing even with the aristocrats of labour. Uninhibited by any reluctance to engage in political action, they established in 1898 their own Employers' Parliamentary Council to carry forward political resistance to strikes. Major court decisions since 1896 had challenged the right to picket.[1] In 1897–8 the engineering employers organized a national lock-out against the engineering unions to smash the attempt at winning an eight-hour day. Whether as cause or effect, the unions generally were now electing more militant leaderships, and entering into politics. The ILP scored impressive successes, notably in the election of the top leadership of the Amalgamated Society of Railway Servants, an industrial-type union. The Railway workers, because of the special nature of the industry, and the additional vital fact that the employers refused to accord them recognition, seized on the offer made to the Trades Union Congress in 1899 by Keir Hardie on behalf of the ILP for a conference on parliamentary representation. By a narrow but historic vote, Congress agreed to initiate a conference of TUC affiliates, socialists and co-operative societies looking towards greater representation in the House of Commons for labour.[2]

The ASE had managed to win a significant degree of recognition after the lock-out. By the 1898 *Terms of Settlement* with the Engineering Employers' Federation, the ASE and kindred unions accepted as a general principle that 'managements have the right to appoint men they consider suitable to work . . . [the machines] and determine the conditions under which such machine tools shall be worked'. In return the Employers' Federation recognized that trade unions 'have the right to exercise their functions'. A multi-level system for handling disputes was created, beginning at the shop level, proceeding to district conference, and culminating at a Central Conference of the two national executive bodies. With some changes adopted in 1922, this sytem of conciliation survived through the 1960s.

The continuing general climate of hostility towards unionism induced a continuing though half-hearted interest by the ASE in narrow forms of political action in all areas except those concerned with legal survival. Although the ASE was not present at the 1899 Congress it did take an active role at the Labour Representation Conference (LRC) in 1900 and in the formation of the Labour Party.

The Engineers' role in the LRC reflected a carefully defined,

[1] H. A. Clegg, Alan Fox and A. F. Thompson, *A History of British Trade Unions Since 1889* (London, Oxford University Press, 1964), Vol. 1, Chap. 4.

[2] *Ibid*, Chaps 6 and 7; Pelling, op. cit., pp. 114–17.

defensive political purpose; it also illustrated a close interplay between political activity and internal bureaucratic needs. The Society was represented at the original LRC London meeting in 1900 by George Barnes and John Burns. Both men articulated the moderate approach which the ILP had adopted in order to win a permanent alliance with the unions. When the SDF delegates proposed that the Conference back a 'distinct party based upon the recognition of the class war . . . and socialization of the means of production, distribution and exchange', Burns gave his famous speech against labour 'being prisoners to class-prejudice'. The Conference voted merely to seek greater labour representation in Parliament without regard to the class origins of the candidates. Indeed, the final resolution was not all that different from the 'reward your friends, punish your enemies' strategy which the American Federation of Labor had begun to develop to protect its bargaining position from court injunctions. The LRC coalition voted merely to back any candidates who were 'sympathetic with the aims and demands of the Labour movement'.[1]

Taff Vale Judgement: 1901–1906 Political Action

This judgement, as is well known, placed union funds in jeopardy and threatened their officers with contempt of court for the actions of members. 'It was', as Cole has written, 'a matter of life and death . . . [and] brought the Trade Unions into politics much more rapidly than any amount of persuasion by the Socialists could have done.'[2]

Barnes now explained to his membership in a series of articles that the Judgement against the Railway Servants, as well as those that followed against the Engineers themselves, endangered the very functioning of the Society. Thus, in May 1902, he urged members to back a resolution for the restoration of the legal position won by the Act of 1875.[3]

The strike against Taff Vale had been an unofficial one (although subsequently made official) and, since many ASE strikes were also now unofficial, Barnes warned that legal security was being endangered by such 'unauthorized and irregular proceedings'. In asking for support of the legislation he said it would 'protect ourselves from the consequences of acts of scatter-brained and irresponsible members'. He reminded members of the limited aims

[1] Ralph Miliband *Parliamentary Socialism* (London, Merlin edn, 1964), Chap. 1.
[2] G. D. H. Cole, *British Working Class Politics 1832–1914* (London, Labour Book Service, 1941), pp. 167–8; cf. Clegg *et al*, op. cit., Chaps 8 and 9.
[3] *Journal* (May 1902), pp. 2–4.

of the new move towards parliamentary activity, however: 'The aims of the LRC may be expressed in a single proposition, namely, the representation of labour.'[1] What Barnes and others took from the Taff Vale incident was first, the need for legislation to assure legal security, and second, the need to strengthen the national leadership within the Society.

The union voted in 1903 for the maintenance fund of the LRC but Barnes remained concerned about the strikes. Paradoxically the Fabians were invited to help strengthen the national union leadership position on the strike issue even though, as previously mentioned, the leading Fabians, Sidney and Beatrice Webb, had reached the conclusion that collective bargaining was not conductive to rational social advance. For example, the *Journal* of May 1902 contained an article by Frank Humphries, a well-known Fabian who argued the need for greater centralization and less unco-ordinated unofficial action: 'I believe in the first place we should depend less on the militant and more on the diplomatic leader in the future than in the past.'[2]

The Webbs were at this time 'regarded with mistrust by practically all the leaders of the trade union movement'; they had even disagreed with the Parliamentary Committee's decision to seek legislative remedies for the Taff Vale decision.[3] Barnes had been a member of the Parliamentary Committee, and had supported new legislation. Nevertheless, he found it expedient to give over a full page of his own three pages in the *Journal* to Sidney Webb, who urged the restless membership to ratify the Head Office's negotiation of a premium bonus system.[4]

After 1906: Resistance to Political Action

Barnes himself stood for Parliament and was elected under the auspices of the LRC in 1906. The modern literature of the AEU attempts to portray this as part of a 'revolt', but the goals of the ASE and other union-sponsored MPs continued to be limited to the restoration of legality. Indeed, after the Trades Disputes Act was passed in 1906 and legality assured, Keir Hardie complained about the indifference of all the union-MPs to broader social issues. For his part Barnes now projected a Fabian approach to industrial relations, foreseeing '. . . peaceful arrangements being made with

[1] *Journal* (June 1902), p. 3.

[2] Ibid., (May 1902), pp. 19–21. Humphries also wrote articles in June and July issues, 1902. Barnes was the Editor as well as the General Secretary.

[3] B. C. Roberts, *The Trades Union Congress, 1868–1921* (London, Allen and Unwin, 1958), p. 178.

[4] Sidney Webb, 'The Bonus System', *Journal* (October 1902), pp. 2–4.

employers . . . wherever possible, so that we can the more effectively cement the labour force and focus them on Parliament. . . . We shall probably find that we need not strike at all except through the ballot box'.[1]

This was hardly a move to the Left, or to real reliance on political techniques. It seems likely that Barnes' interest in Parliament was partly a bureaucratic diversion: to obscure the failure of the national organization to cope effectively with the 1898 Terms of Settlement. In the year 1905–1906, for example, most of the disputed questions ended without agreement. Whether as cause or effect, the failure of the agreed procedure to settle work-place problems was accompanied by an increasing number of wildcat strikes. After the threat represented by the Taff Vale Judgement was lifted there was actually an increase in such unauthorized strikes, and bitter exchanges between national officers and members over what Barnes considered strike benefits 'illegally paid by the Districts'. Barnes resigned as General Secretary in 1908 following the refusal of the North East Coast membership to accept an Executive Council order to end a District-authorized strike.[2]

The centralized structure that had made the ASE a New Model was already showing informal devolution to the Districts and to work-place bargaining. Officially, the functions of the shop stewards were limited to checking that members remained in benefit, but increasingly in Glasgow, London, Manchester, and other large cities, they were assuming such functions as rate negotiation, determining the amount of work produced per man, and the establishment of shop rules.[3]

To an extent difficult to document, workplace leaders were responding in those years to the appeal of syndicalism, which saw the trade union itself as the essential unit of production and government. The ASE's Tom Mann had now achieved an international reputation as a spokesman for revolutionary syndicalism and his tactical ideas—open unionism, low contributions and 'direct action'— all contrary to both parliamentary politics and to the market philosophy of the ASE, struck a responsive chord among many work-place leaders of the Society and other craft unions. The profound influence of Mann, and the ambience of syndicalist thought at the Engineers' is reflected in the following excerpt from a Hundredth Anniversary booklet—issued, paradoxically, in 1951, a year which will be seen as a landmark turn towards greater official involvement by the Engineers in the Labour Party:

---

[1] Quoted by Jefferys, op. cit., p. 161.   [2] Barnes, op. cit., pp. 56–7.
[3] Clegg *et al.*, op. cit., pp. 431–2.

But it was Tom Mann who did most in these years to arouse British Trade Unionists for more militant struggle on the industrial field. Tom formed the Industrial Syndicalist League to conduct a scientific war against capitalism and launched a paper called *The Industrial Syndicalist* which, together with a stream of pamphlets, aroused great interest in trade union circles. He urged the superiority of strike action over parliamentary methods of reform, and the need for union amalgamations.[1]

To summarize: in the early years of this century the Society moved in counterpoint in two somewhat contradictory themes. No doubt the major factor in its shift towards politics was the attack on legal status represented by the Taff Vale Judgement and earlier court attacks. It was also pushed towards affiliation with the Labour Party by socialist influence. It was highly influenced also by revolutionary and syndicalist philosophies, striking a response from worker resentment of employer domination. Yet it seems probable that the Society's entry into politics in these years was at least partly a temporary substitute for needed structural change.

The engineering workers followed the general pattern of growth in both union membership and militancy that began well before and continued during the First World War. Payment by results, which became the prevailing mode in the industry, gave strength to negotiations based on the particular shop, and carried on by shop stewards; and this tendency was reinforced by production requirements during the war. Commitments of national union leaders to Government planning policy, though largely based on the priority accorded to increased national output, took their attention away from the changes needed at the level of the individual work-place. This gap was filled by the shop stewards, whose functional advantage—aided by conditions of full employment—was translated into a decentralized system of authority.[2] While the national leaders necessarily became more closely identified with the Government, and generally concurred with the coalition Government's impatience with unofficial strikes, the National Shop Stewards' Movement, still under strong syndicalist influence, frequently fought the Government, and these local leaders became increasingly anti-Parliamentary in their views.[3]

---

[1] AEU Centenary Souvenir, 'The Story of the Engineers' (1951), pp. 20–1.

[2] Clegg *et al.*, op. cit., p. 271. See also A. I. Marsh and E. E. Coker, 'Shop Steward Organization in Engineering Industry', *British Journal of Industrial Relations*, reprint, Vol. I (undated), pp. 170–99.

[3] Jefferys, op. cit., p. 190. The influence of syndicalism in British unions is more carefully considered by Clegg *et al.*, op. cit., *passim;* Miliband, op. cit., pp. 34 f; Pelling, op. cit., Chap. 7, *passim.*

1920: The Amalgamated Engineering Union

Amalgamation Committees, made up of rank and file delegates from the different engineering unions, had been active since 1915, and had been fused with the National Shop Stewards' Movement in 1917. Here too the push was adverse to political action: these *ad hoc* organizations were largely influenced—according to the official historian—by the 'idea that the trade unions could, when sufficiently strong and well led, take over the whole industrial system'.

The Engineering workers did achieve a certain amount of horizontal combination among national engineering unions as well as closer co-operation of various unions at the work-places. While not quite the vertical integration envisaged by syndicalism, it was a step in the direction of the syndicalists' 'one big union'. When the ASE combined with nine other craft unions in 1920 to form the Amalgamated Engineering Union, the new structure strongly reflected the syndicalists' influence. Although Tom Mann was elected General Secretary and a moderate, J. T. Brownlie, was named President, collective leadership and decentralization were officially recognized: shop stewards were to have quarterly meetings within each district and policy-making power by means of representation on District Committees. At the top, executive authority was divided among a seven-man Executive Council (EC). Elected by direct ballot on an area basis, the EC was given the constitutional responsibility for the general government of the AEU. The President and General Secretary were to meet with the Executive Council. By presiding at all national policy meetings and at the EC, and by casting his union's block votes, the President was given considerable power, but it was clearly limited. The General Secretary enjoyed a lesser authority than in most British unions, being confined largely to internal administration.

Legislative policy-making was placed in the hands of a small National Committee (NC) of 52. Rather than the customary 'annual conference' or 'national convention', the small group of Committeemen annually elected was from the start considered equal in skills and authority to the executive. As indicated in Chart I, the National Committee was constituted from 26 Divisional Committees, each selecting two of its members for the national body. The Divisional Committees, in turn, are elected by the District Committees within the division. This elaborate system, borrowing from the syndicalist Industrial Workers of the World (IWW) and from the Constitution of the United States,[1] was not to eliminate the conflict between the full-time bureaucracy and the lay policy-making body, as will be seen in Chapter VI.

[1] Interview, George W. Aitken, Research Officer (2 December 1964).

The AEU Between the Wars

This was a period of generally diminished union interest in politics despite the 1921-2 engineering lockout, the 1926 General Strike and the fact that by 1922 the Labour Party was the second largest party in Britain. The 1931 confrontation between the TUC and the MacDonald Government, which is discussed in Chapter VII, demonstrated that the union movement could beat off government attacks on vital union interests. The TUC and the Labour Party entered protests against mass unemployment which reached close to 3 million in 1931-33;[1] but, in Britain as in the United States, the popular protest for adequate relief was usually led by Communists; and the Communist Party of Great Britain (CPGB), which in these years created and directed a number of direct action bodies, attracted many AEU militants—some as followers, some as members.

Tom Mann who had been, successively, a major leader in the new unionism of the 1890s, the socialist movements, and the syndicalist movement, became a foundation member of the Communist Party in 1920, the same year that he was elected General Secretary of the union. Retiring in 1922 on account of age, he remained a prominent figure in the CPGB until his death in 1941.[2] At this time the Communist Party could accept Mann despite his continuing faith in syndicalist ideas. 'Such ideas', he wrote in his *Memoirs* published in 1923, 'still hold the field as against the theories and methods of the Labour Parliamentarians.'[3] The National Minority Movement (NMM) which he presided over at its launching in 1924, ignored parliamentary politics and sought union structural changes. Although the Labour Party's concept o 'workers' control' was made an ultimate goal, the NMM's central demand was for a 'real' General Council to 'direct, unite and co-ordinate struggles for immediate demands'.[4]

Wal Hannington who was elected one of the three National

---

[1] Miliband, op. cit., pp. 210–15. Noreen Branson and Margot Heinemann in *Britain in the Nineteen Thirties* (London, Weidenfeld and Nicolson, 1971) feel: 'The gradually-rising standard of those in steady employment also helps to explain to some extent the relative passivity of the trade union movement, at a time when the unemployed were engaged in bitter and massive conflict with the state authorities.' (p. 4). In the early 1930s '. . . the movements of resistance . . . were outside the range of the official labour movement [revealing] a pattern which was to dominate the thirties' (p. 18).

[2] Tom Mann Centenary Celebration (London, Tom Mann Centenary Celebration Committee, undated).

[3] *Tom Mann's Memoirs* (London, Labour Publishing Co., 1923), p. 315. The strongly syndicalist views of CPGB members and leaders are also reflected in Willy Gallacher's *Revolt on the Clyde* (London, Lawrence and Wishart, 1948).

[4] Allen Hutt, *The Post-War History of the British Working Class* (New York, Coward McCann, 1938), p. 76.

Organizers during World War II, was a toolmaker member of the AEU who had been blacklisted as a result of his leadership as a shop steward during the 1922 lock-out. Like Mann, he was a founder member of the Communist Party of Great Britain and became a member of its National Executive. With Tom Mann and Harry Pollitt of the Boilermakers' Union (later Pollitt became the General Secretary of the CPGB), he shared leadership of the Minority Movement, which 'played a great part', as Hannington thought, first 'in preparing the workers for the General Strike' of 1926, and in stiffening the unions generally against employer attacks. For him, as for Mann, there was—even in 1965 when he was interviewed—no confidence in 'constitutionalists', whereas 'direct action' by unions offered hope for improvement and 'changing the damn system'.[1]

Wal Hannington headed the National Unemployment Workers Movement, which has been widely recognized as the 'one body which agitated fiercely on behalf of the unemployed as such'.[2] The marches, which brought Hannington innumerable arrests and beatings, were begun without the backing of the AEU, the TUC or the Labour Party. The objective was to eliminate the means test and, later, the cuts in unemployment benefits. Tom Mann acted as Treasurer of the Unemployed Workers' Movement and served a short term in jail in 1933 for his agitation.[3]

Union Philosophy: World War II

Direct action in the work-places, the rise in the power of shop stewards, the actions of such non-parliamentary organizations as the National Minority and the Unemployed Workers' Movements, all combined to build up a significant unofficial power structure within the unions. As our account makes clear, the Communist Party was an important but by no means the only significant element in this development. The CP and others on the Left had backed for some years the charismatic Jack Tanner, former syndicalist, and war-time President of the AEU. Tanner had risen to leadership as a shop steward during World War I and had expanded his influence as an Executive member of the Minority Movement. He was a militant, but opposed to the Labour Party. In 1921 he had written: 'Imagine a Labour majority, a Labour Government composed of the present crowd of reactionaries, swindlers and traitors.'[4] The

---

[1] Interview with W. Hannington (12 November 1965). See his *Unemployment Struggles* (London, Lawrence and Wishart, 1936) and *Ten Lean Years* (London, Gollancz, 1940).

[2] Pelling quoted by Miliband, op. cit., p. 211.   [3] Ibid., p. 213.

[4] Robert McKenzie, *British Political Parties*, revised edn (London, Mercury, 1963), p. 410 n. The quotation is from *Solidarity*, 'official organ of the Shop Stewards and Workers' Committee Movements' (25 March 1921).

thought was perfectly consistent with its syndicalist roots. There is no reason to doubt the proposition that his opposition to political action stemmed from syndicalist views. Lenin—already persuaded that even militant unionism required political and intellectual guidance for revolutionary advance—grouped Tanner with 'the other comrades of the Industrial Workers of the World (from the United States) and of the Shop Steward groups'. All were represented at the Second Congress of the Comintern in Moscow, 23 July 1920. At this Congress Lenin advised the British delegates to join and work for revolutionary goals, but found the shop militants suspicious: 'The only difference that exists between us is the sort of mistrust which the British comrades entertain towards political parties.'[1] Lenin had written earlier (1912) that the 'opportunist conduct of the [Labour] Members of Parliament is, as is usually the case, giving rise to syndicalist tendencies among the workers. Happily, these are not strong.'[2] Contrary to Lenin's desires, however, they did remain strong, especially among the Engineers.

Tanner and his colleagues co-operated extensively with the Government during the Second World War, but he continued to have small faith in the effect of parliamentary action. Even in 1945, in his Election Address for the Union Presidency, neither the Labour Party nor the General Election is mentioned. We have the testimony of Fred Lee—an AEU Convenor until his election to Parliament in 1945—that this attitude continued to flow from the general ambience of syndicalist thought at Head Office. Lee would soon help alter the forms of political action, and himself become Chairman of a revived AEU Parliamentary Group. But he was convinced that the 'stand-off' position of Tanner and his colleagues with respect to his own 1945 campaign, and the continued indifference of Tanner's successors to any 'real' politics in 1965—long after the formal turn towards Labour—was rooted in the lingering syndicalist thinking within the union.[3]

This syndicalist current, while gradually losing its character as a rallying cry for a new kind of social and economic order, retained its vitality as an influence in support of rank and file initiative and independent decision-making at the shop level. Syndicalism thus found itself living in harmony with a *laissez-faire* approach in general and with market bargaining at the workplace in particular. While the Communists in Britain, as in the United States, for a brief period envisaged trade union co-operation with 'progressive capitalism', there was no great decline in Supply and Demand bargaining.

[1] V. I. Lenin, *Lenin on Britain* (New York, International Publishers, 1934), pp. 263–6.
[2] Ibid., p. 107.   [3] Interview (11 April 1965).

The economy remained predominantly private. While the post-war Labour Government was in some respects a symbol of the full flowering of parliamentary government, and would continue to espouse planning, it too accepted what one student has described as 'a private enterprise type of syndicalism'.[1] Except in war-time crises the Engineers had not relied on Government. Now the unions as a whole sensed that their real power rested on their bargaining strength. Even Professor Beer, an admirer of the Labour Party and a firm believer in parliamentary politics, has said of the British trade unions after 1945:

> In a limited, but important sense, the old syndicalist thesis was vindicated, for it was initially not by their votes but by their control over the instrumentalities necessary to carrying out vital national purposes that the organized working class raised themselves from their old position of exclusion and inferiority. The Labour victory of 1945 and the consequent adaptation of Conservative policy were later phases of this general process.[2]

The AEU's officers and staff were no doubt fully conscious of the new status of the Engineers. One finds abundant references to this in the *Journal*. And in a collective *Foreword* to the official history, *The Story of the Engineers*, all the top officers, as well as the Executive Council, clearly sensed that they had reached an historic moment— the end of a desperate war in which the Engineers had played so vital a role. Yet, although they were writing in 1945, on the eve of the General Election, the Labour Party is not mentioned; and the union itself proposed neither reform nor social transformation. The officers all concurred that, in essence, the AEU was prepared to resume the traditional business unionism of the founders:

> [We] are concerned to leave—in the words of the Preface to the Rules of the ASE of 1851—'to a future generation not only a trade but the means of maintaining its best interests until some more general principle of co-operation shall be acknowledged in society, guaranteeing to every man the full enjoyment of the produce of his labour'.[3]

Of course, the Communist Party faction—then pursuing a world-wide 'United Front' strategy—and no doubt others as well, were

---

[1] Robert Lester Weinberg *Workers' Control: A Study in British Socialist Thought*, unpublished Ph.D. thesis (University of London, 1960), p. 248.

[2] Samuel H. Beer, *British Politics in the Collectivist Age* (New York, Knopf, 1966), p. 215.

[3] Jefferys, op. cit., Foreword.

deeply concerned with the General Election. The former had sufficient strength on the National Committee in 1945 to produce a 'United Front' resolution urging 'an arrangement with the progressive Parties at the General Election'. Duly transmitted by Jack Tanner, the President, to the Labour Party Conference of 1945, the motion was defeated.[1] Considering his own views of the inefficacy of politics, Tanner's advocacy of such an alliance reflects, surely, the strength of Communist influence rather than his own conversion to parliamentary activity. In any event. Tanner joined the other TUC leaders in rejecting the Labour Government's approach to manpower planning, which the Government considered the key to its over–all planning.

General Council's View After the War

This comes very much closer to Tanner's view, and the policy which became operative in the AEU in the post-war years. Only four months after the Labour Party Conference of 1945 Tanner seconded at the Trades Union Congress a motion by Arthur Deakin, General Secretary of the Transport and General Workers' Union, on 'Wages, Hours, and Conditions of Employment', and spoke for a business unionism perfectly consistent with the central tendencies of the union's history. He and Deakin, while urging full employment as top priority, joined in the General Council's rejection of a proposal for a Government-planned wage incentives system, designed to direct labour towards the urgent needs of the coal mines, and otherwise rationalizing the distribution of manpower. Tanner and other Council members preferred, they said, traditional collective bargaining and the maintenance of traditional wage differentials.[2]

Once it became clear that there would be no large-scale unemployment in the economy and the Labour Government showed it could govern, the AEU's attitude towards governmental intervention was aloof. It did remain nominally committed to 'plans' of left-wing origin, but the union's and the TUC's operative policy would continue to remain distinctly voluntarist or market-oriented.

A bellwether of the post-war union leadership's rejection of planning and social change has been the checkered career of the *Plan for Engineering*. Originally drafted during the war by Communists in the Head Office of the AEU, as the Engineers' contribution to the TUC's post-war proposals, it has continued to undergo changes that broadly reflect ideas of Communist and ex-Communist

---

[1] *Labour Party Conference Report* (LPCR) (1945), p. 81. The NC had passed a United Front resolution at its 1944 meeting (*Report, p.* 293).

[2] *Trades Union Congress Report* (1945), pp. 256–9.

intellectuals associated with the engineering industries. Like the TUC plan, the *Plan for Engineering* grew originally out of fear of mass unemployment following demobilization. From rather mild proposals for regulation it then expanded into a series of pamphlets embodying ideas for public ownership and workers' control. These changes broadly mirrored the Communist Party's change of line from support of 'progressive capitalism' in 1944–5 to the far more militant posture of the late 1940s and early 1950s.

On the other hand, even after the CP adopted its strong parliamentary emphasis in 1956, which meant much closer co-operation with Labour, the *Plan*—as shown in later discussion—continued to be a focus for Left-Right confrontation, with ex-Communists in the smaller engineering unions preparing the pamphlets and devising paper victories from time to time.

When Tanner repudiated this *Plan* in public in 1951, it was a public signal of his break with the Communists and the Left Wing members of the Labour Party within his own union. It also marked a far more positive AEU commitment to the Labour Party. He had already split with the CP faction in about 1949, some three years after the Communist Party activists had come into direct conflict with both the Trades Union Congress and the Labour Party.

This is no place to evaluate the various explanations given for this particular split, which—whatever the personal motives involved—must be seen as part of a general polarization taking place within the entire movement. With the Cold War, the war-time honeymoon with the Left was over; it was no longer convenient to maintain connections with the Communist Party, or Party-backed causes. The Communists were now reasserting revolutionary political doctrine. The Left Wing of the Labour Party was pressing for changes in foreign policy, and for more active reform and nationalization. However, the predominant trade union leadership, as well as the Labour Party Executive and its leaders, had decided against further legislative reforms, and for the *status quo*.

The AEU's adaptation to these changed conditions was reflected at the 1951 Labour Party Conference in a confrontation between Tanner and his own Left. Before the Conference, the Engineers had been linked with Labour's 'fundamentalist' wing and against the 'revisionists' on the question of nationalization, and the *Plan for Engineering*. When Norman Dinning, a union activist and Conference delegate, rose to challenge the Prime Minister, Mr Attlee, for omitting nationalization from the Party Manifesto for the 1951 General Election, he seemed to be merely reiterating AEU policy. He asserted he wanted the Party's '. . . National Executive to take particular care, and to take notice of the expressed opinions of the working class voiced through the Unions, who support nationalization and its extension . . . [against] the strain imposed by the surrounding capitalist world'. He held up for Conference an AEU National Committee Report with 'no less than seven resolutions', urging 'nationalization of the engineering industry itself with priority for machine production'.[1]

A day after Dinning's attack on the Party leadership, Tanner explicitly repudiated his colleague and threw AEU support solidly behind the Party Executive, after first polling the entire delegation. Their stand, he explained, was not a departure from union official policy for nationalization. He acknowledged his National Committee's adherence, and the Confederation of Shipbuilding and Engineering Unions' commitment, to the *Plan for Engineering*, but observed: 'That industry is the largest in the country and it is perhaps the most complex and involved. . . . It is a broad outline of what the engineering workers desire, but certainly it is not yet at a stage where we can come forward and say, "These are our practical proposals. They form a long-term policy."'[2] In the same speech Tanner hailed the achievement of full employment under Labour and announced that the Centennial of the union would witness a massive AEU support for Labour in the General Election.

Thus, one hundred years after its founding as a national trade union, the national officers of the Engineers had apparently at last renounced their ambiguity about politics—in at least two senses: they appeared to be embracing parliamentary politics as such, and at the same time they rejected informal alliance with the Communist Party and the Labour Left. Seemingly the goals were now broadened, however. 'Socialism' received a new apparent emphasis. Unlike their public stand on the eve of the 1945 General Election, in which the officers simply re-affirmed the ASE founders' objective of serving the 'best interests' of the trade, Tanner and the General Secretary, Ben Gardner, declared in their *Foreword* to the official Centenary booklet that a 'Socialist Britain' was now attainable:

We of the present generation are faced with different problems from those of our forefathers. Thanks to their work the trade unions are now strong and powerful and the working-class movement is responsible for the Government of Britain. We have the possibility of establishing in our generation the Socialist Britain of which they could only dream. But we shall do so only if we have the same courage and determination as they had, the same faith in our fellow workers and in the power of the working class.[3]

[1] *LPCR* (1951), pp. 90–1. [2] Ibid., pp. 99–100.
[3] *Centenary*, op. cit., p. 2.

The actual meaning of the contemporary Engineering Union's general adaptation to 'different problems from those of our fore-fathers', as well as the implications of their apparent commitment to socialism and political activity, are critically examined in the four chapters that follow.

Chapter III

The Engineers' Sponsoring of MPs, 1950–1965

In 1951, the political conversion of Jack Tanner—and through him the union—to parliamentary socialism was both pragmatic and ideological. On the one hand, his common sense explanation for shelving the socialistic *Plan for Engineering* could be read as a version of Machiavelli's dictum: 'We are confronted with a condition, not a theory.' But Tanner also took pains to assure his colleagues in the union, and in the Confederation of Shipbuilding and Engineering Unions as well, that the AEU was not rejecting the *Plan* or repudiating socialism. In years to come the union would again officially endorse nationalization and other sweeping reforms. Indeed, in 1951 Tanner and the General Secretary—both of them close to retirement—had announced the possibility of achieving a 'Socialist Britain' in their own generation.

To the accompaniment of familiar socialist slogans, the union implemented the line taken by the top officers. As seen in Appendix I, the sums paid to the national Labour Party for affiliation fees leaped from £3,597 in 1945 to £14,715 in 1951; 'other direct grants' rose from £2,629 to £3,875, respectively. However, the most spectacular form of increased political activity was in the area of parliamentary sponsorship, which became the main focus of the political action programme.

(The political levy, the source of all political disbursements, is analysed in the next chapter.)

The analysis in the present chapter of the extensive, highly regarded sponsorship of MPs should illuminate the cloudy relationship which exists between the Party and the sponsoring unions. However, the central argument of the four chapters dealing with the post-World War II activity of the Engineers, is that political action as conventionally understood—to supplement collective bargaining, to achieve social reform or social transformation—was not a significant purpose of the closer identification with Labour.

The fundamental goal of the union movement, collective bargaining, was now achievable—at least in immediate terms—without significant resort to political action. Moreover, the practical men at

D 49

the head of the union were not interested in advancing ideological goals.

These moves by the model union towards Labour during the late years of the first post-war Labour Government grew partly out of the general trade union fear that a radical leader might be elected to head the Party and a potential new Labour Government. The expanded commitment to Labour by the AEU also provided an opportunity to the Executive to enhance its bureaucratic image and security *vis-à-vis* the membership.

Theoretical Potential from Parliamentary Representation

Some theoretical considerations are useful to judge whether trade union political commitments could, or were planned to, produce in post-war Britain either ideological or practical advance. The 1951 Labour Party Manifesto, *Labour and the New Society*, attacked the capitalist system and glorified socialism: capitalism 'degraded humanity' while for socialists 'the true purpose of society is to promote and protect the dignity and well-being of the individual'.[1]

Despite this ringing rhetoric, most scholars of the Labour Movement seem agreed that, after 1947, change of the economic system was no longer on Labour's agenda and that there was little to choose between Labour and Tory policies. Ralph Miliband's study, *Parliamentary Socialism*, depicts the Party as content to stress its past achievements, particularly the achievement of full employment.[2] Richard Crossman, the Labour Party's most distinguished political theorist, has noted that in 1945: 'the conditions in Westminster and Whitehall and the whole political climate of the country outside were extremely well-suited for a big and sustained advance towards a socialist planned economy'. But only two years later, 'the Government was manifestly losing both its coherence and its sense of direction . . . so that in 1950 there was no programme for a second stage of socialism . . . many Labour voters were quite unable to name any difference between the Conservative and Labour policies'.[3] Samuel Beer, a warm sympathizer of the Labour Party, who emphasizes a 'fundamental' gap between the two major parties with respect to ideology and inner democracy, sees in this period a convergence with respect to the 'Welfare State and the Managed

---

[1] *Handbook for Socialists, 1951* (London, Labour Party Research Department, 1950), Appendix, p. 413.

[2] Ralph Miliband, *Parliamentary Socialism* (London, Merlin Press, 1964), p. 315.

[3] Richard Crossman, MP, 'The Lessons of 1945', written in 1963 for the *New Statesman* and reprinted in Perry Anderson and Robin Blackburn (eds), *Towards Socialism* (London, New Left, 1965), pp. 150–8.

Economy'. And the resistance of the TUC General Council to man-power and wage planning by the Labour Government in the years 1945–47—already mentioned above—is given by Beer as 'the princi-pal cause' of the switch in policy by Prime Minister Clement Attlee from physical planning towards 'indirect control by manipulation of the market'. This approach, Beer observes, is 'quite compatible with private ownership, competition and profit-seeking'. And by 1950, he adds, the Tories, 'had accepted the basic framework of the "Welfare State and the Managed Economy" that Labour was administering, and in the following years the Conservative scheme of social and economic priorities was so close to those of Labour's public declarations at election time that the policies of the two parties could seem to be well on the way to convergence.'[1]

Robert McKenzie disputes the idea of an ideological gap alto-gether, and has repeatedly welcomed what he sees as a continuing and healthy trend of the two British parties towards the American model of basic identity of interests and the shedding of ideological differences. In his classic *British Political Parties*, first published in 1955, he sees agreement on 'fundamentals' between the two major British parties and 'furious arguments' about comparatively minor issues.[2]

It is quite clear, then, that the AEU was not seeking ideological goals in 1951. In 1945, when the potential for social change was great, this major Labour affiliate was relatively passive. Now, in 1951, when the union and the Party were both agreed that nationali-zation and other 'socialist' programmes were not feasible, we find the union hotly embracing the Party. What was its real intention? The socialist promise in the Centenary booklet (above) if not disin-genuous, was so close to what the American 'Wobblies' called 'pie in the sky' that it can be discarded as an operative concept.

Was the Party tie, then, utilized for more limited reforms, in the fields of welfare and education; or for labour legislation? There remained a long list of unfinished reforms even after the 1945–51 social achievements by the Labour Government. But by 1951 the formal legislative demands of the entire British trade union movement had been satisfied and 'the unions were no longer agreed as to what their future demands were to be'.[3] The thrust for recent labour

[1] S. H. Beer, *British Politics in the Collectivist Age* (New York, Knopf, 1966), pp. 200–16, 386–7.

[2] Quoted by Beer, op. cit., p. 386. For a brief discussion of U.S.-U.K. Party differences, see exchange of letters between this writer and McKenzie in the *Observer* (27 September 1964).

[3] William Pickles, 'Trade Unions in the Political Climate', in B. C. Roberts (ed.), *Industrial Relations: Contemporary Problems and Perspectives* (London, Methuen, 1962), p. 35.

legislation has in fact come from the government—both Conservative and Labour—as part of the general pattern of governmental guidance of the mixed capitalist economy.

AEU Sponsorship Plan

The Engineers showed no dissent from the TUC's stand for the legislative *status quo*. Yet, the union demonstrated its new Labour Party concern by a greatly expanded parliamentary sponsorship. In 1951, a circular letter, signed by the General Secretary, pleaded for general support of Labour and specifically for a continuation of the political levy payments for the purpose of gaining more MPs: ' . . . [the] wisdom evinced by the great majority of our members by not contracting out and thereby building up the Political Fund and its consequent inestimable value to the Union politically is clearly demonstrated by the fact that the Union was enabled to sponsor ten AEU members as candidates.'[1] In the General Election of that year the union succeeded in getting eight of its ten sponsored candidates elected. These men, the Executive Council told the union, would 'undoubtedly regard it as an important part of their duties in Parliament not only to safeguard but also to promote the interests of engineers generally'.[2] Like all Labour-affiliated trade unions, the AEU was governed by the terms of the Hastings Agreement first worked out in 1933 and revised in 1957. Under the terms of this Party arrangement financial limits are placed on sponsors to avoid the fierce competition which had grown up between trade unions and the Co-operatives for a declining number of safe seats. The candidature of a sponsored candidate is endorsed by the National Executive Committee of the Party only after the latter is satisfied that the election expenses of the candidate are guaranteed.[3] Of the Labour candidates sponsored in the 1966 General Election by the Co-ops and the unions, totalling 162, only 24 were Co-op sponsored; 138 were trade-union sponsored, and 18 and 132, respectively, were elected.[4] (Details of the Hastings Agreement, as well as some financial details of AEU's sponsorship plan, are shown in Appendix II).

In its economic work, this union was successfully pursuing, at both the shop level, and at the national level, Gompers' classically *laissez-faire* economic demand of MORE. In the political field, too,

[1] Published in AEU *Report* from Executive Council (EC) to National Committee (NC) (1951), pp. 170–2. The annual *Report* consists of both an EC account to NC for their year's activities, and the new decisions made by NC. Unless otherwise indicated, *Report* will be used here as the EC account.

[2] AEU *Report* (1952), pp. 167–8.

[3] Labour Party, The Constitution and Standing Orders, Clause IX.

[4] *LPCR* (1966), p. 5.

they now expressed their demand in simple quantitative terms—MORE MPs. Both before and after their major break-through in 1964, when the AEU Group in the House of Commons jumped from 10 to 17 MPs, there was an insistent call on the membership to support the expansion. Jim Conway, who managed the programme then, wrote in 1963: 'We want more AEU members of Parliament. The objects of our Union cannot be achieved in their entirety unless we have adequate representation in Parliament.'[1]

In the union's most important statement of several generations, the elaborate 1965 brief submitted to the Royal (Donovan) Commission on Trade Unions and Employers' Associations, the traditional theory of labour representation is repeated and updated by a rather Galbraithian immediacy:

> Labour early recognized that only by Parliamentary representation could its activities have a hope of success in a democracy as we know it. Hence the trade unions [sic] belief in the intervention of Government to curb excesses in the combined forces of capital. . . . Labour's representatives in Parliament supported by the trade unions provide a countervailing balance which it is hoped will eventually remove anti-social anachronisms from our life.[2]

These strong statements suggest, if not a commitment to social change or a comprehensive legislative programme, at least a determination to articulate and advance the sectional needs of the organization by enlarged parliamentary pressure politics. *And yet current theory of pressure politics in Britain emphasizes non-parliamentary channels, rather than the sponsored Member envisaged by the LRC and the Party in earlier years.* Beer and McKenzie agree that since World War II: 'Class and ideological contours faded, while interest groups appeared as more prominent features of the political scene. . . . "Pressure groups, taken together, are a far more important channel of communication than parties for the transmission of political ideas from the mass of the citizenry to their rulers." '[3] These pressure groups—unions included—are accepted in Beer's classification as a part of a 'vast, untidy system of functional representation' which has grown up alongside the older system of parliamentary representation; and through them 'the powers of advice,

---

[1] Jim Conway, 'Trade Unions and Politics—Why? (2)', AEU *Journal* (August 1963). Conway was then Assistant General Secretary (AGS), and was elected General Secretary in 1964.

[2] AEU, *Trade Unions and the Contemporary Scene, Submitted to the Royal Commission on Trade Unions and Employers' Organizations* [sic] (London, 1965), pp. 42–3.

[3] McKenzie, cited by Beer, op. cit., p. 318.

acquiescence, and approval are brought to bear on public policy'.[1]

As will be seen from later discussion, *the unions were not interested in serious instrumental use of the representation they obtained on planning and industrial training boards.* They were aware, also, of the limitations imposed on their parliamentary channels by governmental processes at Whitehall and Westminster, but quite apart from those limitations, their ineffectiveness in politics was a function, primarily, of their own disinterest in affirmative political goals and their almost exclusive reliance on market bargaining.

The AEU's post-1951 emphasis on parliamentary representation had been given earlier statutory legitimacy by adoption of a Rule change proposed by Fred Lee, MP, who sought to rebuild the AEU Group in Parliament. He felt that centralized control of the Parliamentary Panel at Head Office was necessary in order to obtain the type of candidate who would win approval of the Constituency Labour Parties. What were his reasons for wanting MPs? Lee's printed account to the union members of his first nine months in the Labour Parliament showed a great appreciation for the recovery and reform measures won by Labour. Rather than urging greater union involvement in parliamentary politics, for either pressure or ideological purposes, Lee stressed the national union's status requirements, along with the need for a voice to give the 'A.E.U. point of view' at the work-place. The status argument is plain: 'the Union has grown to the position of being the most powerful force in British industrial life. On the political front we are absurdly weak.' Because he 'went to Westminster direct from the factory and shop stewards' movement', he apparently felt he could on that account clarify for the House of Commons the function of union bargaining in general, and skilled worker bargaining in particular. Thus, he quoted from a House speech he had made on production and wage differentials: 'We do not oppose the idea of increased mechanization, we merely oppose the object of employers which is in many cases to dub the workers on the machines semi-skilled and to pay them lower wages.'[2]

In his interview with this writer in 1964 during the second post-war Labour Government—he was then Minister of Power—Lee gave more stress to another symbolic but significant motivation for pushing sponsorship, namely, that the Party's health required an injection of authentic manual workers: 'The Party in 1945 was beginning to look like the Continental variety of social democratic party—a bourgeois set-up.'[3] Other AEU MP's, notably Mr Charles

---

[1] Beer, op. cit., p. 337.
[2] AEU, 'The Month in Parliament', *Journal* (May 1946), p. 139.
[3] Interview (17 March 1965).

Pannell, Secretary of the entire Trade Union Group of the Parliamentary Labour Party, also stressed the importance of this cloth-cap concept.[1] Although it had no more operative meaning in the Trade Union Group than it did in the Engineers', there can be little doubt of the significance of this image in the etiology of the AEU parliamentary programme. It will be seen that all factions concurred, in essence, with the cloth cap rationale.

Tests and Training

Lee's suggested change of Rule, adopted by the National Committee in 1947, substituted for the direct balloting of Panel members in branches an appointive centralized system administered by the Executive Council.

Shortly thereafter the EC created its own Political Sub-Committee, which has administered the MP programme to date. Although the National Committee was nominally given a veto power over EC choices by the Rule, it appears to have accepted the EC's decisions without debate. This authority will be seen to have served a bureaucratic function, but it has been the means for the AEU becoming a significant factor in the Labour Party nomination process. The Executive developed a training and testing method to choose AEU members who proved able to compete successfully at Party selection conferences.

The EC began the training of people it appointed to the panel sometime in 1950 with a series of weekend mock selection conferences. This proved inadequate; an increasing number remained on the panel without winning adoption by the Constituency Labour Parties (CLPs). In about 1957 the EC began to evolve the present combination of tests at a week-long 'school' for all aspirants for the panel, and additional training for those accepted. The tests, extending over three days, are administered after each change of government. They consist of (1) private interviews with prospective panellists by a committee of three Executive Council members who ask questions about AEU and Party history and policy, and also judge 'appearance and demeanour';[2] (2) delivery by each nominee of a ten-minute address on a Labour Party major social policy position to the audience of panellists—augmented, on occasion, by planted outside 'hecklers' (the candidate is given his topic only ten minutes in advance of this ordeal); (3) impromptu discussion by each aspirant on a subject introduced by an incumbent AEU-MP; (4)

[1] Interview (8 December 1964). The point is also developed by Pannell in 'The Quality of the Commons' *Statist* (12 January 1962). See Chap. VII, below.
[2] After the 1966 General Election, the EC decided to add three journalists, nominated by the National Union of Journalists, to the examining committee.

writing of an essay, under examination conditions, for a maximum of two hours, after having been given ten days before their test to do research on the assigned subject. These essays are sent to the Labour Party's national agent for grading, without identifying the applicant. Only after they pass the test and are placed on the panel do the hopefuls go to the union 'finishing school'—a week's stay at a London hotel for professional speech courses, seminars with Labour Ministers or Shadow Ministers and for 'smoothing out their rough spots'. Candidates who succeed in passing the EC selection tests and completing the week's training will go forward to the Labour Party's 'A' panel list of prospective candidates sponsored by trade unions, which the Party in turn circulates to Constituency Parties that are in the process of choosing candidates.

Having chosen its own prospective candidates, the Executive was confronted with the problem of getting their panellists approved—or adopted—by CLP selection conferences. To help achieve that vote, the General Office mailed letters to the District Committees urging them to seek affiliation of the branches with local Parties. Prestige and more immediate considerations were featured in these appeals:

> The strength of our representation at Labour Party selection conferences could become considerably more effective if District Committees would stress the importance of branches affiliating to their appropriate Labour Party so that this Union may obtain representation in Parliament that is commensurate with our membership, and to ensure that the political interest and aspirations of our members are adequately represented.[1]

(A branch, of course, cannot send delegates to a Party selection conference unless it is affiliated to that Party.) National officers as well as the MPs and the Districts were asked to keep an ear open for by-elections, especially where the incumbent Labour MP was retiring.

In the 1950s only about one in eight panellists was being selected. In 1962, in anticipation of a General Election, the Executive decided on more rigid tests, and required all men already on the panel, but still unsuccessful in their efforts at winning adoption, to take the new examinations and submit to interviews. After an extended 'weeding out of the dead wood', the remaining panellists were then given the week's extended training or 'finishing school'. To further assure electoral success, the EC also decided to sharply reduce the number of 'duds' or 'showing the flag' contests it entered by limiting its sponsorship to constituencies with a Conservative

[1] Circular letter (15 August 1963) from General Secretary C. W. Hallett (retired in 1964).

majority of no more than 3,000. Between the end of 1962 and the General Election of 1964, only 28 men remained on the panel, and as many as 11 of these won adoption. Ten were elected in 1964, making a total of 17 MPs in the AEU Group.[1]

As will be seen from later references to writings and interviews, this success within the Labour Movement became a rather important factor in the image being sought by the contemporary AEU.

The AEU-MP

The impact of the AEU system on the selection process may be greater than has been realized. Harrison's *Trade Unions and the Labour Party* appeared in 1960, when the AEU procedure was still in process of development, but he observed that it 'may be showing the way the rest of the movement will have to follow'.[2] Ranney's 1965 study of the nominating process merely notes the fact that the AEU, like a few other unions, uses weekend schools. In describing the sponsored MPs Ranney, who made no attempt to analyse any particular union group, made the general point that 'a union's most respected and able members are seldom included' because most unions prohibit their permanent officials from being MPs and officers at the same time. 'Consequently', he concluded, 'many sponsored MPs—especially from the blue collar unions—are men who did not quite make it to the top of their unions, men for whom seats in Parliament are a kind of consolation prize.' In general, 'names on the panels change only slowly with deaths and occasional withdrawals'. Consequently, the age of the sponsored Members is generally considerably higher than comparable Labour candidates sponsored by the Co-operatives, the CLP candidates, or the Conservative candidatures.[3]

The AEU panellists and Members of Parliament have shown a marked departure from this stereotype of blue-collar MPs. Entering relatively late into the business of serious sponsorship, and constrained from competing in monetary terms by the Hastings Agreement, the AEU has managed to win a great increase in its representation, due largely to the following: (1) they begin with a large body of skilled and literate members holding cards in a highly respected union; (2) they did change their panel to eliminate 'dead wood'; (3) they put them through the more rigorous tests indicated,

---

[1] *Minutes* of Political Sub-Committee, EC, 1959–64. This remained the total until 1970 when it was reduced to sixteen.

[2] Martin Harrison, *Trade Unions and the Labour Party* (London, Allen and Unwin, 1960), p. 285.

[3] Austin Ranney, *Pathways to Parliament: Candidate Selection in Britain* (London, Macmillan, 1965), pp. 223–4, 236.

and also added the week at the 'finishing schools'. In the event, they obtained a number of young, dedicated and able Members who created excellent public images.

The nine new AEU adopted (and elected) candidates in 1964, with one exception, were all under forty. They had been, of course, even younger when first put on the panel by their union, and many had been work-place activists.[1] One of the better known AEU-sponsored MPs, Mr Stan Orme, when asked how he happened to become interested in politics, related his early years as a skilled worker and his Second World War experience:

> I was an NCO in the R.A.F. At training school we were thrown together, people from all classes. We started as equals. It was a revelation to me that I could keep up with 'them'—men who had had public school or university training. It was the first time I had ever come close to such people. In classes my eyes were opened not only to new ideas but to the fact that I had missed so much. The possibilities of education were now before me. When I came home on leave, I joined the Labour Party. I was 21; I campaigned in my uniform in 1945.[2]

Despite the trade unions' high status in post-war Britain, even the relatively privileged working man in 1945 still lived in a society bisected by a distinct education line, on one side of which were the privileged and on the other side the vast, largely working class sector of the population denied opportunity for higher education.[3] To Orme, his union and the Party provided him with what seemed the only opportunity for upward mobility, and also an outlet whereby he could project his resentment against special privilege and social injustice. His advanced views, however, would place him in conflict with his union when he sought to implement them in the House of Commons.

Orme for some years was active both in his plant as a shop steward and in his local Party. Early in the 1950s, however, he decided that he had reached a 'fork' in his career: he could choose either 'the union path' or 'the political path'; he decided on the political path. For some years he was a Party officer before seeking to get on his union panel. This seems to be a fairly common career pattern among many post-war AEU–MPs, some reaching the fork at the shop steward level, others at the District Committee level.

A contrary decision taken by a successful union careerist, Mr

---

[1] AEU 'Parliamentary Panel Members of Parliament', undated; mimeographed.
[2] Interview (1 December 1964).
[3] Cf. J. Blondel, *Voters, Parties and Leaders: The Social Fabric of British Politics* (Harmondsworth, Penguin edn, 1965), Chap. 2.

John Boyd, confirms—indirectly—the great potential for upward mobility in some trade unions through the sponsoring process. Boyd, when he first stood for the Executive Council in 1952, told his AEU constituency in Scotland that he had been '... invited to accept nomination for "safe" Labour parliamentary seats and have declined these in order to give my members my undivided loyalty and attention'.[1]

Although only two sitting MPs in 1964–5 had been full-time, secondary officers—and these had been elected prior to the 1962 tests—all but one of the entire group of seventeen had once been either convenors or shop stewards. As illustrated by Lee's comments many of these men remained quite conscious of their skilled status, as well as their past experience in workshop bargaining and related union problems. Indicative of the strong role that the skilled men still play at both the Executive Council and District Committee levels is that fifteen of the seventeen MPs in 1964 were members of AEU Section 1—although this category (chiefly skilled and apprentice-trained) makes up only about 35 per cent of the general union-type membership.[2] This would make them quite union-conscious, but few were as class-conscious as Orme.

With its impressive gain of seven new Members in the 1964 General Election, the Engineers' programme became a considerable factor in the trade union and general Labour selection process. Other unions showed active interest in the tests, two of them even sending observers to the 1965 'school'. The Party's National Agent told this writer that the AEU men added 'practicality' to the entire Parliamentary Labour Party.[3] (The sponsorship by unions is important to the Party, among other reasons, because the unions generally finance more campaigns than they win—even where, as in the case of the AEU, they have tended to withdraw from contests they know are doomed to be 'duds'.)

The union's placing of additional carefully selected members on the panel after each general election constituted an announcement to the Labour Party, to other unions, and to AEU districts, that the AEU would continue to seek a substantial increase in adopted candidates. The union aimed, as of April 1965, for a total of some thirty-five to forty MPs, or all their Rules permit, according to Boyd, then Chairman of the Executive Council's Political Sub-Committee.[4]

[1] General Office, *Election Addresses*. By Rule 2, all candidates for General Office may submit such addresses for publication and distribution to branches.

[2] AEU 'Parliamentary Panel', op. cit.

[3] Interview with Sarah Barker, National Agent of the Labour Party (26 February 1965).

[4] Interview (8 September 1965).

Sponsored Members at Work

The quantitative goals reached and the quality of its men at Westminster proved a source of pride and satisfaction; more MPs were being sought. However, the union did not succeed in defining the functions which it expected its MPs to perform. This anomaly rested on changed power relations within the Government and within the union as well.

For trade unions as for other major economic institutions the very growth of the post-war system of guided capitalism—without regard to the particular party in power—has produced an enormous scope for political pressure. Eckstein, in his valuable study of the British Medical Association, has shown that many organizational pressures have come in direct response to governmental policy decisions.[1] While there was an absence of legislative initiative by the Trades Union Congress in this period, there is no doubt, as the TUC asserted in the opening paragraphs of its brief to the Donovan Commission in 1966, that it is 'universally recognized as the spokesman for employed people in Britain on a wide range of national issues. Consultation takes place between the TUC and Government Departments—often at Ministerial level—on all aspects of working life and on other national or international problems upon which the TUC has a viewpoint.'[2] But for all these interventions the General Council members are quite aware that they no longer need intercession by Members of Parliament. Thus, at the very time when the union was ostensibly developing a great new instrumental concern for parliamentary activity, on the substantive level it was increasingly by-passing parliamentary channels. The AEU officers had demonstrated their own direct access to the highest circles of Government during the war and after the war. This was one of the more significant developments in their wartime experience. Under Tory rule, or Labour rule, they were quite aware—as President Carron of the AEU would soon prove—of their ability to pick up the phone and win a ready 'I'll have the kettle on' invitation from a Minister or his Parliamentary Private Secretary. This of course nettled the MPs, who regarded it as poaching on their functions. Fred Lee, Chairman of the Engineers' Group (1951–64), recalled making a formal complaint on behalf of the group of MPs to the Executive Council that the union's officers were going directly to the Ministry of Labour under the Churchill Government. In 1965,

[1] Harry Eckstein, *Political Pressure Groups* (Palo Alto, California, Stanford University Press, 1960), p. 27.

[2] Trades Union Congress, *Trade Unionism*, Evidence to the Royal Commission on Trade Unions and Employers' Associations (1966), p. 1.

when Lee spoke of the conflict, he was already a Minister in the Labour Cabinet, but he still clearly retained a resentment over this slighting of the MPs: 'Winnie was pretty smart. He told Monckton [Sir Walter, later 1st Viscount, the highly regarded Tory Minister of Labour] to keep the door open so the unions could go directly to the Ministry and ignore us.'[1]

Such access and acceptance, even while Lee and other sponsored MPs bemoaned it, was, of course, a demonstration of the new status accorded to trade unions in the highest levels of Government. However, for the man—no women were sponsored as of 1966—who entered Commons through his national union's programme, it was often a shock to be confronted by this bewildering indifference from his sponsors. The resulting grievance of many of the newly elected MPs against their union was summed up by one of them in the plaintive comment: 'They go all out to get us here, and then don't seem to know what the hell to do with us. They let us scatter to the winds.' At the same time, the vast majority found themselves under the tight discipline and direction of the Parliamentary Labour Party: as long as their vital interests were not threatened the AEU and other unions were content with this arrangement, both under Tory and Labour rule. Of course the unions and the MPs recognized also the strong restraint of Party discipline. They knew also the constitutional limitation against a sponsoring organization dominating a Member, who remained the representative of his constituency. Crossman also questions, in his introduction to Bagehot, whether there is room for the back-bencher to carry out his own will, attend to his constituency's needs, or his sponsor's wishes, while the current dominance of both Cabinet and Parliament by the Prime Minister continues.[2]

Within those drastic limitations on all contemporary back-bench Members, however, the individual sponsored MP may fulfill valuable functions for a trade union—provided the union is actively seeking tangible change through the legislative process. With a large block of Members, a union might be able not only to influence the choice of the Party Leader, but also policy decisions made in the Parliamentary Party meetings, which are held three times per fortnight. In addition to these channels, the Parliamentary Party's 'Area Group' and its special groups; the House of Commons Select Committees and Standing Committees; the Question Time and debates—all these provide MPs, who have knowledge and expertise, an opportunity to exert pressure on behalf of their sponsors.

[1] Interview (11 April 1965); cf. Harrison, op. cit., pp. 296–7.
[2] R. H. S. Crossman, MP, Introduction to Walter Bagehot, *The English Constitution* (London, Fontana, 1965), pp. 19–22.

Some of the AEU–MPs did bring their knowledge to bear in the House of Commons on general trade union and engineering problems, but they were apt to do so contrary to the union's plans, and without union authorization or even knowledge. The Executive Council exercised, in practice, a minimal legislative or ideological direction over their own MPs.

Yet, the two Left Wing Executive Councilmen, as well as the Right Wing majority, were solidly behind the expanded programme. Hugh Scanlon, the Left's leading candidate for President to succeed Sir William Carron in 1967, told this writer in several interviews that the union had impressed the entire movement by its achievement in MP selection. Even the, by then, lone Communist Party member of the Executive Council, the late Claude Berridge, stressed the 'working class content' given Parliament by such a large group of skilled manual workmen. 'The special value', as Berridge put it, of Engineer MPs arises from 'their tradition of militant unionism, their higher level of education, and their knowledge of industrial skills.'[1] (The Communist Party itself after 1956 had reverted to a generally 'support-Labour' stand and fielded relatively few of its own candidates.)[2] The Right Wing's leading spokesmen were officially committed to a policy of non-interference with the MPs. Yet it will be seen below that both Left and Right found what was to them vital non-legislative uses for the sponsored Members.

Meetings of MPs and Executive Council

There is a formal structure created by the EC for purported liaison with the MPs. It consists of a quarterly meeting of the two groups at the House of Commons, in a private dining room. The minutes afford us an unusual perspective on this little known phase of Labour politics. These documents reflect some of the economic, as well as the political, problems of the union, and the remarkable structural deficiency which has hampered their resolution.

Each year the National Committee 'instructs' the Executive Council to work for dozens of specific legislative and political measures. And each year the Executive Council reports back to the incoming delegate conference substantially as they did in 1954: 'The AEU Parliamentary Group has continued to give its close attention to matters concerning the interests of our Members.'[3] One would assume that the Group would be given the National Committee's

[1] Interview (6 September 1965).

[2] For a view of the Communist Party's 1964 electoral role, see D. E. Butler and Anthony King, *The British General Election of 1964* (London, Macmillan, 1965), p. 355.

[3] *Report* (1954), p. 126.

and the Executive Council's views on legislation at the quarterly meetings. In practice, however, these quarterly meetings are only peripherally concerned with political issues.

An analysis of the minutes for 1962–65 reveals how thin is the legislative gruel which accompanies what one official termed the 'nosh-up' at the Commons. The minutes themselves are unfortunately only a rough guide to the actual discussion: they are based on notes taken by the Assistant General Secretary. He performs the same function for the Political Sub-Committee. Both are summaries rather than full minutes, but they are the only known written record of subjects covered, and give some clues to actual discussion.

About half of the estimated sixty-two separate agenda items discussed by the MPs and the Executive during that period deal with specific redundancies in an area, a plant, or an industry. Most of these problems are disposed of with a notation that a Member would table a written or oral question for the Minister involved. Occasionally, the matter is referred to another Labour MP who is working on a relevant Parliamentary Party or Commons Committee. Fourteen of the sixty-two items deal with the merely technical and largely trivial matters concerning the parliamentary panel and the group itself, such as the role to be played by the incumbent MPs at the school; the nature of the examinations to be given; comparisons of the sponsoring methods of other unions, and, most frequently, the arguments between EC and the MPs over payment for clerical assistance. The financial arrangements, in fact, occupied at least half the time, and accounted for most of the heat, for example, at the post-General Election of 1964 meetings, below. There are only nine items dealing with pending legislation—of varying importance to the unions—introduced by the Conservative Government. Later in this chapter, and in succeeding chapters, we will discuss the more important of these measures, giving the AEU's and some individual MP reactions.

Of the total of sixty-two, three industrial items—a strike in one instance, and wage problems in the other two—were raised by MPs, only to be politely shelved after an EC member paternalistically observed that such items were of no concern to them (the MPs)!

There is no evidence in these minutes of the union utilizing this political channel for advancing general economic proposals *or* specific legislation; although it will be noted that after the General Election of 1964 a few MPs from the carefully cultivated new crop tried to get the union to move in such a direction.

Also conspicuously missing from the minutes, until the meeting of 10 May 1965, is the *Plan for Engineering*, which was cited in 1951 by Jack Tanner as an abiding article of socialist faith when he and the union delegation laid it aside for the General Election of that year. As suggested previously, the *Plan* was the most persistent *official* legislative programme of the union—made official by virtue of repeated enactment at both the National Committee meetings and the Confederation meetings. When the *Plan* was again brought to the fore at the above-named 1965 meetings, it was only as a defence of traditional bargaining rather than signalling a renewed interest in economic planning.

At the same meeting in 1965 George (later Lord) Pargiter, MP, secretary of the group, departed from the accepted procedure of leaving the EC to draft the agenda, and brought up what he termed 'concern in the workshops [over] ministerial statements regarding restrictive practices and modernisation' in the engineering industry. He proposed that EC 'should endeavour to counter these statements'. From this publicity-orientated suggestion there appears to have followed, first, 'a long discussion' led by John Boyd, the EC member in the chair, regarding exchanges that had been held between the union's leaders and the employers; second, a 'general feeling' that EC 'should be looking at a National Plan for engineering'. By coincidence, apparently, Mr Boyd was able to say that at the CSEU annual meetings scheduled for June (the following month), the Executive of that body would be bringing in 'a Plan', adding that 'this could be a useful document to assist MPs in this regard'. This appears to have been the only reference ever made to the *Plan* in the EC–Group meetings!

The Plan for Engineering, in revised form, was in fact brought before the CSEU by the same white-collar union officials who had been piloting it for many years. It again won unanimous approval, both at the CSEU meeting and at the National Committee of AEU. The AEU officers, now the most powerful force in CSEU, seemingly allowed such resolutions to win unanimous votes rather than pointing out economic or technical flaws, or questioning ideological implications, knowing that it would never be taken as a serious goal of the union by the TUC or the Labour Party. Nor, as shown by later analysis, did other major sponsoring unions, also affiliated with the CSEU, show signs of wanting the *Plan* as part of either legislative or bargaining strategy.

The problem of redundancies pointed up the deficiencies of existing planning. This was perhaps the most familiar and the most perplexing problem for both union leaders and Members of Parliament, but not one which lent itself readily to remedial treatment by legislative steps or by standard pressure-type politics. As will be seen from the discussion below of the Contracts of Employment Bill of 1963, the entire labour movement has had difficulty formulating either industrial or political approaches to redundancies within the context of a relatively full employment economy. The problem may have elicited such frequent discussion inside the group because this provided a safe and non-operational outlet for accumulated pressure within the work-places and areas affected.

The group's value as a pressure-release for the Executive Council may be seen from the case of a 1963 redundancy resulting from a shutdown of a factory following a take-over in the private steel sector. The matter had been brought to the attention of the Executive Councillor in the area who had in turn presented the problem to the entire EC. The Group Secretary then was advised of this problem by the EC in advance of the regular quarterly meeting, with a note reading in part: 'members dismayed and angry, [and] are already seeking a method of protesting'.

'It was felt that the three [non-AEU] local MPs had done all that was possible', the minutes note. Despite the apparent finality of this observation, it was agreed that 'the AEU Parliamentary Group would assist and co-ordinate with the [same] MPs on the problems raised by this issue'. In the event, the AEU Group's Secretary merely sent a letter to the Minister concerned; nothing further is reported to have come of it. Clearly, as this brief minute suggests, it was not expected by the MPs or the union that anything *could* come from such an action, but it did give the Executive Council members an opportunity to show 'action' to the Divisional Organiser; and he in turn could say to the District Committee, shop stewards, and the branch involved that the matter had been taken up with the Executive Council, with the union's own MPs, and even with a Minister.

For some years an item for the Members' agenda, and for the National Committee as well, was the question of the banning of an elected District Committee Secretary, Mr Pat Farelly, from the Aldermaston Atomic Weapons Research Establishment. As a member of the Communist Party, he was barred by the Government from negotiating there because CP members had been classified as security risks. The National Committee protest noted that Farelly was a 'democratically elected Secretary and should be allowed to negotiate on their behalf as he does in other places where the Union's members work'. The NC protest had been duly passed on by Executive Council to the group in 1965 as it had in 1964 and 1963. Both Labour and Conservative Governments enforced the security ban on Communists at atomic installations. The minutes indicate, nevertheless, that the MPs went through the motions of protesting in 1965 as they had in previous years. Neither the MPs nor the Executive Council seem to have expected results. This action was apparently perceived as a log-rolling gesture by EC not only for the branch, the

E

65

District, and the National Committee, but also—and especially—for their lone Communist colleague on the Executive Council. 'Claude [Berridge] knows we can't buck this, but at least he can tell his Commie friends something's being done,' explained one of the veteran MPs.

To sum up the documentary phase of the evidence: formal liaison between the Executive and the MPs suggests little pay-off to the union for its costly efforts—either in short-term or long-term economic or ideological goals.

Informal Pressure by MPs

In a series of formal interviews and frequent informal conversations in 1964–5 with Mr Jim Conway, then General Secretary, this writer sought elucidation of his reasons for increased AEU Parliamentary representation as given in the *Journal*, above. Conway stressed, as did others at Head Office, status and symbolism: 'It's a matter of prestige. We are the most important union in Britain. And the men we send to Parliament are *authentic* working-class men.'[1] He was also very much aware that the image of the AEU needed to be brought 'up-to-date'. He had taken office in 1964, after having won election on a platform of modernizing the structure and services at headquarters. He never intended, nor could he have implemented, a programme of change that included an acceptance of work-place bargaining, a shift towards greater authority for the TUC, or a significant alteration of traditional attitudes towards the State. As already indicated, the General Secretary in this union has but very limited authority. In any event the union, as will be seen from its brief to the Royal Commission and its approach to incomes policies, was not deviating from *laissez-faire* policies, even though it did pay lip service to planning.

When pressed for information on concrete use of the expanding MP programme Conway claimed some sectional gain. He said MPs were able to intervene with Ministers, especially Tory Ministers. He could, however, think of only one specific service performed: getting needed home telephones from the Postmaster General for the members of the Executive Council during the post-war shortage!

A more impressive if equally antiquated example of MP intervention at Executive level was given by Executive Councillor John Boyd, Chairman of the Political Sub-Committee. He mentioned a 1952 effort of Charles Pannell, then Secretary of the AEU–MP group, to secure for North British Locomotive Works in Glasgow

1 Interviews (8 December 1964). Conway's emphasis; this was meant to contrast the AEU approach to the T & GWU's reaching out for professional people to sponsor—a point discussed in Chap. IX, below.

track space from British Railways for trying out a diesel locomotive. The union's objective was to help sell the locomotive to the publicly owned British Railways and thereby retain the jobs of 6,000 locomotive workers who had been employed in the production of now obsolescent steam locomotives. Recounting the incident, Boyd showed a wry awareness of how internal pressures can conflict with long-term planning or socialist goals: 'Charlie Pannell got on the radio to boast of our success. But I got flooded with protests for helping a private enterprise against the [nationalized] workshops of British Railways.' Grinning at Conway, who was present at the informal conference, Boyd added: 'That theory is fine, but jobs come first, eh laddie?'

The extemporaneous and job-orientated quality of these interventions is suggested by a conflicting bit of pressure applied by the Executive Council. At the very time of Pannell's achievement for the private enterprise shop, the EC had referred to the group a National Committee resolution with an opposite purpose: the NC had asked, and the EC in turn now asked the MPs, to take up with a Parliamentary Committee dealing with Road Transport matters the possibility of getting more diesel locomotive-building work for the publicly owned shops of British Railways! One of the two MPs assigned to that matter by the group was the same Charles Pannell, who had also earlier that year boasted of helping to win the scarce locomotive orders for the private shops. For the latter effort the MPs even asked for assistance at the Research Office, which was a rare involvement of the union's staff in parliamentary work.

In seeking to ascertain political purpose of a union, pressure on the government is but one of several dimensions. Conway was asked also about the group's role in pending legislation, and the union's interest in new legislation. He replied by citing the helpful contributions of John Robertson, an AEU–MP, to the debate on the then recently enacted Contracts of Employment Bill (1963). Ironically, as our discussion of the Bill in the next chapter suggests, Robertson used the occasion not to transmit his union's views, but to unfold an analysis of the inadequacy of the existing structures to cope with modern industrial relations. The Bill is again cited in our analysis of the Trade Union Group's activities (see Chapter VIII), to illustrate the political passivity of the union movement as a whole during the period.

Was the union hoping for new legislation to emerge from the group's activity or from other channels? Conway's response to this question came with a marked uncertainty that was in striking contrast with the clipped incisiveness he displayed on the mechanics of the parliamentary panel or on trade union economic questions:

he 'supposed' bills on safety and vacation pay might be helpful. His tentativeness on such legislation was understandable: the TUC General Council and successive British Governments have avoided statutory solutions to general safety problems, except for a few 'safety supervisors' in some industries on the ground that the voluntary spirit in industrial relations might be stifled;[1] holiday pay in engineering industries is largely a subject for industry-wide bargaining.[2]

Direct Pressure

The nebulousness of the union on political matters as previously shown is not constant. When a central union interest such as a break-away is involved, the union can intervene with the Government directly, and forcefully. For example one of the more precise positions of the AEU President before the Donovan Commission in 1965—a statement that will be seen as noteworthy for its ambiguity on strikes—was his assertion that the union, which otherwise deplored 'unofficial strikes', would look with favour on them if they were directed against 'splinter organizations'.

The normal concern of a national union leadership about an outside challenger might have been heightened for the AEU by the shift towards work-place bargaining. For the case at hand, General Secretary C. W. Hallett, early in 1964, wrote directly to Denis Healey, Shadow Minister for War, giving him a precise summary of the break-away threat by a group of technicians functioning under the banner of the Aeronautical Engineers' Association (unaffiliated to the TUC) and employed in the War Department. Hallett explained that when the break-away first occurred, in 1961, the AEU had been assured by the War Office that no action would be taken to threaten the interests of the AEU.

When some members of the break-away Association had decided to work to rule in 1963 the War Office asked the AEU to carry on, and they evidently agreed to maintain their regular work schedule. The occasion for the AEU letter to Mr Healey was a report sent in to the Head Office by the District Secretary at York, where the Association was centred, reporting that some of its members had been present at a political rally addressed by Healey and had interested him in their 'alleged problems'. The Shadow Minister was now warned against becoming involved 'quite innocently' with the rival

[1] W. K. Wedderburn, *The Worker and the Law* (Harmondsworth, Penguin, 1965), pp. 170–1.
[2] Milton Derber, *Labor-Management Relations at the Plant Level Under Industry-Wide Bargaining* (Champaign, University of Illinois, Institute of Labor and Industrial Relations, 1955), p. 35.

group. A prompt reply came from Healey's office announcing that the War Office had been contacted and that they had no intention of dealing with the rival union. While this transaction with the Conservative Minister and the Labour Shadow Minister underscores the dispensability of the MP, if and when the union elects to use its own power, a key analytical point is that the union was here depending more on its industrial power than on its political power—as it had all through the period.

Chapter IV

Measuring Grass Roots Commitment and Activity

To what extent did the Head Office commitment represent, and influence, the political thinking of the membership? Answering this question requires some analysis of the levy payments; of the nature and degree of branch affiliation; and of the District Committees' affiliations and activities.

The *a priori* inference from the AEU literature quoted, and from customary trade union practice is that the union, or at least its leaders, decided that they needed more MPs, and this need became the incentive for the members to pay, and the leaders to disburse, the needed funds. We have seen from the foregoing, however, that the familiar ideological goals embodied in the Labour Party Constitution and also in ceremonial literature of the AEU formed no significant part of political purpose in the years of intensified, nominal political commitment. Moreover, the men sent to Parliament, although they represented a significant addition to the union's representation—both quantitatively and qualitatively—were not assigned substantive legislative goals by the responsible Executive Councilmen. Indeed there was really no expectation of direct economic or long run political return from the heavy commitment of funds and energies. *A posteriori*, there were several autonomous variables in the shift in emphasis from a rather formal relationship with the Labour Party to the close and warm stand taken by the union after 1951.

The Levy

The growth of the political fund may itself have been an independent influence in the EC's decision to enlarge the group. 'Parkinson's law' states that expenditures rise to meet income. Here, as in other unions, growing amounts of unexpended funds helped to create a demand for political expression. This accumulation of funds, in turn, was primarily the result of union growth and cannot be equated with a high degree of political interest and commitment.

It is common knowledge that union affiliation funds supply the Labour Party with financial stability. The collection and disbursement of these funds is governed largely by the Trade Union Act (1913). That Act affirmed the right of a trade union to engage in political activity along with any other lawful activity, after approval by a majority vote of the membership voting, and provided also that the political rules are approved by the Chief Registrar of Friendly Societies. Political activity has to be paid for out of a special fund, and members must be advised that they may *contract out* of the fund.[1] In 1927 the Conservative Government, in the Trade Unions and Trades Disputes Act, reversed the contracting-out process: members of unions affiliated to the Party desiring some part of their dues money to go into the political fund were required individually to sign a 'contracting in' form.

In 1946 the Labour Government once again reversed the collecting process: since then, in general, members of unions with political funds pay the levy which has remained the main source of Labour Party funds. After analysing records of the Chief Registrar and other relevant data, Harrison concluded that while there are no reliable official statistics on either the number of people actually signing the official contracting-out forms, or the number paying the political levy, the number of contributors between 1945 and 1947 had risen by two million. The rise, according to Harrison, is to be attributed to the simple administrative change from contracting-in to contracting-out.[2] The Labour Party's own figures on affiliated and individual memberships reveal that at the end of 1963 the total of union-affiliated Labour Party members was 5,507,232; by contrast, the overall total of individual members of the Party—men and women, union and non-union—totalled only 830,346.[3]

In the AEU, as shown in Appendix I, the number of members credited with paying the levy increased from 172,395 in 1945, to 208,344 in 1946; it then leaped to 608,721 in 1947 (the first full year in which contracting-out was effective)—or 25 per cent, 29 per cent,

---

[1] B. C. Roberts, *Trade Union Government and Administration in Great Britain* (Cambridge, Mass., Harvard University Press, 1956), Chap. 17.

[2] Harrison, *Trade Unions and the Labour Party* (London, Allen and Unwin, 1960), pp. 34–6. See also McKenzie, *British Political Parties*, revised edn (London, Mercury, 1963), pp. 483–4 and Roberts, op. cit., pp. 370–1.

[3] LPCR (1964), p. 51. For 1970, according to Harry G. Nicholas, Party Secretary, the sixty-seven affiliated unions paid the Labour Party affiliation fees for 5,518,520 members—virtually a stand-still since 1964. The individual membership figure was down to 680,191; Nicholas stated that the actual figure would probably be less than 500,000. The larger figure, which appears each year in Conference *Report*, is based on the presumption that all parties paying the £75 required for attendance at the Conference collected it at the rate of $7\frac{1}{2}$ new pence per member, or 1,000 members. But many CLPs that pay the £75 have fewer than 1,000 members. They simply tap sources other than the individual membership fees. Interview (2 July 1971).

and 82 per cent respectively of the entire United Kingdom membership. By contrast, in Northern Ireland, where the contracting-in feature has been retained, the members continued to pay at about the pre-war rate which has stayed close to the rate paid in the U.K. before the change in law. Thus, in 1950, for example, the rate was 23·3 per cent in Northern Ireland, whereas the U.K. members were then paying at the new norm of about 81 per cent. (In *most* years the Executive Council omits the Northern Ireland data. As explained in a 1950 *Report*, 'an introduction of their figures into the comparison would be extremely misleading'; this was a reference to the annual printed report on levy payments, which then merely mentions 'little change' for the Northern Ireland District Committee fund.)[1]

Once affiliated, collection of the levy tends to be automatic. It takes knowledge and initiative, at the very least, to contract out. The AEU Rule book contains the elaborate model rules approved by the Registrar to make sure that the individual member both knows his rights, and is given a clear procedure for exercising his rights to withdraw. However, largely because of high turnover since the end of the 1939–45 war, the typical AEU member has been a member for only about a year; he rarely goes to the branch office where the contracting-out forms are located, and he isn't likely, in any event, to read the complicated 196-page Rule book. He may not even know that there is a distinction between his regular contribution and the levy since the bureaucracy-enforcing general practice among collectors at the work-place or the branch is to 'compound' the two to arrive at the combined sum which the member pays out weekly as a total contribution—the weekly dues and the pro-rated quarterly levy. Thus bureaucracy is strengthened in the name of fiscal efficiency. An AEU member may find out about the fact that he is paying a levy that is not obligatory only when he has become in arrears in his regular contribution, and faces 'exclusion'.[2]

---

[1] NC *Report* (1951), p. 205; NC *Report* (1950), p. 170.

[2] John Robertson, AEU Assistant Divisional Organizer (now MP), *Report on Membership, Mid-Lanark District* (1953) (mimeo). Goldthorpe *et al* found in their 1962–4 interviews of 'affluent workers' belonging to AEU and other unions in the motor car industry that about 70 per cent were contributing to the levy, but that 'in all [occupational] groups except the craftsmen from a third to a half are making their contributions without realizing this; that is to say, either they do not think that they pay the levy but have not contracted out or they admit to having no knowledge of the levy at all . . . only among the craftsmen [do] a majority of the unionists pay . . . and know that they do. . . .' In these samplings the levy and union dues were 'compounded'. John H. Goldthorpe *et al.*, The *Affluent Worker: Industrial Attitudes and Behaviour* (Cambridge, Cambridge University Press, 1968), pp. 110–12.

Table I. *Contracting-out Trend in AEU*

| Year | Contracting-Out | |
	Number	Per Cent
1947	131,749	17·8
1948	135,803	18·1
1949	104,271	15·2
1950	123,992	19·1
1951	136,360	19·2
1952	144,390	19·9
1953	161,866	21·8
1954	189,305	23·3
1955	170,898	20·8
1956	191,469	22·4
1957	192,675	22·3
1958	191,840	21·6
1959	202,933	22·3
1960	205,801	21·2
1961	208,791	21·3
1962	207,375	21·0
1963	212,889	21·7
1964	236,608	23·4

Source: Calculated from data supplied by AEU Finance Department.*

We have seen the persistent Head Office exhortations linking the levy with union ambitions for an enlarged representation in Parliament. Were the members responding to this as a need of their union? If the added MPs had been an important incentive to the membership, *ceteris paribus*, there should have been some corresponding rise in the percentage of members paying the levy after 1950, when the Parliamentary effort became so prominent a part of the union's national activity. The absolute numbers paying into the political fund increased steadily, as shown by the 'total income', as well as by the total number of members paying, in Appendix I. But this table also shows a small but steady decline in the percentage paying the levy. As a rough approximation of the numbers and percentage contracting-out we assume that all who did not make the

* A set of supplementary figures for the years 1964–70 supplied (and rounded out) by the General Office indicate a mixed trend. On the one hand the 1964 figure used above, based on preliminary data (see Appendix I), was corrected from a 76 per cent payment rate to 82 per cent, leaving only an 18 per cent figure for contracting-out that year. From 1965, through 1968, however, there was a steady decline in the collection rate—from 77 to 72 per cent. The rate rose again in 1969 to 76 per cent, and in 1970, to 78 per cent. For the latter year, the membership had reached 1,130,668, and the imputed figure for contracting-out would be 249,110. Letter (16 September 1971) from J. Conway, General Secretary.

payment effectively withdrew, even if they did not sign the official contracting-out form. On this basis, as shown in Table I, there has been a rather steady upward drift in the number and percentage opting out of the political fund. Indeed the highest percentage increase of withdrawals from the fund took place between 1963 and 1964—when the union made its large advance in electing its own MPs. Since this was also an exciting period of Labour activity— the year of Labour's preparations for what appeared to be a good chance for electoral victory after thirteen years of Tory rule—there should have been more than normal incentive among the rank and file for maintaining the levy payments.

These figures on the number contracting-out, as well as the increasing rate of such withdrawal, strongly suggest that the MP programme has not been seen by the average member—whatever his attitude towards the Labour Party—in the same light as the officers presented it, i.e. as representing 'the interests of engineers'; nor has he responded to the more general appeal sometimes voiced of 'the political interests' of the Union.

Even the National Committee, whose proneness to political resolutions is famous in Britain—a phenomenon we explore in Chapter V—apparently did not regard its sponsored members as relevant for political action: of 204 political resolutions introduced at the 1964 delegate meeting—those resolutions requiring implementation by Parliament or by a Ministry to achieve their purposes —only four so much as mention the MPs.[1]

In sum, we have the official policy-making body (NC) virtually ignoring the MPs for political policies it considered important for the union, the governing body (EC) indifferent to new political policies despite a heightened interest in greater union representation, and an increasing proportion of members demonstrating their desire to contract-out of the political fund. But the total sum available to the Executive for political action was increasing. This increase was attributable to membership growth, especially after 1951: in rounded sums from 711,000 in 1951, 907,000 in 1959, to over 1,000,000 in 1964.

In 1961 the EC, citing a report prepared by the Political Sub-Committee on the accumulation of unexpended balances in the political fund, decided to direct more money into the parliamentary programme. The Executive Council, according to the minutes of its Political Sub-Committee (PSC), gave no consideration to alternative uses of the fund, such as greater grants to the Party or for more political propaganda. Nor did it weigh the possibility of reducing

---

[1] Calculated from NC *Report* (1964), pp. 148–227.

the levy, in spite of the fact that the PSC had established, first, that there had been annual unexpended political funds of about £6,500; second, that the total unexpended balance for the year ending 1962 would be £113,500. Instead, in 1962, when the Labour Party informed the AEU of a general increase in trade union *per capita* affiliation fee from 9d to 1s, the union took the occasion to double its own levy from 2s to 4s per member per year.

The decision made in 1961 to enlarge the MP strength was thereby given an added financial cushion. The already large balance, it was pointed out by the PSC, would now be supplemented by 'an overall financial gain of 75 per cent'.[1] It was then calculated that a further expansion could be undertaken in the sponsorship plan. (See Appendix II for the financial calculations for this expansion.)

Branch Participation

Having decided on a parliamentary push, the national office advised the branches that the increased levy was needed for 'strong representation in Parliament which assists us in safeguarding the interests of our members'. While such centralization was a quite logical adaptation to Labour Party selection procedures and the evolution of Government at Westminster and Whitehall, the EC found it difficult to develop a strategy for its implementation within the existing AEU structure, at either branch or district level.

It is obvious that the successful pursuit of adoption plans, and meaningful participation in Labour Party politics generally, requires grass roots activity. The grass roots link between organized workers and the political wing of the Movement is at the level of union branch affiliation to the local Constituency Party. The levy is generally collected from the member (usually along with the regular contribution) by the branch. (National affiliation of a union, as we have seen, is no reliable guide to actual involvement or interest of the rank and file member of that union in the Party.) Strangely, however, neither the national offices of trade unions nor the national Labour Party maintain records of branches affiliated, the number of people from branches for whom local Party dues are paid, the amount of the contribution per trade union member paid to the Party constituency, or the aggregate union financial contribution at local Party levels.

The AEU national office receives all levy payments along with regular contributions. The Districts are allowed a third of the levy—enough for branch affiliation to local parties, for District Committee affiliation to the regional parties, and for support of candidacies for local public bodies (city and county councils, urban

1 PSC files, undated memorandum, 'Political Activity, Future Policy'.

councils, and parish councils).[1] Branch affiliation is decided by vote at the branch, but the DC not only finances the affiliation, it also decides how many to affiliate from the branch. The DC, which is considered a bridge between Head Office and the branches as well as the shop stewards (see Chart I) was therefore a key for successful operation of a political programme at the grass roots level. District Committee political operations, however, were considerably less than optimal, as we will see from our examination of (1) branch affiliation to local Parties; (2) the DC affiliation to Regional Parties; and (3) the number of PSCs the Districts established to co-ordinate their political work. (Some scattered data are available for another assigned function, namely, backing local government candidates, but these are inconclusive and beyond the present study.)

AEU Branch Survey of Affiliation

Although some districts made a blanket affiliation of all their branches without waiting for the branches themselves to take the initiative, the total number of branch affiliations appears to have remained rather static. Martin Harrison, in demonstrating that the unions are in a general state of withdrawal from the Labour Party, cited an AEU 1949 survey—possibly the first ever done by them— showing that of 2,034 branches, 1,667 or 82 per cent, were affiliated to their local Parties.[2] In 1963 another rare union survey of branch activity was undertaken by the AEU's national office. By comparison with the 1949 data, there were now reported to be 1,857 branches affiliated out of 2,252 reporting, or again 82 per cent.[3] The 1963 questionnaire sent by the General Secretary to all District Secretaries cited the possibility of an early General Election as the occasion for 'ensuring that candidates with the right qualifications and of the necessary calibre are nominated. . . . EC feels that this concept may be materially assisted by our District Committees nominating and supporting AEU members at Labour Party Selection Conferences.'

Clearly, the proportion of branches affiliating suggests that at this grass roots level, after fifteen years of steadily growing emphasis by the national office, there had been, on the basis of this true measure, little or no progress. It is equally clear that a mere quantification

[1] AEU brief to Royal Commission, op. cit., p. 20.

[2] Harrison, op. cit., pp. 102, 111.

[3] AEU 'Report to the Executive Council on the State of Political Organization within the Twenty-Six Divisional Organizers' Divisions', by C. W. Hallett, General Secretary (17 April 1964) (mimeo). All references, unless otherwise indicated, to affiliation and payments, in this chapter, are from the survey or from the files of the PSC.

at the branch level of affiliation is inadequate for measuring the full depth or significance of the association of the union and its sub-structure to the Labour Party. The adequacy of the branch affiliation figure is limited by the fact that AEU branches range in size from 28 members to 1,500, and the reports mentioned make no breakdown on affiliation by size of branch. Perhaps because the local parties are generally considered to be more interested in the money received from the unions than in the number of people represented by them, the amount of payment per branch to a Party, or the number of members per branch affiliated—either of which would give a better clue to actual strength of the affiliation—were only loosely reported even in this special survey. The EC did receive a total of branches affiliated and a total of members for which affiliation fees were paid but these were rough aggregates from the Districts' reports.

The Districts' returns were summarized at the national office for the Divisional Organizers, who 'provided additional information and amended the figures given by the District Secretaries' in their territories. The responses of the Divisional Organizers ranged from incisive, knowledgeable comments on their Districts, to 'Bro.——— is at a loss as to the type of information we are seeking. He (the District Secretary) does not think he could add to what we have already sent him.' The comments from the District Secretaries themselves, added to the Divisional Organizers' comments, suggest a complex array of union–Party relationships—from virtually total indifference, and even outright hostility, to an intimate matrix of joint union–Party co-operation. From various internal inconsistencies, as well as comments heard at Head Office, however, it appears that for this survey some reports were partly 'filled in' by organizers who could get *no* response or unsatisfactory replies only from their districts.

One basic problem in obtaining either reliable information or standardized procedures has already been indicated in our discussion on structure: the lack of central authority. 'We can't order the Districts to do anything; that's the trouble. So we just have to be satisfied with what we can get out of them,' said one national official when questioned about one of the more obvious discrepancies. (During the 1950s, Head Office had tried to 'proscribe' some DC officers from political work with the union, and this no doubt further complicated the already attenuated relationship. This effort is examined in Chapter V.)

The Districts' determination of how many branches, and how many branch members to affiliate from a branch—even where a branch decides on its own to affiliate—seems to depend only partially on the amount which is remitted to the DCs as their one-third share of political income. According to the National Political Sub-Committee, DC payments to local Parties averaged, in 1962, 6d per levy-paying member. The Tyne District, however, reported in 1963 that it pays the several Parties in the area varying sums, ranging from 3d to 6d per member; in Ipswich and Stowmarket District a flat payment of £2 per year was made to one borough Party, £1 per year to various Constituency Parties. These latter sums were independent of the number of members affiliated: 'I wish to inform you that a fixed affiliation-payment [for each branch] has always been made to the various Labour Parties,' wrote the latter District Secretary.

A branch's payment of fees is not always a sign that it is represented at the Party to which it is nominally affiliated. The Greenwich Labour Party Secretary, for example, complained to the AEU General Secretary in 1963 that three affiliated AEU branches hadn't paid any dues for a year, and that he could get no response to his own letters. In replying to an inquiry about this matter from the General Secretary, one branch secretary said: 'The Branch have had little or no connection with the Party as it is impossible to get a delegate. I have, however, paid the affiliation fee.'

The branches' withdrawal is sometimes attributed to political dissent, but the dissent may originate in the District rather than in a branch. Thus a District Secretary, responding to one of the General Secretary's 1962 letters asking for greater levy collection to support the MP programme, said the contracting-out was increasing because of 'discouragement at the D.C. . . . much of it the result of apathy and disillusionment with the Labour Party in Parliament'. On the other hand, many appeals were received at Head Office from branches and DCs for funds, over and above their affiliation fees, to help some particular parliamentary or local campaign, or the general activity of a Party.

District Committee Activity

Thus far we have focused on the branch-Party link. However, this discussion also suggests how centrally important District Committee co-operation is for political success in any area. Yet the link between the DC and Head Office with respect to political activity has been marked by a surprising display of ambiguity and ambivalence on the part of the latter, and a sometimes ebullient display of autonomous power by the former. The 1947 Rule, centralizing the parliamentary programme in the EC, was implemented by constituting at the Peckham Road headquarters the Political Sub-Committee previously mentioned. While the District Committees were central to the success of the programme, it wasn't until seven years later, in October 1954—and then only with marked hesitation—that a parallel instrumentality was proposed by the EC for the District level. How does one account for this seven year delay? Again, one must look at union structure.

We have seen that on industrial matters the DCs have been traditionally oriented towards the work-place. This identification has become stronger as work-place bargaining has superseded national union bargaining for the determination of wage rates, and conditions of work. This is reflected in the make-up of the District Committees, which include, in addition to annually elected representatives from the residence-based branches, the shop stewards. The latter are elected on the basis of one shop steward for every 5,000 members. These Committees are given the vital 'duty [of] regulating rates and wages, hours of work, terms of overtime, piecework and general conditions affecting the interests of the trades in their respective districts'.[1]

While their economic role and their ties to the membership made the District officials of key importance for successful political work, these leaders did not always see eye to eye with the EC on national Labour Party work. Some were indifferent. Some were in competing political parties,[2] and some were combatting the established Labour leadership by joining in the Bevanite and other left-wing groups. Consequently, in applying the new political rule, the national leaders seem to have been torn: they wanted and sought DC help in getting affiliation of the branches to local Parties, and affiliation of the DCs to the Regional Labour Parties; they also wanted the co-operation of the DC for nomination of suitable panellists, and for finding and winning more House of Commons seats. But because the national officials in charge of the political work had no pressing affirmative political objectives and no control over the selection of members of the District Committees, and little control over their conduct, they moved with great caution. Their ambivalence remained, apparently, even in 1954, when for the first time the Executive Council took a cautious step towards resolving the dilemma. An EC circular letter announced that the governing body were responding to requests from several DCs and 'permitting' (not urging) the creation of PSCs 'in view of our affiliation to the Labour Party . . . and in order to ensure that the interests of our members are fully

---

[1] Royal Commission brief, op. cit., p. 11.

[2] The DC's non-Labour political commitments may influence its decision on affiliating branches to the Labour Party. Thus, according to a national officer closely involved with the political programme, one major DC waits for the *branches* to take the initiative before making the affiliation, largely because the DC officers feel this leaves greater scope for their own District-wide Communist Party activities.

represented'. The anticipated District PSCs were told, however, that they must limit discussion to 'such matters as are consistent with Labour Party national policy'.[1]

This language reflected the well-known fact that the AEU was divided, at least as much as any other union, by the right-wing versus left-wing positions in the Party. The Districts' delegates to the AEU National Committee and to other official meetings were often challenging the orthodoxy of the national leadership of their own union, of the Party and of Congress. The injunction to the largely autonomous DCs was rather obviously Canutean. A more realistic limit was the EC's reminder to the District Sub-Committees that while they were to affiliate to Regional Councils of the Party, they were not 'permitted to mandate delegates': the Party itself bars its Regional Councils from discussion of policy decisions.

Five members of the District Committee, including the President and Secretary, were to be chosen by the full DC; by Rule, the two officers were *ex-officio* members of *all* committees. However, for the PSC the District officers were to be disqualified and others appointed if they did not meet the test of Labour Party membership eligibility. This ambivalence and divided authority no doubt partly accounts for the fact, disclosed in the 1963 survey, that only 49 out of 212 'eligible'[2] DCs in the United Kingdom had established the instrumentality of a PSC for carrying on political activity—some ten years after the national centre had finally 'permitted' it!

The national survey, which was meant to help prepare the union for an effective role in the 1964 General Election, revealed a serious weakness at the District Committee, shop-steward and branch linkage. Although the DCs' formal function as bridges to the shop stewards and the branches would soon be reiterated to the Royal Commission, the tenuous connection for the political function is revealed by examining at closer range several of the major Districts.

Scottish Division

Observing that the Districts vary in the degree of their political activity, the managers of the national programme offered the Districts of the Scottish Division as models of 'political-minded

[1] Circular letter, by General Secretary Ben Gardner (6 October 1954), addressed to 'the District Secretary'. Reflecting the altered factional balance in both the Party and in the union, a circular letter to District Secretaries dated 8 January 1971, makes no attempt to bar DC officers from the Political Sub-Committees, provided only that they pay their political levies to the Labour Party.

[2] An added fifty-five DCs were in Eire, N. Ireland and Scotland, all of which were excluded from the totals. Eire's exclusion is obvious. We have cited the AEU's reasons for excluding N. Ireland. The omission of Scotland is discussed below.

Districts'. Both Conway and Boyd cited the 100 per cent affiliation of all its DCs to the somewhat autonomous Scottish Regional Council of the Party. This optimal figure for the DCs would also suggest a high affiliation rate for the branches, *ceteris paribus*. In actual performance, from what can be learned from the raw returns sent by the Scottish affiliates and from interviews at Peckham Road, this relationship was not so much a display of grass roots political power as it was a manifestation of oligarchical decision-making. It is commonly known that the AEU has been a bulwark of the Party in Scotland for many years; but this decision to affiliate was not an act of volition by the Scottish membership or the DCs in Scotland. The decision was made formally by the Executive Council in the early 1960s, during one of the more critical phases of the Labour Party leadership struggles. The Executive Council had acted on the initiative of John Boyd, the Councillor for the Scottish Division and also the union's representative on Labour's National Executive Committee. As previously mentioned, Boyd had accrued immense authority on such matters, as Chairman of the EC's Political Sub-Committee.

To finance all the Scottish Districts' affiliation to the Regional Council, the General Political Fund of the union was drawn upon at the rate of £1 per 1,000 members. Boyd, in explaining this arrangement, said there were three principal factors: (1) blanket affiliation was simplified by there being no over-lapping Regional Parties, as in other parts of Britain; (2) such affiliation would enable the Scottish membership to rotate the popular position of paid delegate to the annual Scottish Party Regional Conference among all the Districts, rather than confining the 'plums' to those DCs that had formally voted affiliation; (3) a blanket affiliation would maximize the voting power of the AEU in the block voting.[1]

While such affiliation, and the dues payments contributed to the Regional Party, helped strengthen the Party and also constituted evidence of confidence at the national AEU centre in the role of Labour, it hardly established a high degree of organizational support within the union for the Party at branch or DC level. What does emerge from Boyd's comments is that the Regional Conference was viewed at least partly as a means of patronage, without regard to the particular Labour Party strengths in the various districts; and—as later discussion will make clear—the union wanted to maximize its voting strength, not for the purpose of advancing substantive political goals, but for the decisive battles that were shaping up in the Party's leadership crisis.

In any event, the blanket affiliation did not penetrate very deeply

[1] Interviews (December 1964); PSC files.

into the Scottish structure. Officially, the Scottish survey returns were ignored because affiliation on a blanket basis made unnecessary any examination of their branch and district data: 'It was a misunderstanding for those Districts to do that,' Boyd explained to this writer. Thirty-one DCs from Scotland opted to submit returns, individually, however, despite the fact that they had been affiliated on a blanket basis. These individual DC returns disclose that only four of the thirty-one had PSCs.

The number of branches within these four DCs affiliated to local Parties, and the membership on which fees were paid, as shown in these unpublished DC reports, add up to be so negligible a percentage of the total potential that one is led to question the quantitative, or qualitative, meaning of the 82 per cent affiliation credited to the total of U.K. branches. Out of the thirty-one only six—the four above with PSCs, plus Paisley and Ayrshire—show *any* significant branch and membership affiliation. (The AEU Parliamentary Group includes three MPs from these six Districts.)

The quantitative evidence from this survey is patently inadequate for a definitive measurement of the affiliation, although it does point to a serious defect in the over-all DC-party *nexus*. Scotland, despite the official satisfaction expressed, confirms the general withdrawal from the Party at the branch level, even in what Boyd and Conway term a 'political' sector of the union. We now seek to analyse more closely two other major AEU districts, London (South) and Manchester, both of which are known to be relatively active in Labour politics.

London (South) District Committee

This large District, with a full-time Secretary, was extensively involved in the 1964 General Election. It showed a high rate of co-operation with the Regional Party at the DC level. Moreover, London (S.) took a step which is not normally encouraged in the AEU's literature or practice, namely, formally involving the shop stewards in a political mobilization. According to the District's paid secretary, Mr S. Hill, the DC circularized not only all branches, but all AEU shop stewards. The latter, in turn, were requested to make 'a joint approach' to the joint multi-union works committees wherever such bodies functioned; and the joint stewards, it was proposed, should offer the Labour Party Election Agent general assistance and, specifically, 'to see whether workers in the factory would assist by using their cars to take people to the polling booths'. The District Committee, as a whole, voted that overtime should not be worked on polling day, October 15, 'thus ensuring that everybody has ample time to record his or her vote'.

The greatest amount of activity among AEU operatives in this area occurred in the Woolwich Arsenal, the largest employer in the area. The effort inside the Arsenal was carried on outside the orbit of the national union, however, and under the direction of the inter-union Woolwich Arsenal Joint Shop Stewards' Committee. Hill, the AEU's paid official, supplied the name of the secretary of this committee, as the person who knew the political activity that had been carried out in that work-place for the General Election. *Qua* shop stewards, according to the Secretary of the Arsenal Joint Shop Stewards, that body had not conducted political functions before this election. The latter cited possible saving of the Arsenal by a Labour Government as the incentive that had brought about (1) extensive recruitment of canvassers in the work-place for 'knocking up' voters in the constituencies; (2) polling day transportation; and (3) repeated propaganda effort in the joint shop stewards' mimeographed 'Monthly Report'.[1]

For Hill and for the District Committee, on the other hand, apart from the possible momentum generated at the District Office by the steward-led Woolwich Arsenal spurt of activity, the incentive —as far as one can judge from Mr Hill's approving comments about Labour, and his disparaging remarks about Communists, whom he regarded as less than helpful in Labour political effort in this traditionally strong area of Communist Party strength[2]—was their ideological affinity to Labour. It was in response to a communication from the London Regional Officer of the Labour Party to Hill that the District Committee decided to (1) communicate with all shop stewards; (2) plan factory gate meetings for candidates; and (3) get cars and manpower allocated to all the wards in the constituency parties.

The parliamentary programme of our model, if not an actual disincentive, was largely irrelevant to the District Committee secretary and to his District Committee colleagues. While Hill voiced general approval of his union's system of training and choosing members for the panel, he was blunt in asserting that some of his District's nominations for the panel were rejected by the EC because 'they just were too far Left for some people doing the questioning'.[3] He also felt that even after some of his more left-wing Labour

[1] Interviews (17 December 1964); London (S.) District Committee Political Sub-Committee minutes and files.

[2] Interview; cf. C. Berridge, the Executive Councillor for the District National Committee 1964 *Proceedings*, (1964), unpublished, p. 450.

[3] The obverse of this complaint is the same DC's rejection of the request by Charles Pannell MP for their endorsement when he first sought to win a place on the parliamentary panel.

Party members won approval from the Executive Council examiners, and thereby won a place on the AEU panel, they failed to win adoption because Transport House was not co-operative.

Two significant points emerge from this District's pattern of political behaviour in 1964: (1) major electoral action came through the joint stewards' mechanism, which is beyond the control of the national AEU leaders; (2) because of a job threat Party victory may have become the District's central concern. But the District Committee and the stewards were largely untouched by the elaborate AEU Parliamentary organization.

Manchester District

For the same 1964 campaign, unlike London (S.), Manchester's District Committee asked Head Office to co-ordinate activity at the District level. Although complications arose from this proposal, the task was fairly simple: to get the maximum number of workers in all engineering shops transported to the polls on election day. No less than sixteen parliamentary constituencies were reported in the territory covered by the District. Six of these were marginal and in one of the six an AEU-sponsored candidate had been adopted by the Constituency Party. The District proposed to the national Political Sub-Committee that all union strength in the shops should be concentrated on the six marginal seats; and that each shop should be studied for a residence breakdown, 'to direct the workers into the correct constituencies, with the assistance of the Labour Party itself'. A meeting of representatives 'from all workshops and branches' was proposed to 'lead to selection of a General Election officer at each factory'. It was also proposed that District Committee literature be published in conjunction with the Manchester City Party 'directly related to engineers and the General Election'.[1] The District Secretary asked the Executive Council for approval to spend the accumulated District funds for the purpose of such meetings and literature. The response to this request was peremptorily negative: several AEU Rules were cited by the General Secretary to prohibit either political or general funds from being used for the proposition.[2] As indicated in the Scottish discussion, there was no dearth of District money at Head Office.

Such a co-operative plan is quite common among American unions interested in presidential or other national contests. Indeed, without this co-operation by the major national unions concerned, and their assignment of full-time staff, or 'task forces', the official

---

[1] Undated letter, E. Frow, District Secretary, to C. W. Hallett.
[2] Letter, C. W. Hallett to E. Frow (29 January 1964).

co-ordinating body for political activity—the local and state Committees on Political Education (COPE) of the AFL–CIO— would regard their own efforts as less than optimal. In Manchester, however, while the six marginal constituencies proved to be decisive for Labour's majority in 1964, and Manchester is a traditional Engineers' stronghold, there were both ideological and organizational disincentives for the National Office to 'buy' the proposal. Acceptance of the District's plan would probably have meant EC'S rubber-stamping a DC-conceived and DC-executed set of meetings and literature. The DC's own position was known to be Left Wing within the union and within the Party. Moreover the prospective Labour candidate who made the proposal for concentrating DC funds among the designated Constituency Labour Parties, although sponsored by the Engineers, was decidedly to the left of the national union leadership. He had been nominated for the Panel by this DC after having taken a prominent part in the Committee for Nuclear Disarmament (CND), the principal rallying force of the Labour Left against Gaitskell, to whom the AEU governing body was firmly committed. And at least two additional candidates were on Labour's Left Wing. Thus, the *ideological* incentive that seems to have motivated the District for the General Election plans was probably matched by a comparable degree of disincentive at Head Office.

Quite apart from the ideological conflict, there was a basic organizational constraint. The national union has no direct control over the DC and would therefore have difficulty, as already suggested, in winning acceptance of its own views and authority. Moreover, the shop stewards mentioned in the plan, whether they were nominally AEU or other union members, were known to function largely outside the orbit of their respective national union centres.

The general constraint on the national bureaucracy resulting from this phase of the structural evolution of the AEU is analysed in some depth in the chapter which follows—where we seek to link the phenomenon of structural weakness with political action. Our earlier description of how the Woolwich joint shop stewards functioned in the 1964 General Election suggests the key importance of such local cadres, but it also suggests the essential irrelevance of the national union membership cards which a steward might hold.

Evidently, the national office's 1963 survey avoided altogether the question of how the branches and districts dealt with stewards on political matters. One delegate to the 1964 National Committee meeting, after crediting the EC with 'having done an awful lot of work during recent months in extending the political aspects of our Trade Union in Branches', implied that while the survey helped jolt his branch into some activity, it would have been of greater value if a circular had been prepared also for distribution to all shop stewards 'for them to get out on the streets'.[1]

An added factor in the EC's reluctance about accepting the Manchester plan may have been the competition between the national AEU and other large national unions for recruiting and mergers. One competitive element rarely expressed in the literature, but implicit in the officers' concern with 'prestige', is the comparative size—and quality—of the respective MP Groups. In the AEU the parliamentary panel had become by the 1960s a significant element in image-building, not merely for the public but for all workers in the shops.

We have cited some common criteria by which a politcal commitment is commonly measured—assignment of manpower, collection of funds, grass roots organization and response. By such yardsticks of political activity one sees no commitment at local levels comparable to the increased national effort made to add to the number of AEU MPs. Primarily, the lag appears to have been traceable to a low priority assigned to political work for the achievement of either planning, or direct instrumental purpose. Neither the membership nor the officials actually expected significant pay-offs from the added MPs and the associated political activity. This paradox is explored in the following chapter: there we seek to examine some *internal* bureaucratic incentives that may have helped bring about the expanded political commitment of the AEU in the post-war years.

[1] *Proceedings*, p. 447, remarks of E. Johnston (Liverpool).

Chapter V

Political Action for Non-political Purposes

We will deal in this chapter with both structural deficiency and governance problems, and relate these to some major political developments in the 1950s and 1960s as seen from the perspective of the AEU national leadership.

We have seen that one central feature of the historical setting in the period was the decentralization of economic functions. In the trade unions in engineering there was a general shift in the locus of bargaining activity from the centre to the work-place, in contrast with the North American trend towards greater centralization of bargaining activity with its attendant shift of administrative power within the unions. The modern AEU, according to a statistically persuasive study, 'meets most of the standards of the criteria for non-oligarchy and for a moderately stringent conception of democracy'.[1] Conversely, the metal-working industries in the United States have produced highly centralized oligarchic models. Thus, Lipset, citing the steel and automobile industries, noted that a 'dictatorial mechanism' has evolved in the major American unions, as an adaptation to developments in industry: modifications in union constitutions come about from the necessity of a single union, dealing with a few large firms, to prove 'responsibility', in return for winning union security. Modifications defended by the bureaucracy of the union as necessary for contract negotiation, however, are also used to eliminate rivals, or potential rivals. For example, in the closest counterpart to the AEU, the United Automobile, Aerospace, and Agricultural Implement Workers of America (UAW), the Executive sought and won the right to suspend local union officers.[2]

The UAW developed a powerfully entrenched national officialdom which eventually eliminated factional politics and negotiated the bulk of agreements in the automobile and other industries through its centralized bargaining system. This centralization was achieved only after some years of decentralized administration. The AEU

[1] J. David Edelstein, 'Democracy in a National Union: The British AEU', *Industrial Relations*, Vol. 4 (May 1965), No. 3, pp. 102–25.
[2] S. M. Lipset, *Political Man* (New York, Doubleday, 1960), pp. 360 ff.

took a reverse path, showing a tendency to centralized control of the bargaining apparatus when it was becoming a mass union in 1918–20 and reversing the process in the post-World War II years. The general trend to work-place bargaining produced a structural and administrative deficiency which is the key to an understanding of the political activity of the labour movement in general and the AEU in particular:

> At the top, British trade unionism has clearly been hampered in the post-war period by the relatively limited authority of the TUC—and particularly by the latter's virtual inability to guide the economic policies of its affiliated national unions. While at the bottom, it has suffered from the relative failure of the national unions to absorb the largely spontaneous growth of workplace union organization into their institutional framework. This organization they now generally recognize, of necessity; but it was in the first place largely thrust on them by unofficial pressure and is even now not usually fully integrated in their structures. . . .
>
> In each case—at top and at bottom—the key to the situation is the reluctance of powerful union leaderships either to accept greater central guidance or to expose themselves to greater rank-and-file pressure.[1]

As our London (S.) example indicated, industrial relations in the engineering industries by 1964 were characterized by a largely autonomous system of bargaining in the shops by Joint Shop Stewards' Committees. Labour market conditions and the traditional wage patterns of the industry, as well as the institutional atrophy of both the national unions and the principal employers association, all contributed to this evolution of a kind of 'parallel' bargaining unionism.[2]

Lipset perceived the British unions' Labour commitment as a deterrent to oligarchical control, believing that this commitment gave to the membership a potential for influencing internal affairs. Yet the empirical evidence available from AEU files on that union's commitment confirms on the contrary that this commitment was in fact what Lipset elsewhere calls 'a primarily adaptive mechanism of a security-seeking leadership rather than the result of the situation

---

[1] H. A. Turner, *Trade Union Growth, Structure and Policy* (London, Allen and Unwin, 1962), p. 352.

[2] Cf. H. A. Turner, Garfield Clack and Geoffrey Roberts, *Labour Relations in the Motor Industry* (London, Allen and Unwin, 1967), Chap. 7. See also Chap. XIII, below, for more recent industrial and political developments relating to workshop bargaining and the engineering unions' economic and political goals.

of the workers'.[1] Indeed, the MPs, as well as the Labour Party affiliation, will be seen as having played a decisive part in the quest for leadership security.

The AEU leaders vary in their attitudes towards work-place bargaining, but all, even those who are most militant, claim officially, that the shop stewards' autonomy is encompassed through the District Committee 'bridge'. Yet from their experience all the Executive have known for some years that the shop stewards and the District Committees, far from being absorbed in the national structure, have been steadily moving away from the centre. Furthermore the National Committee, the official legislative body, has shown little interest in accepting either industrial or political guidance from the Executive. Partly in pursuit of a solution to the resulting dilemma of governance, there have been innumerable unofficial as well as official contacts with the North American unions, especially with the United Auto Workers in Detroit. In reporting on such a 1965 delegation, Executive Councillor Percy Hanley referred to the political work undertaken by both unions:

> But there is one thing in common with trade unions in both highly developed countries and in the less developed areas, and that is no trade union has any real strength and influence unless it can command the loyalty and the respect of the people at workshop level, no matter how intricate the structure of trade unionism, how elaborate it may be on top, and how close its ties may be with people of great political influence, none of this is a substitute for the leadership role which the trade union can and must play at work-shop level.[2]

Hanley here clearly implied that insofar as the AEU was concerned, this political work was to some extent a 'substitute' for 'the leadership role' at the work-place.

'Swanning Around'

Some months before writing the above, Hanley was asked what he saw as the purpose of his union's professed political programme. He was then attending the three-day 1965 'school' for MPs, as an official examiner of panel aspirants. His answer came in two words: 'swanning around'. He could see no industrial role for sponsored Members; indeed, in his special area of work, transport aviation,

[1] 'The Political Process in Trade Unions', in W. Galenson and S. M. Lipset (eds), *Labor and Trade-Unionism: An Interdisciplinary Reader* (New York, Wiley, 1960), pp. 231–7.
[2] 'Learning from American Experience, Part II' *Journal* (March 1966).

he had to occasionally remind them that 'this is industrial, not political stuff'.[1]

By 'swanning around' Hanley is interpreted here to have meant the ego-satisfaction for Executive Councillors attending the House of Commons 'nosh-ups' with the MPs, sitting on governmental bodies, and other activities associated with the union's role in politics. In the pages that follow, we discuss the 'substitute' functions of the MPs—and Hanley's own use of them as a political simulacrum to divert pressure from below. Later we consider the 'swanning around' function of representation on governmental bodies.

In Hanley's presence the 1963 National Committee meeting adopted a resolution instructing the EC '. . . to use its influence to the utmost through the AEU Members of Parliament, and our affiliation nationally to the Labour Party, to bring about the nationalization of all Civil Air Transport, including Cunard Eagle'.[2] Hanley, the EC member responsible for Air Transport, did not oppose the resolution. Instead he opened with: 'We are hoping to do something about this if . . . we can get a Labour Government.' 'Meanwhile', he added, 'Fred Lee leads for the Parliamentary Labour Party on this question [and] has of course raised certain points.' He also noted that Austin Albu, MP, 'who is a member of the Select Committee on Nationalized Industries . . . has this well in hand', and that John Boyd was on the NEC of the Party. 'Our point of view', he concluded, 'is right to the fore all the way through.'[3] But none of this was a sign of the model's involvement in economic planning in general or industry planning in particular.

At this time the Labour Party had already created a Joint Committee on the Air Transport and Aircraft Industries made up of the Party National Executive and Parliamentary Party members, with Fred Lee as Chairman.[4] Clearly, Hanley and the other union officials present at this delegate meeting could not, under the circumstances, declare a firm programme of action to implement the resolution. They could, of course, readily present their thinking to the appropriate bodies of the movement. The naive might reasonably assume, however, from Hanley's language, that the leadership was endorsing the nationalization idea; that the resolution would be implemented through the union's well-placed people.

Had the EC seriously considered legislation they would have referred the matter to the MPs as a first step, but neither in 1962, 1963, nor 1964, years in which similar NC resolutions were passed unanimously, did the Executive place the matter on the agenda for discussion with the MP Group. Nor—as far as one may judge from

[1] Interview (15 April 1965).   [2] *Proceedings*, p. 242.   [3] Ibid., p. 243.
[4] *LPCR* (1963), p. 32. Boyd was a member of the Committee.

the sketchy 'minutes'—did any individual EC member, including Hanley, seek to implement the presumably official political decision during these meetings at Westminster.

In a general atmosphere of institutional inertia, and lack of overall economic or political vision on the part of the union movement as a whole, it was clearly impractical for a single member of the seven-man EC to push innovative measures in the area of his particular responsibility. Militating against such initiative by Hanley was his awareness that he had some authority and considerable prestige in his capacity as national representative of the skilled men on the joint employee side of the air transport industry. He had helped achieve, and he enjoyed, excellent relations with his counterparts on the employer side—in both the public and private sectors of the industry. He was therefore apparently not keen to initiate any substantive moves that might disturb this relationship, as nationalization or public management might have done. He made it clear to this writer that he had as little use for 'meddling' by political figures in this industry as he had for union leaders seeking titles or 'swanning around' on the political scene. One must conclude that it was the generally insecure leadership position of the Executive Councillors in the NC-EC relationship which impelled him to the above-mentioned political charade at the 1963 National Committee meeting.

The AEU's Political Curbs

While no quantitative yardstick exists for measuring whether the opportunities for discussion were increased or decreased by the national leaders' rising political input, we do have evidence that that commitment provided the bureaucracy with *opportunities* to *curb* democratic procedures and discussion—opportunities that were not available to them through regular union channels. If it can be demonstrated that they *attempted* to make use of these opportunities, it will give additional support to the argument in this study that the political plan was only peripherally related to obtaining benefits for the membership; or in Lipset's phrase, the purpose was not 'the result of the situation of the workers'. On the other hand, the present discussion of AEU activities does not support Lipset's generalization on the value of a political commitment to the practice of democracy. Let us summarize how such limitations were attempted at district, at national, and at branch levels.

National Controls

In the previous chapter we saw the Executive Council belatedly sanctioning Political Sub-Committees for the District Committees.

The EC then felt it could impose restraints on personnel and policies. These DCs, having operated with a high degree of autonomy for so many years, were now informed that for work on the Political Sub-Committees they must select only those individuals who were not 'proscribed' by the Labour Party; that elected officers of the DC, although they are *ex-officio* members of all committees by Rule, must stand aside from the PSC if they were 'proscribed'. In addition, there was a multi-pronged effort to limit discussion and participation in the political decision-making, aimed particularly, but by no means exclusively, at the Communist Party element. The AEU did not follow the policy adopted by many American unions and the Transport and General Workers in the late 1940s, of writing a constitutional ban against Communist Party members serving as officers. The Engineers' long tradition of democracy and local autonomy, the strength and prestige of the CP at the national, district and branch levels, and the relatively weak position and prestige of the national AEU leadership, all probably contributed to an uneasy co-existence policy in this union.

With its increased involvement in the Labour Party, however, the Executive Council felt it could no longer keep its CP colleagues in sensitive political positions. The Labour Party's own ban on the Communist Party was enough to keep Communist officials from Party Conferences, which the rest of the EC attended. It was seen (see Chapter II) that during the honeymoon of the war and immediate post-war years, despite this attendance ban, the Communists in practice joined in, and clearly influenced the EC discussions on political policy, including Labour Party resolutions. The 1947 Rule change giving the EC authority to choose the MP panel resulted in a divorce between the EC majority and the Communists at the political level, despite the Communitsts' subsequent conversion to parliamentary methods.

The new political programme, throughout the 1950s and into the mid-1960s, was administered by a sub-committee chaired, and effectively controlled by John Boyd, a likely choice of the Right to succeed the incumbent William Carron as President. Boyd was certain to face a left-wing slate. However, by the 1964–5 period, when the political programme had assumed expanded size and importance, the entire EC was content with Boyd's administration, i.e. dissipation of it: the Right, which he represented; the Labour Left, as represented by Hugh Scanlon; and even the Communists, as indicated by Claude Berridge's approving remarks, above.

By the mid-1950s the Communist Party was back to a parliamentary emphasis. Indeed, the CP was being accused by some of its resigning officials of having 'an obsession with Parliament'.[1] In the AEU, too, they consistently followed a 'defeat the Tories' line, even when they occasionally filed their own candidates against Labour. They generally paid their political levy and often took the lead inside the branches, the districts, and in the broader communities on behalf of Labour candidacies. On the other hand, many Communist activists, like other activists in the union—including shop stewards—became so caught up with the work-place bargaining and its own bureaucratic processes, that they often had little time or interest in politics (see Chapter VI).

Although there was substantial convergence on political ideology between the Communist group and the Labour group (as the Right Wing generally referred to itself) there was no thaw in the factional cold war. A *de facto* 'debarring' of the CP was invoked by the majority of the EC, not only with respect to attendance at Labour Party Conferences, but in overall political policy-making. This rather tortuous process of exclusion is candidly expressed in the following letter from the knowledgeable George Aitken, Research officer from 1962–1965:

> An EC member is not ineligible for membership on it [political sub-committee] any more than a Communist who is a delegate to the national committee is debarred from participating in the political discussions on resolutions for the Labour Party conference. In both cases, that is to say, they are not debarred. In practice, however, a Communist member of the EC is not elected by his fellow EC members to the political sub-committee and that will remain the case so long as the Communists do not have a majority on the EC.
>
> The only bar at present is that Communists, whether EC members or not, are not eligible for election as delegates to the Labour Party conference.[2]

The closely contested elections for all national union positions— even the organizers are elected rather than appointed as in many unions—made for a high internal political temperature. Control of the union was rarely, if ever, in the hands of any one group or coalition. The 'Labour Group' on the EC was in a majority, but was in a constant state of preparation for contests against various left-

---

[1] Peter Fryer, *Tribune* (19 April 1957). The CPGB in 1964 declared its determination 'to defend and uphold the sovereign power of Parliament and . . . the democratic use of that power to legislate for the people'. John Gollan, General Secretary, CPGB, quoting from 'The British Road', their 1964 manifesto, in *Marxism Today* (July 1964), p. 213.
[2] Letter from Aitken (20 March 1966).

wing candidates. The Left Wing was generally a coalition of left-wing Labour, CP and non-political people. With such polarization, and in the absence of positive political goals, it was perhaps inevitable that the 'adaptive mechanism' of the incumbents, rather than actual or potential inputs into the political work, determined the make-up of the political sub-committee and of the meagre political staff.

The two left-wing EC members were Berridge, a known member of the CP, and Hugh Scanlon, a prominent Manchester left-wing Labour Party member, both able politicians. They refrained from seeking election to the PSC, however, because they knew they faced certain defeat by the majority. Scanlon, although not on the PSC, offered—in outside publications—affirmative political programmes, such as the perennial *Plan for Engineering*, nationalization of the aircraft manufacturing industry, and the syndicalist inspired 'workers' control'.[1] Berridge, we have seen, was quite vocal in his support of the Labour Party. Scanlon could obtain an outlet in the higher councils of the AEU for his political views by his automatic attendance as an EC member who was not proscribed by Party rules at the Labour Party Conference. Berridge, of course, was proscribed by Labour because he was a member of the CP. Both of these EC members could attend the meetings at Westminster with the MPs. But, as indicated, the planning of these dinner meetings and other phases of the MP programme were officially left to the PSC, and, in practice, to its Chairman, Mr Boyd. Scanlon and Berridge were virtually excluded from the planning stage, and little active interest was displayed by them or by the remaining EC members.

Boyd was not only the strong man of the union's programme, he was in many respects *the* voice of the Labour Party inside the union. But he could hardly give his AEU political job the close attention that his PSC chairmanship implied. Like other EC members, he was generally out of headquarters on official union duties for four days of each week, and the fifth was largely devoted to the EC meeting. While he retained authority over policy decisions with only minor checks from his peers, details of the political programme were left largely to the secretary of the sub-committee, who was one of two elected Assistant General Secretaries (AGS). The AGS, the union's most frequent contact with the MPs, occupied a distinctly secondary position in the union governing structure, as many MPs complained when discussing their AEU ties. The AGS, however, was not freed of other, often more pressing, administrative duties and therefore assigned most of the actual details of the PSC to a clerk, who was

[1] See, for example, 'Nationalize Aviation', in *Voice of the Unions* (April 1965); Interviews (1964–5).

himself already burdened with other chores. Thus, not a single full-time person was assigned to the AEU's political work!

Clearly, at the national governing centre, notwithstanding the intense ideological debates in the Labour Party, there was greater restriction of discussion and debate, as well as of administration, than there had been prior to 1951. The incumbent Right Wing was willing to dispense with the input that might have been available from the Left (1) because of the traditional factionalism of the two main power groups in a union characterized by close electoral contests; (2) because of the over-riding importance the Right (and the Left) attached to the not unrelated leadership contest within the national Labour Party. The Left Wing seems to have accepted its virtual exclusion from policy-making and administration without visible protest—although such channels of dissent as the National Committee, the sub-structure of branches and districts, and outside publications *were* open to it. At the EC level the Left's tacit consent to such exclusion may have been due to two additional and somewhat contradictory factors: (1) its own acceptance of parliamentary methods without a well-defined programme but with a confidence (expressed by both Berridge and Scanlon) that the addition of more AEU men in Parliament somehow assured social progress; (2) its own lack of faith in legislative solutions—a scepticism they shared with unionists generally.

Limitations on the Branches' Political Activity

The limitations on the branches' political discussion was also taken up by EC. To limit branch discussion of political differences the EC decided to 're-interpret' Rule 3, Clause 1, which reads: 'Branches may also discuss matters concerning Labour interests generally. . . .' The only constitutional or Rules restriction is that the matter 'does not interfere with the ordinary branch business and is not on questions of a religious nature'. In a circular letter dated 9 March 1950, however, the General Secretary pointed to the 1949 National Committee's unanimous endorsement of the Labour Party for the General Election and concluded:

> Quite obviously this meant that all parties opposed to the Labour party, and Labour government, were to be discouraged, and even opposed. To lend the facilities of the Union to the furtherance of Parties, Policies, and Candidates, opposed to the policy and official candidates of the 'Labour' party would have been in opposition to the policy laid down by the National Committee in resolution No. 38. . . .

In this unaccustomed and obviously strained interpretation and

95

implementation of a National Committee's political resolution the AEU was clearly aiming at Communist Party candidacies, but one may reasonably assume on the basis of evidence already cited that the admonition was prompted also by the rising strength of left-wing Labour opposition. The emphasis on 'policies' is clearly a reference to the Labour Party's official policies as adopted at Conference. Branches of this pivotal union were now engaged in mandating, at least in theory, their delegates to the District Committees, the Divisional Committees, and on up to the Party Conference[1]— often in direct conflict with the position favoured by the EC and the established Party leadership. In the above-mentioned policy letter to the branches, the General Secretary took the unprecedented step of instructing branch officers to withhold correspondence and ban speakers from 'opposition bodies':

A responsibility is placed upon Branch Secretaries to give effect to that part of Executive Council's circular that forbids correspondence from opposition bodies to be submitted to Branches. An equal responsibility rests upon Branch Chairmen to see that if such correspondence is on the agenda, or verbal requests are made at Branch meetings for politicians or speakers of opposition bodies to address Branch Meetings, they should not be submitted to the meeting.

Summarily, at the national centre, as well as at the district and branch sub-structure, the Party's leadership and policy schism provided a justification for restriction on debate and, indirectly at least, on political initiative in general.

Political Influence on Industrial Policy

The customary argument for trade union political action is that such action is essential to safeguard and advance the union's economic position. The reverse of this cost-benefit sequence, that an economic arrangement with the employers was needed to safeguard the Labour Party's electoral chances in 1964, was a principal argument advanced by AEU officers seeking ratification of the famous 'Package Deal'. This also had the *appearance* of a conflict between a national leadership timidly seeking adaptation to the mixed economy and a rank and file determination to hold fast to 'free' collective bargaining.

Negotiated nationally in 1963–4 between the Confederation of Shipbuilding and Engineering Unions (CSEU) and the Engineering Employers' Federation (EEF), this national agreement was known

[1] See Chap. VIII, below, describing the EC's later direct conflict with the National Committee and the Labour Party Conference delegation over Bevan's candidacy for Treasurer of the Party.

to provide merely a general framework for local productivity bargaining at the work-place by shop stewards. It also offered a 40-hour week, higher *minimum* rates of pay, and a precedent-shattering—for British engineering workers—three-year contract term. The National Committee of AEU approved the long-term feature but voted unanimously in a separate resolution to demand also a general wage increase.

The long-term contract has become a feature of post-war industrial relations, providing the framework at least for industrial peace needed for an incomes policy. The union's chief negotiators at this national level of bargaining, the President, Sir William Carron and EC member John Boyd, each attributed his willingness to depart from the pattern of annual general wage increases to the needs of the Labour Party in the forthcoming General Election. Said Carron: 'I don't know what the policies of a Labour Government might be, but I conceive that this could be an element in national stability in following out the policies of the Labour Party.'[1]

Boyd also linked the package to a Labour Party incomes policy and management of the economy. With his eye on the dissenting Left, he argued that 'most of us are hoping for a Labour Government . . . to control profits . . . take control of the capitalist class . . . and this most important union must have a policy which is in line with the Labour Party and Socialist thinking'.[2]

In December of 1964—after the General Election—a recalled NC Meeting was presented with a final draft of the CSEU-EEF agreement, for rejection or acceptance. Two delegates interrupted Boyd's renewed defence of the long-term idea with the assertion that the NC had approved that feature with the understanding that it would be combined with 'the need to go forward for an immediate increase'. Replying for the Executive, Boyd showed his acute awareness of both labour market conditions and the new realities of collective bargaining in the industry by noting that AEU members in the shops would be able to bargain beyond the national minima. Even if an incomes policy should be adopted, Boyd remarked prophetically, and in direct conflict with the stability prospect advanced by Carron, such workshop bargaining could break through the minimum standards of the Package Deal.[3]

For this centrally important bargaining policy problem, the

---

[1] NC *Proceedings*, pp. 99–104.   [2] Ibid., p. 102.
[3] Unpublished 'Report of Discussion on Proposed Memorandum of Agreement between the Engineering Employers Federation and the Confederation of Shipbuilding and Engineering Unions' (mimeographed) (Brighton, 13 December 1964), pp. 16–18. See Chap. XIII, below, for a more extended discussion of the trade unions' approach to incomes policies, especially in the 1967–70 period.

political lamp post provided little light; it did, however, provide crucial bureaucratic support. Several EC members considered that the meetings of both the AEU National Committee and the Confederation were carried by the political argument; that delegates would probably have rejected the plan, and thereby repudiated the officers, had the latter not invoked the Labour loyalty argument. Ironically, evidence from the industry indicates that the formal proposal for the three-year contract was made during the negotiations by the employer. It was accepted simply as a good bargain.

In January 1965, at the very height of national concern with 'cost push' inflation, an EEF spokesman expressed the hope that wage drift could be contained, but he made clear that the national agreement, as both sides knew, would merely provide a floor from which wage earnings could rise: 'If increased earnings arise from increased rate of working or increased production per man, it should be encouraged.'[1]

The union itself removed the political haze from around the 'Package Deal' in 1965; indeed, the AEU cited the same contract as a reason for *reducing* reliance on political techniques! The Royal Commission evidence, below, reads on this point:

> This agreement gives every reason to believe that future negotiations may go beyond wage rates and hours worked to look at a whole range of fringe benefits which are often part of settlements in foreign countries but which have played an insignificant part in our affairs. Perhaps this is because we have always considered social welfare a matter for Government rather than industrial negotiations.[2]

Thus, instead of affirmative approaches to planning at the macro level or even suggesting new legislation for 'social welfare' our model union now looked longingly at the bargaining success of the American unions—but did little about it!

MPs and Politics at National Committee Meetings

It has been commented here that the policy-making body of the AEU, the National Committee, was highly political in its resolutions, and, paradoxically, showed only marginal interest in its own MPs as a channel for implementing such resolutions. Let us explore first, the reason for the unusual amount of NC interest in politics, and second, the unofficial role of the MPs at the annual conference.

[1] A. J. Stephen, statement on behalf of Engineering Employers Federation, quoted in full in *British Industry* (8 January 1965).
[2] Royal Commission Brief, op. cit., p. 9.

Harrison and Roberts have held that the well-publicized leftist AEU political resolutions stem from the indirect method (see Chart I) of electing delegates to the NC. Such indirection, Harrison has observed, is 'normally considered undemocratic in other contexts by the Left. The system has shown itself peculiarly vulnerable to the action of organized minorities.'[1]

Writing in 1955, when Communist-inspired resolutions were common, B. C. Roberts also felt 'a disproportionate number of Communists being elected' was due to the indirect election system.[2] This electoral result did occur in many elections in the early 1950s to the NC. One must note, however, that a disproportionate number of Communist Party members and their supporters were also on the Executive Council and other national positions, which were filled by direct balloting. (In 1955, there were two Communists on EC, out of seven, and two or three of the three National Organizers were reported to have been CP members.) One must assume that their electoral success arises chiefly from their greater organization and interest as well as many workers' discontent with 'the system'. Yet, the declining Communist Party influence in the union in the early 1960s, did not result in significantly lower political temperatures at the National Committee meetings.

The ostensible concern of the Committee for political questions must be seen in the context of structural atrophy and substantive political inertia. In this enormously complex institution the policy-making body continues to be a symbol of democratic debate, but its functional role is now minimal. An alternative hypothesis to that offered by Harrison and Roberts might be that the NC, conceived as an elite corps of lay, elected activists on a par with the top officers in ability, and with the power to control these paid officers are now left with only a vestigial role in the fundamental economic policy question—wage negotiations. *The NC's political activity is thus seen to spring from their being deprived of a more solid functional union role.* Similarly the Executive Council itself also injected politics into the NC meetings at least in part to obscure or compensate for their own loss of authority as a consequence of the dispersal of economic power. In other words, by increasing their inputs into non-operational political activity, the EC as well as the NC could presumably strengthen their leadership images.

In current national bargaining, the AEU is a large but by no means controlling unit in the Confederation of Shipbuilding and

[1] M. Harrison, *Trade Unions and the Labour Party* (London, Allen and Unwin, 1960), pp. 142–3.
[2] B. C. Roberts, *Trade Union Government and Administration in Great Britain*, (Cambridge, Mass., Havard University Press, 1956), p. 170.

Engineering Unions, which bargains for the employees' side. The National Committee has no representation in such national contract or procedural work. At their own annual conferences NC delegates make their views heard and may veto a national contract, but they are in no position to participate in final demands. For work-place bargaining, delegates have no role *qua* NC, although some are shop stewards when elected to the annual conference and undoubtedly are influenced by their identification with such local bargaining.

The anachronistic role of the NC delegates was vividly demonstrated during the ratification proceedings of the 'Package Deal', which, as noted above, had been negotiated by the Confederation (CSEU) and the Engineering Employers' Federation (EEF). For the recalled NC meeting on 13 December 1964, arranged for the purpose of voting on the agreement, Carron told delegates that they would be given a half-hour to read and adjudge the 5,000-word memorandum incorporating the terms, and that they could make NO changes: their options were simply to take it or leave it! When the precisely stipulated half-hour expired, he and Boyd spoke at leisurely length. With the authority of Confederation negotiators, they gave the terms and political as well as economic arguments for ratification. Some 10 or 12 delegates spoke, or asked questions. The entire procedure of ratification was completed in one morning including a tea break.

Lacking a significant functional role, the delegates unquestionably found the two-week conference attractive as a paid, away-from-work experience, a suitable springboard for career building and an outlet for venting their frustration. The loosely structured meeting, with its tradition of free expression, no doubt attracted some delegates who merely sought a platform for ideological propaganda. Attacking the officers and the EC may have not only helped assure re-election as a 'militant' delegate; it may also have served for winning notice as a possible aspirant for higher office. In addition, baiting of the bureaucracy—where there was endemic hostility between lower levels and the Executive—was a surefire tactic for winning at least a minimum of locally oriented delegate support.

The typical political resolution posed little danger of upsetting branch or district arrangements, even if it proved awkward for the commitments of the national officers. We have indicated that the national officers usually ignored—and no doubt were expected to ignore—most such political declarations of policy. Only rarely did they put their own power and prestige on the line publicly and oppose the majority of the NC, thereby producing some famous JANUS positions in AEU policy (see Chapter VIII). Sometimes they sought to head off or change an NC vote by bringing in an MP.

MPs at National Committee Meetings

From the foregoing discussion we have seen that the sponsored AEU Member of Parliament, while perhaps financially and emotionally attached to his union, is remote from its major functions: politically he tends to be absorbed by the Parliamentary Labour Party and for economic policy he is irrelevant and plays no official role. Harrison pointed to the national policy conferences to illustrate the fact that British unions find little economic use of 'their' MPs. He cites the Engineers, where 'MPs have no part at all' in the National Committee conferences.[1] Officially, and functionally as well, his conclusion is confirmed by the Rules and constitutional history which characterize these meetings as select; they are to be attended by lay delegates on a par with the officers, called together annually to 'instruct'—as their resolutions usually state—the governing body. Yet in recent years, MPs have attended, unofficially. One learns about such appearances from occasional oblique references in the mimeographed proceedings; or a newspaper might provide the information. MPs' appearances are *not* cited in the official, printed *Reports*, which are issued as summaries of the conferences, nor are they mentioned in the minutes of the quarterly meetings at Westminster.

What are the reasons for these informal appearances? Motivations of the invitees no doubt vary but, insofar as the bureaucracy is concerned, there is little doubt that it has issued these invitations to strengthen its hand against elected representatives in general and the NC delegates in particular. The 1962 Conference is a case in point. This was a year of bitter conflict over Labour Party leadership. It was, perhaps, a period of more than customary tension between the Executive Council and the sub-structure. After several days of bitter, highly publicized conflict between the President and the NC delegates had once again exposed the weakness of the Executive, John Boyd, a supporter of the President, proclaimed the EC's hopes for the outcome of the power struggle:

> The Executives have been elected by the rank and file members to be responsible for the government of the union, and by God we are going to be the government. As an executive we are not prepared to delegate our authority or one iota of it to shop stewards, district committees, national committee or anyone else.[2]

While Boyd was addressing himself at the moment to differences over an unofficial strike, the press had already reported intense

[1] Harrison, op. cit., p. 297.   [2] *Guardian* (3 May 1962).

conflict over a major additional industrial question, as well as several political problems. The Confederation had ordered a strike vote among its affiliates, and because the NC Conference was scheduled to be ended before the balloting results were due, some delegates were complaining that there had been too much delay by the EC and the CSEU.

The political problems at the Conference were the familiar ones of nationalization and defence, as well as two new, and not unrelated issues—the Conservative Government's decision to seek entry into the European Economic Community (EEC), or the Common Market, and that Government's creation of the National Economic Development Council (NEDC) or 'Neddy'. These issues apparently inspired Carron to invite Austin Albu, MP, widely known as a 'European', and an expert on planning. These qualities were subordinated to the major task of reinforcing the Executive. In this instance there was no secret made of either his appearance or the function he was to serve. The *Guardian* story was headlined: MP ASKS AEU POLICY-MAKERS TO TOE THE LINE.'[1]

On all these political issues the President was aligned with the 'revisionist' wing, and the NC seemed ready to go along with the 'fundamentalist' wing. Carron was a leading member of the General Council of the TUC, and a frequent spokesman for the Council at the annual delegate meetings of Congress, which were then beset with substantially the same Right-Left issues dividing the Party Conferences. In addition, Carron had already committed himself in favour of entry into the Market, which was still an open question in the Party and in Congress. Advance votes at the AEU's divisional committee meetings indicated that NC delegates would be voting against entry: ten of the twenty-six divisional conferences (which precede the NC, and choose the delegates to NC) had mandated their delegates to condemn the Conservative Party's proposal to seek entry, and none had endorsed the idea.[2]

EEC: 'Common Market' Struggle

Was the President and his EC majority in this instance furthering political action against a political negativism by the policy-making body? As suggested above, some delegates may have been in opposition for no other reason than to advance their own careers, or simply to assert a role against what they regarded as a competing power structure. Others may have had ideological motives. Whatever the motivation of the National Committee or of the Executive, and despite its far-reaching political implications, support of EEC was

[1] *Guardian* (16 April 1962).   [2] NC *Report* (1962), pp. 179–81.

consistent with the belief in a policy of *laissez-faire*. It was not an ideological advance towards socialism. It did not represent an affirmative use of a political technique to advance the economic goal of the AEU. The appeal of Common Market entrance was widespread: of course a broad spectrum of political spokesmen saw it as a move towards supra-nationalism as well as a possible source of general economic gain by Britain. Professor Nicholas Kaldor, however, observed that the then 'fever which gripped our governing classes in 1961–62' for EEC was especially strong among *laissez-faire* economists, notably Professor Hayek. He also quoted Lord Hinchingbrooke, who told his Conservative colleagues in Parliament that many of them were seeking an escape from 'the fear of nationalization, of loss of business enterprise, and of overtaxation'.[1]

Albu warned the delegates that the actions of trade unions were often interpreted by the public to be the same as Labour Party actions, and this image hurt the Party's electoral chances. In addition to this general caution on political activism he pleaded for an 'open mind' on Britain's entry into the Market, which was then the official Labour Party line, while the line of the Labour Left was outright opposition. In the event, the Conference vote on entry into the Market was sufficiently vague so that the union was not at direct odds with the Party's declared position.[2]

On the issue of NEDC ('Neddy') Albu pleaded against adoption of a widely circulated critical resolution. Since Carron was slated to be one of six 'Neddy' representatives of the General Council of the TUC, adoption would clearly have been a direct repudiation of the President.

The issue of NEDC was not officially resolved. Although two Divisional meetings—apparently determined to maintain their traditional 'free' bargaining—had adopted identical resolutions rejecting NEDC, viewing it 'with grave suspicion' as a means of 'stabilizing the present unjust and inequitable [*sic*] division of the National Income', the matter, significantly enough, was not reached on the NC agenda, and was therefore referred to EC.[3] But the TUC General Council and Congress, as Carron and Boyd observed to the 1963 NC meeting, considered Neddy as a step towards growth and therefore supported it, and voted to participate.[4]

[1] Nicholas Kaldor, 'Escape from Socialism', *New Statesman* (26 July 1963).

[2] *Guardian* (16 April 1962). As is well known, the Wilson Labour Government pressed for entry into the Market, but Wilson later opposed the Heath Tory Government's decision to do so. See Lord George-Brown, *In My Way* (London, Gollancz, 1971), Chap. 11.

[3] NC *Report*, pp. 135, 270.

[4] AEU *Proceedings*, p. 135; TUC *Report* (1963), pp. 266–7, 383, 389, 487–8.

AEU and 'Neddy'

Harold Wilson, during the 1964 General Election, told a union audience: 'Neddy, if it is going to be a reality, is a blueprint for Socialism, which alone can turn an academic exercise into a national plan.'[1] But when the General Council first decided to embrace Neddy, the Conservatives were in power, pursuing now, as all post-war governments had done, a form of indicative planning that was widely prevalent in Western capitalist countries. Since the AEU's involvement stemmed from the Council's decision to participate, it is useful to recall that the latter never intended, when it made that decision, to utilize NEDC for the significant industrial and social changes that the words 'national planning' imply to some. Indeed, the Council's involvement was not in conflict with the General Council's *de facto* philosophy of *laissez-faire*.

Recounting the origins of the NEDC and the General Council's vital role in its formative stage, Andrew Shonfield in *Modern Capitalism* asserts that the Council preferred a 'corporatist character' NEDC, holding out for a 'tightly-knit body of powerful men representing the major interest groups'. The Council, he writes, was responsible for the Government's decision to drop the idea of 'a powerful contingent of independent members' who might have forged initiatives for growth. Almost as soon as the NEDC held its first meeting in 1962, the 'trade union members were complaining (privately) that the employers sitting on the Council were altogether too experimental and bold in the ideas which they put forward: these men, they said, were quite "unrepresentative"—as the trade unionists knew better than anyone from their own contacts with the average British employer'. One should add that according to Shonfield the Government itself gave only the most minimal co-operation to the Council; that information on Government consumption, 'the key element in French economic planning', was kept from them by the Treasury's permanent staff.[2]

It will be seen from later discussion that the Labour Government of 1964 made incomes policy a central feature of its planning effort, creating for that purpose (among others) the Department of Economic Affairs (DEA). The General Council continued its support of NEDC, and gave lip service to wage restraint. It insisted, however, on retaining NEDC as a separate agency, fearing that the unions' underlying objective of maintaining post-war high employment levels

[1] Speech to Biennial Delegate Conference, T & GWU (1963). Reported in *Daily Herald* (9 July 1963).

[2] Andrew Shonfield, *Modern Capitalism* (London, Oxford University Press, 1965), pp. 152–4; cf. Lord George-Brown, op. cit., Chap. 5.

would be endangered if Neddy's separate staff should disappear into the Treasury, via DEA. The General Council could exert influence on an independent agency, but it regarded its influence at the Treasury, which preferred a reduced level of employment, as minimal.[1]

Thus, the General Council had displayed genuine political action with regard to NEDC but it continued to abstain from affirmative social reform or serious planning proposals. The latter would have run counter to the immediate bargaining goals of the various TUC affiliates, including the AEU.

At the AEU in the period 1963–6, under both Tory and Labour rule, the small research staff made 'Neddy' studies and papers a principal task, in order to brief for the central NEDC meetings Carron and several other EC members who took places on 'little Neddies'. Thus NEDC was in fact made a concern of the AEU as well as an official TUC function. Yet, it is interesting to note that Albu, an authority on planning, who had taken the trouble to 'sell' NEDC to the policy-making body, was apparently not consulted at any time by the governing body of the AEU or its research staff, or the Parliamentary Group.[2]

What is the significance of the British movement's connections with NEDC and other important national bodies? The noted North American authority on Britain, Beer, saw in NEDC 'functional representation' by labour.[3]

The most 'social' of American union leaders, UAW President Walter Reuther, cited the NEDC-TUC ties as a model for participatory democracy and consultation at the highest levels of government.[4] Such recognition, largely absent in the planning efforts of the advanced democracies of the United States and France, is clearly a symbol of the British labour movement's high status in society.

Status, indeed, may be the principal residual gain; and it is not altogether clear whether this gain accrues to the individual officers, to the institution or to both. Percy Hanley, the Executive Councillor, was firmly on the Right. Yet in his article for the *Journal*, above, and in his verbal comments, Hanley stressed the lack of significant gain for the institution, seeing only personal triumphs for his Right Wing colleagues then in power from their 'swanning around'. A

[1] Interview with L. Murray, then Research Officer, TUC (13 March 1966); cf. Trades Union Congress, *Report* (1963), pp. 266–7.

[2] Interview with Hon. Austin H. Albu, Secretary of State, Department of Economic Affairs (8 March 1965).

[3] S. H. Beer, *British Politics in the Collectivist Age* (New York, Knopf, 1966). p. 71.

[4] UAW, Nineteenth Constitutional Convention , *Report of President, Part Two, Economic Conditions* (1964), pp. 106–7.

rather different, but not conflicting view, came from a research officer assigned to preparing Neddy papers for the union's leaders. Asserting that little was achieved by such representation, he saw the Neddy-type activity as one phase of a general public relations approach necessary for the union leaders to maintain some sort of unified organization on a national level: 'Let's face it: the National officers can't really do much today; the action is taken in the shops. To keep the organization together it requires a man with connections, titles if you can get them, and respectability.'

The engineering industries were, of course, of pivotal importance in any planning effort. However, the *Economist*, in reporting on the tasks facing a newly appointed full-time professional NEDC executive, declared he would have to 'make contact at the real grass roots of industry, especially in heterogeneous industries like engineering'. To do so he would have to 'liaise with the 80 or so trade associations concerned and secondly to develop closer relationships between [firms that were] makers and users'.[1] Thus, in the Neddy closest to AEU interests, the union, by implication, was considered irrelevant by the *Economist*!

Despite the frequent claim of increment to the nation and to the membership from the MP-type work, and from NEDC activity, the 'swanning around' categorization by Hanley has a wider relevance for British trade unions than has been recognized. We have the testimony of a professional publicist hired in 1964 by our model union in the flush of Conway's modernization wave; he had resigned from another major national union to take the AEU post. He explained why he quit the latter: 'They wanted image-building prestige. They don't want policy.' Asked about the NEDC activity, which was by then a conspicuous part of his and other staff work at AEU, he produced a copy of a memorandum he had prepared on leaving his earlier union post, which he felt also defined the general position at AEU with respect to all government consultation and participation, as well as the MP programme:

If the Union proposed to take seriously its membership of the Industrial Training Boards and the Economic Development Councils, then the work of the Research Department would increasingly be geared to brief our representatives engaged in these fields and evolving policies for the Union. . . . Deficiencies in research stem from lack of policy. Our contribution to the work of the trade union side of the industrial Neddies on which we are represented is nil.

The closest approximation to a considered contemporary, overall

[1] The *Economist* (16 March 1967), pp. 944–5.

policy statement by the AEU is contained in its written and oral evidence of 1965 to the Royal Commission on Trade Unions and Employers' Associations, which had been established to inquire into '. . . relations between managements and employees, and the role of trade unions and employers' associations in promoting the interests of their members and in accelerating the social and economic advance of the nation, with particular reference to the law affecting the activities of these bodies; and to report.'

In the next chapter we consider how the AEU answered this broad inquiry and otherwise adjusted to problems posed by the new Labour Government.

Chapter VI

Political Work of the AEU under the Labour Government, 1964–1966

When the Labour Government came into office in 1964 the union movement had no pressing legislative agenda; its overriding political concern, as we have seen, was to maintain the relatively full employment and successful bargaining that had prevailed since the end of World War II. On the Government side, the chronic problem of deficits in the balance of payments and wage inflation determined its dual strategy: to contain incomes and achieve trade union 'reform'.

The AEU's 1965 responses to the Royal Commission's inquiry regarding the role of trade unions and employers' associations avoided direct discussion of incomes policy for reasons that will emerge in this chapter. But there was extended discussion in its brief on the structure of the union, and at least a conditional acceptance of the need to reform at the level which was of central concern to the Government, i.e. 'parallel' bargaining and associated 'unofficial' strikes at the work-place. This bargaining had become probably the most important single factor in 'wage drift' and therefore the most direct challenge to an effective incomes policy.

The present chapter, which concludes the analysis of the main empirical model, is organized as follows: (1) the adaptation made by the AEU and its group of MPs to a Labour Government; (2) the role of the MPs in the response to the Commission inquiry; (3) how the union and its MPs reacted to the initial stages of the Labour incomes policies; and (4) the union structural problems as seen, first, by the MPs, and then as viewed by the union itself for the Royal Commission.

Adaptation to Labour Government

The Engineering Union could take justifiable pride in its own role in the 1964 Labour victory. The union supplied 17 among the 317 Labour MPs. In addition, the Rt. Hon. Fred Lee was appointed to the Cabinet; the Rt. Hon. Charles Pannell was made a Minister;

Hon. Austin Albu would soon be appointed to be George Brown's deputy and a Minister of State in the newly created Department of Economic Affairs. Several of the remaining MPs in the group would be Parliamentary Private Secretaries and Assistant Whips.

With all the care and expense that went into their election, however, the successful Members *qua* AEU Group received *no* formal guidance by their sponsor on the functioning of Parliament or their relations with the Parliamentary Labour Party, or with the union! Formal rules of conduct might have been helpful under any Government, but now the Members were to serve under Labour after thirteen years of Tory rule, most of the seventeen had never served a Labour Government. Seven were new to the House of Commons. The 'finishing school' did expose the newer Members to front-bench Labour Party leaders; the group also had a small corps of veterans like Lee, Pannell, Albu, and others who could provide informal coaching and help in the integration process. But the most able and experienced men became part of the Government, and therefore had less time for such proctoring; they also had a rather different conception of their roles.

The Executive were quite aware of the symbolic value to the institution of having sponsored a large crop of 'authentic' working class Members of Parliament. However, while some of these Members would create challenges to the leadership of the union by seeking an active role for themselves as union spokesmen in the House of Commons, the union showed no interest in making a change from the general political passivity of the movement.

Under Labour, the first two Group-EC meetings at the House of Commons consisted largely of financial details. The MPs had won a substantial increase in salary early in the Labour Government. Relations then became quite bitter over EC's decision to cut off funds for secretarial help, which had been for years supplied by the General Office political fund. The men who had gone into the Government did not need the union's money for office help. Some of the less active back-benchers, especially those from safe seats, decided they could dispense with such assistance, but others, especially the newer MPs who were pressing for an industrial role, insisted that they needed secretarial help and could not afford the expenditure out of their Parliamentary salaries. Some also implied to the officers that they construed this cut as a sign of Members' derogation in the eyes of the union leaders. At the 9 November 1964 meeting, several of the Members, to support their contention that the union should continue the secretarial subsidy, asserted that their work with the Labour Ministers would be increased by the unrest in the engineering trades resulting from the Government's cancellations of major aviation contracts. At this point, according to several present at the meeting, President Carron angrily told these Members: 'I can pick up the phone and get any Minister I damn please!'

Aircraft Cancellations

The sharp point of Carron's riposte was brought home within a few weeks. The danger of immediate redundancy had become a major concern to the AEU and other unions in the Confederation which had membership in the plants working on the already cancelled military TSR-2 and on other, threatened, plane cancellations. Not a single MP, however, was in sight when Carron and Boyd led a Confederation deputation in February 1965 to the Ministry of Aviation to discuss the future of the industry. The far-reaching implications for the economy and the aircraft industry in this cancellation, and the proposed purchase by the new Government of the less costly American planes, made major news headlines for weeks, but 'it was strictly union so no MPs were needed', Boyd explained to this writer.[1]

The formalities of consultation on this Government decision were apparently enough to satisfy the top leaders. Carron verbally informed the 1965 National Committee meeting in April–May that the decision to cancel TSR-2 was a difficult one, but emphasized that the new Government did communicate it to the Confederation and thereby showed 'an earnest of the Government's intention of consultation at the earliest possible moment. . . '.[2] However, the non-sponsored Labour Member of Parliament from Coventry, Mr Maurice Edelman, the well-known novelist and a knowledgeable spokesman for aircraft workers, criticized the Prime Minister, Harold Wilson, and his Government precisely for their failure to consult the unions and the workers involved.[3]

The absence of MP participation as well as the decision of the Labour Government to consult with the key unions only after the fact may well have been at least partly a function of the latters' lack of policy. There was certainly a readiness on the part of the AEU-MPs to respond to union policy. This was indicated to the present writer by Mr George (later Lord) Pargiter, then Secretary of the Group. Asked on the very day of the Confederation delegation to the Ministry—27 February—about Group reaction to the job crisis, he replied that EC had issued 'no orders'; there was 'no policy conveyed to us'.

While Fred Lee, the AEU-MP, had become Shadow Minister of

---

[1] Interview (8 February 1965).
[2] NC typescript of *Proceedings*, pages not numbered.
[3] *Hansard*, Vol. 706, c. 293.

Aviation in 1962, and, as we have seen, the AEU was considered to be well placed throughout the political movement, this major affiliate of the Confederation had neither coherent policy nor adequate information on aviation development. As early as 1962, the MP Group had asked for guidance and information on the already serious problem of aircraft lay-offs. The EC had replied that it would 'look into the possibility of our Research Department studying the position with a view to preparing a report setting out the facts'. Evidently no such position paper had been prepared, illustrating the point made by the AEU's disenchanted professional *supra* that 'deficiencies of research stem from the lack of policy'. One of the younger MPs, the newly elected Norman Atkinson, formerly employed by the University of Manchester as a design engineer, demanded from EC both factual data and policy guidance. At the above-mentioned November 1964 meeting, which he considered the first opportunity to discuss with his union sponsors both policy and procedure under the new Government, he had asked Boyd: 'What skills do the displaced men have? Those working on hydraulics, on engine-fitting, might be able to function successfully in the manpower-short machine tool plants. But the airframe fitters ("skin people") could not readily fit into other work of a skilled or semi-skilled character.' Atkinson proposed that he put forward the policy adopted by the National Committee, criticizing the cancellations on the ground that the Government should reduce its overall military commitments rather than economize by transferring expenditures to American firms and thereby risk losing valuable technical skills. Most of the MPs at the meeting were in general content to leave the matter to the Cabinet. When Atkinson persisted, and won some support from new Members, it appears that John Boyd announced 'the position': 'It's the Tories and the manufacturers that got us into this mess. The union shouldn't be putting the Party into a bad light.'

At this meeting Atkinson advanced two other proposals. He asked that the MPs be consulted by the union in whatever evidence it prepared for the Plowden Committee, then investigating the aircraft industry. This was refused. (The trade union position was presented by a joint General Council and Confederation statement.)[1] Atkinson also proposed—and again was rebuffed by EC—that the AEU Group could help the reallocation of jobs for the displaced aircraft engineers by pressing the Government to give London Transport, a publicly owned industry, the right to build its own vehicles at the Oldenham plant. This plant had been used for building of LT buses before the war, when it was taken over by the Air Ministry. At the

[1] TUC *Report* (1965), pp. 212–13; cf. 'Plane Truths', Talking Points No. 3 (April 1965), Labour Party Publication.

moment, it was reported by Atkinson as being used merely for repairs are rebuilding.[1] This latter proposal will be recognized as basically similar to the referral made by the Executive Council to the group in 1952, in the pursuit of job opportunities for railway equipment workmen (see Chapter III).

What is a plausible interpretation of EC's negative response in 1965? First, the Confederation itself sponsored no MPs: only individual unions in the CSEU did. There was no organization, then, of MPs parallel to the structure evolved for national bargaining. Second, Atkinson raised the matter, not only because of pressure for jobs by the rank and file, but because—and, possibly, primarily because—of his own determined effort to find a positive role for himself and his colleagues in the group, consistent with what he regarded as the major ideological goal of the union and the Party— an extension of public ownership. The AEU has been shown to have had no such ideological goal or incentive. Moreover, as the private job market continued to be generally favourable, neither the Engineers nor the more left-wing affiliates of the Confederation pressed for legislative solutions.

Mr Stan Orme, citing national economic policy requirements, supported Atkinson's thrust for a more active role for the MPs. He had campaigned in 1964 for public ownership of steel and other industries. His House of Commons maiden speech repeated Bevan's famous stand for controlling 'the commanding heights of industry'. Orme's own proposal to his MP and union colleagues was now more limited in scope: as the union most directly concerned with machine tool production the AEU should develop a plan for advanced machine tool design and production at Government-operated pilot plants. He felt this would aid the Government's quest for technological advance and also assure job continuity for many members. EC gave him no encouragement. He subsequently decided that he should cultivate a specialized knowledge of machine tools, but realized he would find it unprofitable to seek either research aid or political assistance from the union in developing that speciality. Notwithstanding its accumulation of MPs the union was content to rely on market forces to assure technical progress.

Mr Harold Walker of Doncaster, in a 1964 maiden speech that was a marked departure from the customary banalities of such occasions, vividly described the ancient equipment in use at the engineering firm where he had been employed only recently, and cited it as evidence for the need for a greater public role in the technologically strategic machine tool industry. The new Minister of Technology, Frank Cousins, is reported to have cited the speech to

[1] Interview (8 February 1965).

a Parliamentary Party meeting to illustrate the failings of British industrial technology generally. Members on both sides congratulated Walker on the 'solid knowledge' of the metal-working industries the speech had shown.[1] This writer called Walker's speech to the attention of the Research staff of the AEU a few weeks after its delivery. They were delighted with its earthy and informal account of the workmen, the machines, and the employers in a firm well known in the trade. They subsequently extracted it for the officers—who until that moment had been unfamiliar with the speech. The point here is that a new union-sponsored MP, speaking on what was presumably the most pressing problem of the new Labour Government—planning and the productivity of industry—had not considered going to his union for information, or for policy guidance.

Incomes Policy

After Fred Lee became a Member of the Government he was invited into the union debates on the vital issue of incomes policy. This extension of hospitality to Lee, after so many years of relative isolation from official industrial and political policy, did not represent a change towards acceptance of the MPs for policy-making, however. Instead, the invitation is better viewed mainly as another manifestation of insecurity at the top—this time over the national leaders' ambiguous position on wage control.

An effective incomes policy is known to be difficult to achieve under conditions of relatively full employment—in any modern market economy.[2] In Britain, and especially in the huge engineering sector, the 'parallel' bargaining system had shifted economic power to the work-place, where it functioned largely outside the scope of the national unions. Even after the TUC had joined in approving the 1964 'Joint Statement of Intent on Productivity, Prices and Incomes' there had been no significant change made in the two levels of bargaining: the national unions, as seen in our discussion of the 'Package Deal', continued to negotiate through the Confederation on the national level, while the shop stewards negotiated at the work-place level.

When the Government in 1965 asked for statutory advance notice of all wage claims, consent was obtained from the TUC. Within the AEU, however, this proposal of Labour created a serious split. On the one side were the national officers and a majority of the EC, who gave at least nominal support to the Government. On the other side

[1] Interviews with Walker (1964–5); also letter from Walker to writer (7 April 1965).
[2] Murray Edelman and R. W. Fleming, *The Politics of Wage-Price Decisions: A Four Country Analysis* (Urbana, Illinois, University of Illinois, 1965), Chap. 6.

was the contending minority of the Executive Council which was basing its forthcoming campaign for control of the union on an appeal to the shop stewards, whose numerical and strategic position had been steadily growing. In this struggle neither side was seeking substantive programmatic political or ideological goals: the basic conflict was over internal power.

Having announced support of the Labour Government, the national leaders were now faced with the problem of winning approval for a Governmental role in wage determination. In an institution founded on and sustained for over a century by the market concept of collective bargaining, the leaders found this to be awkward and risky. To help solve their dilemma they called on their MPs. For example the officers provided Fred Lee with several channels for reaching the membership: he argued before the National Committee, on invitation of the President; his photograph was given the entire front cover of the *Journal* and his speech lengthily summarized in the same issue—a rare and possibly unprecedented public acknowledgement of MP participation in the NC debates. He was also credited by some with being the most persuasive of the Executive Council's supporters within the badly split AEU delegation caucus at the 1965 Labour Party Conference.

Addressing the 1965 National Committee, Lee argued that the Government was controlling prices, as well as stimulating the economy, and warned that a defeat of the Government would mean 'a free for all, stop-go economy which presupposes insignificant growth rates and high unemployment'.[1] The Minister was, naturally enough, speaking in defence of the Government as well as for 'rational' wage policies. He was also defending the now moderate leadership of Harold Wilson and George Brown against a small but vocal Left Wing in the Party who argued for 'free collective bargaining'. He was, of course, also defending the publicly declared position of the top officers, although the latter were only nominally supporting planned wage policies.

In addition to Lee, other AEU-sponsored MPs in the Government —and the Prime Minister himself—were brought into the National Committee meetings and other union channels by the officers to help swing the union membership behind the Party Leader, the Government and the incumbent Executive majority.

[1] 'Straight Talk from Brother Lee', *Journal* (June 1965), pp. 231–2. Lee was then Chancellor of the Duchy of Lancaster. The planning function of NEDC 'was lifted bodily' out of it in December 1964, and put inside the Department of Economic Affairs, under George Brown, the Minister, thereby becoming 'very largely an adjunct to the Labour Government's drive for an "incomes policy"'. A. Shonfield, *Modern Capitalism* London, Oxford University Press, 1965), p. 154.

By contrast with Lee's shift towards support of the Executive, some of the able young MPs, products of the innovative training programme, began to put additional pressure on the Executive majority. During the caucus discussions on incomes policy at the 1965 Party Conference for example, both Messrs Orme and Atkinson dramatically demonstrated a reversal of their intended institutional role in the union. Instead of helping the national leadership to persuade the dissidents to 'toe the line', these MPs assumed leadership of the opposition. They, too, played dual roles: they were defending traditional unionism and were also affecting the union leadership contest.[1]

At Conference, the AEU held the centre of attention for its possibly decisive block vote. The elected lay delegates were deeply divided on the issue. Councillor Hugh Scanlon, presumed left-wing candidate for the Presidency to succeed Carron, had been arguing, alone among his EC colleagues, for rejection, and for 'free collective bargaining'. (Berridge, the Communist EC member, was of course ineligible to attend.) The prolonged, bitter AEU caucus meetings were attended by Lee, Pannell and Albu—all in the Government—and back-bench MPs. The Government group, led by Lee, argued of course for the pending legislation. The back-benchers present, except for Orme and Atkinson, were reported to have remained silent. Exercising their right to speak—no MP had a vote—these two MPs appear to have been the decisive force in swinging the entire lay delegation, who constituted a majority, against the EC majority stand. One lay delegate told this writer after the vote: 'Without Stan and Norm, Hughie [Scanlon] could never have lined up the votes.' Thus, the MPs were used by both sides for factional purposes even though they had been deemed essentially irrelevant for substantive legislative functions.

Structural Problems: The MPs' View of the 'Procedure'

The MPs, without a recognized role in either economic or political policymaking in the union, thrust themselves into the structural problem. Again, however, this took on a largely factional character, and was not part of a volitional political or economic policy.

The heart of the structural problem and the resultant conflict between the national bureaucracy and the shop stewards was the

[1] Orme and Atkinson, however, joined in promoting informal meetings at Westminster of university economists and Labour MPs, to discuss economic policy. Beginning in 1965, these discussions culminated in September 1966, with a printed pamphlet issued after the July 1966 'freeze', and entitled 'Beyond the Freeze: A Socialist Policy for Economic Growth', and signed by six economists and twenty-one MPs (London, Goodwin Press, undated).

'procedure', which officially governed the conciliation of disputes in the engineering industry. Ever since the end of the nineteenth century, the agreement between the organized employer group on the one side (now the Engineering Employers' Federation (EEF)), and the unions on the other (the Confederation of Shipbuilding and Engineering Unions) had been a symbol of British voluntarism. We will briefly describe the agreement in its contemporary industrial and political setting, and then show how the MPs became involved. This four-step agreement between the CSEU and the EEF provided for all disputes arising at the work-place to be first handled by shop steward and management representatives; the second phase required a works conference; the third was a reference to the Confederation and the Federation district representatives; the final stage, calling for meetings between the national representatives at York for the settlement of disputes remaining unresolved at local levels, gave the 'procedure' its name—the 'York memorandum'.

Because of the weakness at the national level of the employers' and employees' institutions, an informal means of settlement of disputes evolved: short 'unofficial 'strikes which had taken place for years amid complaints of delay and inefficiency. These strikes were often unannounced and unapproved, and sometimes even unrecorded by union, employer or government officials.[1] Largely conducted outside any national, recognized institutional framework, these 'strikes' were frequently ascribed to political activists.

Like his predecessor, Jack Tanner, President Sir William Carron believed that charges of delay and inefficiency under the 'procedure' were politically inspired. Shortly before his official appearance on behalf of the AEU before the 1965 Royal Commission, where the issue of unofficial strikes was the paramount question, Carron defined the 'Tasks and Problems' of his union for an academic audience at the London School of Economics. While the 'procedure' was summarized and said to be generally satisfactory for the bargaining system, 'unofficial' strikes were attributed to:

cases where the shop stewards in a factory usurp authority which is in excess of that allowed by the rules of the Union concerned. . . . This is not always the outcome of industrial reasoning but is, in fact, very often evidenced in an endeavour by the steward concerned to further the concrete interests of a movement which, at the very greatest stretch of the imagination, cannot be classified as industrial. It is certainly not based upon trade unionism either. I think you know what I mean. This, of course, is a major problem, which all

[1] H. A. Turner, Garfield Clack and Geoffrey Roberts, *Labour Relations in the Motor Industry* (London, Allen and Unwin, 1967), Chap. 2.

Unions have to meet and the solving of which can determine whether the Union is an industrial organization or a vehicle for conveying the propaganda stemming from a political movement....[1]

In an important sense the shift to work-place bargaining does represent a political process with crucial policy implications: by development of a power structure at the work-place level that negotiates and settles disputes directly with employers, the workers may have evolved an improved industrial democracy. While this process of bargaining has been given little formal recognition by either employers or national unions, the *de facto* recognition of the work-place bargaining—by workers, by unions and by management —has proceeded, largely because the existing institutions and procedures were inadequate to encompass the potentials for collective bargaining in an economic climate of full employment and a social climate of higher worker expectations. However, the conspiratorial political view suggested by Carron is widely held, namely, that politically inspired shop stewards are fomenting the 'unofficial' strikes for ulterior purposes. Yet, the shop stewards' movements are in fact localized, have been unable to achieve a viable national organization or a national horizon, are largely outside the formal parliamentary political work of the union, and have been only peripherally involved in informal political work, including radical politics.

In their definitive study of the strike-prone motor car industry, Turner, Clack and Roberts found no general evidence to support the charge of political motivation.[2] The Communist Party itself has anguished about the inattention to politics by 'the NCO's of the workers' army'. This invocation of Wal Hannington's term appears in a more recent Party analysis which nostalgically recalled the 'campaigning spirit' of the Clyde shop stewards' movement in 1914–18, which resulted in the election of some shop stewards to Parliament, and urged that as a model for 'wider participation in the Labour Movement as a whole'. The article went on: 'The very success of shop stewards at job level on wages, conditions, etc., has often given rise to the idea that attention at the branch is no longer necessary.'[3]

It is at the branch, and not at the work-place, that the decision on

---

[1] AEU President's office; the speech draft was prepared for delivery in Lent Term 1965, but was not presented because of Carron's illness. This was not only Carron's view, but had been expressed in more explicit accusatory terms by President Jack Tanner before his retirement in 1954: 'Extracts from the President's Address to the National Committee, 1952', *Journal* (June 1952), pp. 168–9.

[2] Turner *et al.*, op. cit., p. 212. See also Chap. XIII, below.

[3] Dennis Goodwin, *Marxism Today* (April 1964).

117

Labour Party affiliation is made. Resolutions on political activity provide a forum for many ideologues and others interested in stating their views. But the shop steward, steeped in work-place functions, may not feel willing or able to stretch himself to cover the political work at the branch. He can of course become caught up in political campaigns at the work-place, as we have seen—when the issues are directly related to job interests. He has, in any event, little security against punishment by the employer, and less so for such totally unrecognized work as political activity.

A Left organ, *The Week*, in 1966 considered the 'lack of politics' a 'central weakness of the contemporary shop steward organizations'.[1] The *Financial Times*' well-informed 'Observer' wrote in 1967: 'The very model of a modern unionist—devoted, intelligent and well in command', but also 'disillusioned with politicians of every colour', and believing in 'trade unionism pure and simple'—that was his profile of the AEU convenor of shop stewards, John Weakley, at the British Motors Corporation plant in Llanelly.[2]

Although the shop steward system has come to operate largely outside both the formal disputes procedure and the formal political programme of most Labour-affiliated unions, this structural phenomenon did receive significant attention from the union-sponsored MPs, who brought the question to the floor of the House of Commons under both Conservative and Labour Governments. A common practice of the UAW and other American trade union lobbyists is to persuade a friendly Member of the House of Representatives or the Senate to speak on behalf of the union's side of a labour problem. The purpose of the intervention is generally to supplement the union's bargaining power, by seeking public support or governmental assistance. However, this was not a recognizable purpose of the AEU-MPs who introduced the 'procedure' on the floor of the House. A major purpose, apparently, was either to defend or criticize this basic, voluntarist bargaining machinery, and to pose thereby the familiar problem of the ability of the national leadership of the AEU and associated unions to cope with the mixed economy and modern-day industrial relations.

As far back as 1958, Mr Charles Hobson, later Lord Hobson, discussed the York agreement, giving it as his 'whole purpose' in entering the debate on the 1958 'pay pause'. Arguing against any 'government interference' in the bargaining system, he gave an extended defence of both the engineering 'procedure' and the national union leadership. The Tory Government had aroused a

[1] *The Week* (26 August 1965).
[2] *Financial Times* (26 August 1965). This would seem to support Clack's view, below.

furore in the union world by imposing on employees in the public sector a freeze on wage awards which had been achieved by previous negotiations—a 'pause' attributed by the Government to the foreign exchange crisis.[1] In this instance the 'pay pause' affected relatively few AEU members, and the disputes machinery between the CSEU and the EEF was not directly affected, but Hobson appeared to think that the Government's action might encourage the critics of the 'procedure' and thereby help foment 'unofficial' actions.

He conceded that the last stage of the procedure was a 'favourite butt of speakers for many years', and that 'it is tedious [and] puts issues through a very fine sieve indeed'. 'But', he warned, 'it will be very difficult for the trade union leaders to maintain' if the Government should interfere with the arbitration awards. A principal objective of his intervention was to establish that incumbent 'trade union officials, particularly those in the engineering industry [who] are often criticized about the sloth of the negotiating machinery', have been successful in gaining a procedure that is 'the envy of the world'.[2]

Ironically, one of the most serious parliamentary critiques of the 'procedure'—and, indirectly, of the national leadership—came from John Robertson MP, whose intervention in the 1963 Contracts of Employment Bill debate was cited by James Conway as a justification for the expanded MP programme. That Act, as passed, requires an employer to give each employee 'written particulars' of certain terms of his employment: date of commencement; terms of remuneration; hours, holiday, sick pay; pensions and pension schemes. In cases of lay-offs, or redundancies, the employer must give notice of one week after twenty-six weeks' service, and up to four weeks after five years of continuous service. However, the employee is required to give one week's notice before quitting.[3]

Because the AEU Executive Council, the TUC General Council and the Parliamentary Party had all decided not to oppose the bill, the AEU Group as a whole was neutral on the matter. The larger Trade Union Group, through its Secretary, Charles Pannell (AEU-sponsored), expressed that group's neutrality benevolently: 'The measure, let us face it, confers no substantial rights. Still, it is at least a start. It probably registers a principle.'[4]

The MPs' vagueness may have reflected the union's own lack of policy. The British trade union movement had not been pressing for legal job rights. Job rights of individual workers and the individual

[1] V. L. Allen, *Militant Trade Unionism* (London, Merlin Press, 1966), pp. 62–3.
[2] *Hansard*, Vol. 581, c. 1422–8 (6 February 1958).
[3] TUC Congress *Report* (1964), p. 154.
[4] *Hansard*, Vol. 671, c. 1547.

employer's rights to hire and fire were covered, legally, by the common law, with no special code of law for labour matters as there was in the United States. The problem had been a subject of constant debate among the various national union centres, including the Confederation affiliates, but they were unable to reach agreement on a common policy. Within the AEU as in British industry generally, the subject was not covered by national agreements; the workshop bargaining system conducted under shop stewards filled this vacuum.[1]

This Bill, then, might have been an important legislative precedent. Marked suspicion, however, was shown by some labour legal experts, and others who feared that the employee notice provision of the Bill might be construed by the courts to outlaw 'unofficial' strikes. In 1964, after the Rookes-Barnard judgement, in which the House of Lords held that a union official could be liable for the tort of conspiracy for inducing some other person to break a contract of employment, the General Council of the TUC saw a threat to vital union interests; it decided that 'perfectly proper, legitimate trade union activities might be impeded' by such an interpretation of existing law; that the judgement made it 'possible to regard merely the giving of a strike notice in itself as constituting a threat to break a contract of employment'.[2] The General Council then won from the Labour Government an amendment that restored legal protection. This was achieved by language added to the 1965 Redundancy Payments Bill, amending the Contracts of Employment Act and overcoming Rookes-Barnard by stating that continuity of an employee's period of employment is not broken if the employee takes part in a strike.[3]

In deciding to oppose the Contracts of Employment Bill, despite the willingness of AEU and the TUC General Council to go along with it, John Robertson felt the bill might endanger the system of unofficial bargaining at the work-place—including strikes in breach of the agreed 'procedure'. Robertson reflected the feeling among engineering workers that they were still suffering from the procedural terms of settlement imposed after the 1922 lock-out, despite the recovery of union strength. Thus he made a strong point of the fact

---

[1] NC Proceedings (1961), pp. 147–60; W. K. Wedderburn, *The Worker and the Law* (Harmondsworth, Penguin, 1965), Chaps 1 and 2; see also Frederic Meyers, *Ownership of Jobs*, cited in Andrew Shonfield, *Modern Capitalism* (London, Oxford University Press, 1965), p. 116.

[2] *Congress Report* (1965), pp. 58–9.

[3] *Hansard*, Vol. 716, c. 1770. Foreshadowing 'Fair Deal at Work', the Tory policy document of 1968, the Conservative Shadow Minister of Labour, Mr Godber, charged that the amendment was 'an encouragement, if not an incitement, to people to break their contracts of employment'. Ibid., c. 1757.

that federated employers retained the right—under the existing 'procedure'—to act on such basic matters as work-loads (exercising traditional 'managerial functions').

Robertson told the House he saw in the individual contracts provision 'a great deal that is dangerous' to the legal right to strike, especially to strike unofficially. He then criticized the official 'procedure', asserting that under it the employers had been able to make basic changes without prior consultation with union representatives. The trade union at the work-place, he told the House, will 'continue to be a defense mechanism. . . . We have heard of the power and influence of shop stewards. That power and influence extends . . . into unofficial channels.' He went on to cite his own experience as a National Organizer for AEU when he had regularly sanctioned unofficial strikes. While such strikes were nominally in breach of procedure, the union generally gave its approval, unofficially, because 'no other approaches [i.e. the four-step formal "procedure"] were listened to over a period of months. . . . People go on strike in order to get a just grievance settled quickly.' And, as though anticipating the short-lived proposal soon to be made before the Royal Commission by his own President for written, enforceable agreements, to bar 'unofficial' strikes, Robertson said that most of the workers were dependent upon informal pacts achieved by joint shop stewards' bargaining at the work-place: 'Negotiations are always going on about [wages] and I can see a danger in trying to put it all down on a piece of paper.'[1]

Hobson's speech to the House in 1958 was plainly a defence of centralized leadership. Robertson on the other hand was justifying publicly the new form of 'parallel' bargaining while at the same time questioning the ability of the national leadership to cope with such bargaining. Several of the 1964 crop of AEU–MPs dealt with the 'procedure' and other institutional and leadership inadequacies. These interventions, like Hobson's and Robertson's, were quite clearly *not* the result of volitional policy decisions of the union or of the Parliamentary Party.

Debating the Government's Redundancy Payments Bill in 1965, Mr Harold Walker, above, invoked his experience as an AEU convenor to conclude that the official procedure made extended delays inevitable and created 'ill-feeling and ill-will which so readily lends itself afterwards to further strike action'. The procedure had become 'anachronistic' and had 'little relevance to the conditions of the 1960s', while shop-inspired unofficial action had brought rapid and fair settlements of disputes.[2]

---

[1] *Hansard*, Vol. 671, c. 1576–80.   [2] Ibid., Vol. 711, c. 135–7.

The unusual emphasis on anachronisms was carried further in the maiden speech of Mr Ben Ford, MP, also an AEU convenor of shop stewards before his election in 1964. His 'message to trade unions' was to 'pull trade union structure our of the horse and buggy period', alter the 'procedures originating in rule books more applicable to the age of itinerant journeymen', and 'look closely at their methods of [officer] selection'.[1]

Political and Economic Policy of the AEU as Reflected in Testimony for Royal Commission on Trade Unions and Employers' Associations

Because of the broad scope of the questions submitted by the Commission to all national trade unions, their responses are central to a consideration of union political purpose in contemporary Britain. In the remaining pages of this chapter we will focus on the AEU's brief, which is relevant not only for its substantive evidence but also for the methodology used in its preparation. In later chapters (IX and X) we will consider how two rather different types of national unions responded to the Commission.

The AEU was the keystone of the Confederation of Shipbuilding and Engineering Unions, which had been dealing with the Engineering Employers' Federation for some seventy years under the most important procedural agreement in British industry. Here was certainly an occasion for 'representation in the interests of labour'. Yet the minutes and other evidence indicate that neither the inquiry from the Commission, nor the union's responses were discussed with the MP Group! Indeed, the seventeen members of Parliament did not receive their copies of the printed, official AEU testimony, *Trade Unions and the Contemporary Scene*, until the very day it was issued to the press! In this brief, nevertheless, the AEU not only reaffirmed the traditional theory of labour representation to justify the sponsorship, but related its own parliamentary effort to both economic objectives and to social goals: 'to curb excesses in the combined forces of capital'; and to remove 'anti-social anachronisms from our life'.[2]

How account for the apparent contradiction of giving the MPs great prominence in such a vital public statement and at the same time ignoring them during its preparation? One finds this at first glance even stranger when it is understood that legislation was expected to be a likely outcome of the Commission's inquiries. Moreover these MPs, in addition to possessing legislative expertise useful in the consideration of such legislation, had shown first-hand acquaintance with the system of industrial relations. They had also shown some ability to relate their experiences to the broader problem

[1] *Hansard*, Vol. 705, c. 1479–80.
[2] AEU, *Trade Unions and the Contemporary Scene*, p. 43.

of getting trade unions to function for what the Commission termed 'the social and economic advance of the nation . . .'.

The rather obvious interpretation is that the organization was observing the traditional 'voluntarism' of the British industrial relations system. There is considerable evidence in the union's own brief, below, to support such an interpretation. But even as a voluntarist policy the new situation confronting the union and the Commission required some serious re-thinking since the Government had made plain its intention to consider reform of trade union structure and to curb wage income.

The union cited in the brief its affiliation with the Confederation, which embraced 35-odd federated unions in order to illustrate its own attempt 'to modernize the [national] structure of the trade union movement'.[1] In addition, it cited the existence of Confederation shop stewards, as well as the control by the national AEU of its own stewards through the District Committees, to assert that integration of work-place bargaining was achieved. Our analysis of the political work of the District Committees, however, has already indicated that the District bridge that officially connects the shop stewards to the national structure is not a major means of communication. The Confederation did permit a high degree of co-ordination for the purpose of national bargaining, and represented a great union achievement. But it had minimal importance at the workplace, and was wholly inadequate for the formulation of relevant economic policies at the national level. Confederation stewards constituted a mere handful of the thousands of stewards in the industry, and few of these had achieved recognition by their employers, or by the workmen in the plants.

Clack's description of the 'shop floor democracy' by which a typical shop steward was elected underscored the continuing devolution away from the centre. He noted that the particular national union to which a worker belonged was frequently of no interest to his fellow workers, or to the shop steward involved. An AEU steward, for example, served non-AEU members, and the AEU operatives' own steward often held a card in some other national union. 'Shop floor respect' was the key to the elections. While a convenor of shop stewards of a particular union had somewhat closer links to his union, even for him 'factory interests took precedence over trade union interests'.[2]

[1] AEU, *Trade Unions and the Contemporary Scene*, p. 38.

[2] Garfield Clack, *Industrial Relations in a British Car Factory* (Cambridge, Cambridge University Press, 1967), pp. 30–5. For the typical car worker's attitude towards his work-place leaders see Goldthorpe *et al.*, *The Affluent Worker: Industrial Attitudes and Behaviour* (Cambridge, Cambridge University Press, 1968), Chap. 5.

On the other hand, the overworked paid officials of the national unions in the area are:

> . . . rarely observed at the factory, and almost never on the shop floor. Most factory workers probably saw their union officials only at strike meetings—at which it was more likely that they were being exhorted by the officials to return to work. . . . To the worker, the shop steward was the union, and his interest in union affairs was largely confined to work-place problems.[1]

Ignoring these structural lags, the union referred to the nationwide collective bargaining agreement with the EEF and declared it was 'satisfied with the general operation of the Agreement'. It gave credit to the 'present equable industrial climate [full employment]' for the 'more cordial and co-operative atmosphere'. Some uneasiness was suggested, however: 'This change of heart on the part of employers, generally, may well be a function of economic prosperity and perhaps will disappear,' but the union '. . . hope that this would not be the case and perhaps the new mood may, in itself, be self-perpetuating as both sides come to see the advantages of negotiating in an atmosphere of mutual trust.'[2]

The hope for expanding market bargaining at the company level was reflected also in the bargaining agreement cited by the AEU as a model for future behaviour, the famous Fawley Agreement with Esso Petroleum. In language which recalls the business unionism of William Allan, as expressed before the 1867 Royal Commission in a *laissez-faire* era, the modern AEU declared:

> The reward was commensurate with the far-reaching effect of the new arrangement and thereby an easy transition in new work relations was easily achieved. It is this kind of agreement we are ever seeking throughout industry, and wherever we find it on offer, or we can get it accepted on our suggestion we are always ready and willing to make the deal.[3]

After all this reaffirmation of faith in free collective bargaining the union proceeded to offer to 'outlaw' unofficial strikes and approve discharge of unofficial strikers—in return for a legalized 'closed (i.e. union) shop':

> If legislation was considered necessary to enforce the closed shop

[1] Garfield Clack, *Industrial Relations in a British Car Factory*, p. 26.

[2] Brief, op. cit., pp. 23–4.

[3] Ibid., pp. 5, 44; cf. Allen Flanders, *The Fawley Productivity Agreements* (London, Faber & Faber, 1964). See also Chap. XIII, below, where we discuss some recent aspects of productivity agreements in relation to incomes policies of the Labour Government.

and the check-off the unions may well have to redefine their attitude towards recalcitrant members. . . . They (unions) would probably agree also to outlaw forever unofficial strikes, i.e. strikes about disputes that had not been through any procedure for the avoidance of disputes.

The union then asserted that it would have the power to: 'discipline their members—for with expulsion the ultimate sanction leading to the loss of a worker's job would be more than a sufficient deterrent to an individual thinking of ignoring his union's advice'.[1] How—and if—the various unions commonly found in the British work-place would agree to share or allocate the closed shop was rendered moot by the TUC's 1966 testimony which dismissed the idea of punitive or other legislation—indeed it directly rebutted the highly publicized AEU proposition: 'In fact, some people argue that the establishment of the union shop should be supported by employers for the very reason that unions would then be in a better position to control and discipline their members. This approach represents a grotesque parody of trade unionism.'[2]

The quest for bureaucratic security by the central leaders to offset the shift to the work-place had led one officer to seriously contemplate (in private discussions with this writer) a recommendation for a supervised government election of the kind used in the United States, to determine the exclusive bargaining agent in place of the present joint union arrangements. 'Then with a check-off', he said, 'we could afford a well-paid set of branch officers and get a disciplined and loyal organization.' This hope for strengthening the tenure of the incumbents and eliminating factionalism by a sort of 'Civil Service' at the branch level based on a Wagner Act election procedure apparently did not formally reach the Executive Council, and is not in the brief. While the check-off and certification have helped to entrench the national leaders in the United States, the basic consideration behind the American unions' campaign for securing and retaining the National Labor Relations Act was the widespread refusal of employers to recognize and bargain with legitimate trade unions. This was not a general problem for British trade unions. The AEU itself stated that point plainly: 'The recognition of the AEU by individual employers is not generally a problem.'[3] The situations, in short, are not analogous.

The press reporting of both the printed testimony and Carron's comments at the press conference prior to his official advocacy of the 'outlaw forever' legislative swap understandably produced a

<hr/>

[1] Brief, p. 26.   [2] TUC Brief, op. cit., p. 151.
[3] AEU Brief, op. cit., p. 26.

wide range of interpretations of the AEU's real purposes. *The Times'* industrial correspondent, who seems to have read the printed brief as well as having listened to Carron at the press party, cited his remarks that the AEU was not asking for closed shop legislation, but only describing 'what they would have to do if legislation was introduced'. This correspondent's story, nevertheless featured, as did a *Times* leader, the 'bargain which would transform labour relations in Britain'.[1]

However, the union's transitory political solution to this issue was withdrawn by Carron when he gave his oral testimony. The Executive Council had in the interim voted to reverse the stand it had taken in the written document. Repeatedly pressed by members of the Commission for some expansion or clarification of the proposal to 'outlaw forever unofficial strikes', Carron made a *volte face:* 'We are opposed to legislation.'[2] Carron's switch included a statement on the union's distaste for all forms of compulsion and a reminder of the limits of a voluntary organization on the disciplining of members. This, taken with the TUC's more carefully reasoned brief against legislation, would seem to have left intact the voluntarist philosophy of British unionism.

Yet the closing, impromptu remarks of Carron on acceptable and unacceptable forms of 'unofficial' strikes indicates how centrally important this issue was in the philosophy of the model union during the period. Such strikes, he told the Commission, were perfectly proper, 'procedure or no procedure, or even somewhat in defiance of our rules', if the members at the work-place were striking to eliminate a 'splinter organization' (the Toolmakers' Union).[3]

On the other hand the President offered to the country an unreconstructed view of the now standard variety of 'unofficial' action. His closing oral testimony might possibly be dismissed as the personal pique of a 'trade union knight'. He was about to retire because of age and enter the House of Lords. However, Carron now expressed the central concern of much of the trade union hierarchy in the post-war years, namely, that *recognition might be given by employers, and by the workers, to the unofficial movement.* The mild-mannered President departed from his own prepared script and from the probing of the Commissioners, to present his fears about the inroads being made on the national union institutions by the new form of bargaining. After levelling some criticism at employers who are 'making nonsense of the "procedure"' by accepting work-place

[1] *The Times* (9 November 1965).
[2] Transcript of oral evidence (15 February 1966), prepared by AEU as 'correction of Note taken by Treasury Reporter'.
[3] Ibid., p. 14.

settlement of disputes in response to local pressures, he directed the Commission's attention to one of Dr Clack's articles which had attracted considerable attention. In his brief account of a 'downer', in which sixty storemen in a car assembly plant downed tools for a few hours, Clack contended that such unofficial actions actually were beneficial to management and labour because they propel management towards mutually acceptable agreements. This point had also been made by Robertson and Walker, above—to the House of Commons. Carron's questioning had been ended, but, waving the magazine, he gratuitously added:

> If I might mention unofficial strikes, you may perhaps be interested in the discourse given by an academic, Dr Garfield Clack of Cambridge's Department of Applied Economics, who tells the world of unofficial strikes in industry. If this kind of literature is written and distributed by academics generally, presumably of repute, it might be that some of our members take notice of it.[1]

This calamitous though amusing finale of the performance by the Engineers' chief spokesman (and a member of the General Council's inner power structure as well) before the Royal Commission symbolized the alienation of the national leaders from the rank and file and the inability of the union to formulate a coherent policy even for its own fundamental interest—the bargaining system itself. The union had not sought to develop significant national economic or political policies during the period, despite its acceptance of the employer-initiated three-year 'package' agreement. It preferred to rely on its market power. It was slowly accepting the State's participation in the management of the economy and its involvement in the industrial relations system, but basically in practice it resisted both institutional adaptation and significant social or political change.

The Labour Party tie remained solid. It was still a sort of insurance policy for retention of both legality and full employment, but real political action seemed unnecessary and perhaps dangerous since both the major parties accepted these two policies during the period. The great increase in nominal political commitments arose largely out of a complex of interacting historical, social and bureaucratic factors. Given the continuation of the Labour alliance, the increased flow of political funds would in itself have provided the leadership

[1] Transcript of oral evidence (15 February 1966), prepared by AEU as 'correction of Note taken by Treasury Reporter', pp. 5, 44. Phelps Brown cites Carron's anger at employers on this occasion as an example of the national union leaders' loss of authority in a period of full employment: 'the individual member depends less upon the national officers . . . has less fear from repudiating their authority', op. cit., pp. 161–2.

of the national union with increased influence in the Party. Thus, the growing Labour commitment was in part a manifestation of such an inertia factor, insofar as the union leaders continued to maintain the historic tie without having immediate or visible goals. In addition, one may reasonably conclude that they channelled considerable energies, in addition to funds, into the programme because (1) it enhanced their bureaucratic image *vis-à-vis* the membership at a time when they were losing negotiating power to the work-place leaders; (2) it helped assure the maintenance of a non-revolutionary leadership of the Labour Party. In any event, pure and simple unionism remained the prevailing philosophy, conforming essentially with the Perlman model, despite the historic changes that were making that *laissez-faire* philosophy obsolete.

Chapter VII

The Trade Union Group of the Parliamentary Labour Party: Its Make-up and Philosophy

Like any empirical model, that of the AEU has it limits as a basis for conceptualization and generalization. In the absence of definitive statistical and other quantitative evidence, ascertaining political purpose of Labour Party-affiliated unions requires some comparative analysis. In this and the following chapter we focus on the make-up, philosophy and functions of the Trade Union Group of the Parliamentary Labour Party (TUG), the official organization of sponsored trade unionists in the House of Commons, which has accounted for about one-third of the Labour total in recent years.

The Group is an accurate mirror-image of the General Council of the TUC insofar as it is simultaneously representative of all TUC unions and is dominated by the manual unions. To be eligible, however, an MP must be sponsored by a trade union affiliated to the Labour Party and to the TUC.[1]

Manual Tradition

Trade unionists in Parliament are very conscious of the fact that it was the Trades Union Congress that took the decisive step towards constituting the present Labour Party by its 1899 vote calling a Labour Representation Committee meeting for the purpose of 'securing a better representation in the interests of Labour' in the House of Commons. At the turn of the century 'labour' meant manual workmen. Even today all elements of the Party, and even the principal critics on the Left, the Communists, continue to see in manual union representation not only the very heart of the Labour

---

[1] The Group does not accept trade union MPs who are unsponsored. Thus, the Chairman of the PLP in 1968, Mr Douglas Houghton, MP, was excluded from the Group even though he was General Secretary of a national trade union affiliated with the TUC, and a member of the General Council: 'But I was not a sponsored MP, and that decided it.' 'Trade Union MPs in the British House of Commons', *Parliamentarian* (October 1968),p. 218. His union, the Inland Revenue Staff Federation (IRSF), is not Labour-affiliated.

Party, but a *sine qua non* for social advance. And the present Trade Union Group embodies the tradition of strong representation in the House of Commons of 'workers by hand'.

Group activists have been predominantly manual union leaders; they tend to use such terms as 'authentic' and 'real working class' to designate colleagues who spent their lives prior to being elected to public office on hourly rated, blue-collar work.

Current Rationale

It will be recalled that Fred Lee of the AEU Parliamentary Group, who had been influential in enlarging that group, gave as a principal rationale for adding more union MPs the need to counter-balance the trend towards middle-class dominance of the Parliamentary Labour Party. Lee was a man of the Left. Mr Charles Pannell, the Secretary as well as organizer-spokesman for the entire Trade Union Group during the years 1954–63, was strongly on the Right. He voiced the same need for keeping in the House of Commons 'men who have earned the rate for the job'. Writing in 1963 for the Labour Party, Pannell said:

> We must still bring here the men who have earned the rate for the job, who have used the tools, who really know what it is to go out on strike and walk the stones. If we fail to bring them here in sufficient quantity then something fine will leave this place; that earthiness, the commonsense that broadly makes the greatest appeal to the wonderful people of these islands, the most mature democracy in the world.[1]

In more authentically earthy terms, a year later, after he had become Minister of Public Building and Works in the 1964 Labour Cabinet, Pannell summed up the thinking of many union MPs: the Party 'might turn out to be a bloody lot of lawyers' he said, if sponsorship were ended.[2] While this conviction cut across factional lines, it will be seen as serving to legitimize a public claim of a proprietary interest in the Labour Party by the group during the 1959–62 'crisis' stage of the Party Leadership struggle. It is therefore useful to recount some relevant recent history of the unions' relations with the Parliamentary Party.

While there has been virtual unanimity about the need for a proletarian content, the actual make-up, as well as the formal and informal work of the trade unionists in Parliament has changed over the years. There is a substantial recorded history of union activity in the House of Commons. A trade union group made up

[1] 'Unions and Politics', *This Week* Union Special, pp. 1–2 (undated, mimeographed).

[2] Interview (8 December 1964).

largely of Liberal Miners' MPs functioned even before the Labour Party was born. We have seen that already in the 1860s, parliamentary political action was a major weapon of the still defensive unions. The Trades Union Congress' Parliamentary Committee was created in 1871, three years after the TUC's founding, to help the already active London Trades Council watch over the pending Trade Union Bill.[1]

When the Labour Party in 1918 adopted its socialist constitution, it also became a party of mass size for the first time: constituency parties were formed and individual memberships invited. The trade unions, however, then enjoying considerable power and status, as well as numerical and financial strength as a result of their World War I acceptance, became the most stable element of the Party. They provided most of the funds and the bulk of the candidacies, and they were counted on for caution. As a member of the Labour Government in 1930, Sidney Webb dismissed the constituency parties as 'frequently unrepresentative groups of nonentities dominated by fanatics and cranks, and extremists'. Speaking of the policy debates at Party Conferences, Webb added that if the 'block vote of the Trade Unions were eliminated it would be impractical to continue to vest the control of policy in Labour Party Conferences'.[2]

Only a year after voicing such confidence Webb referred to the General Council leaders as 'pigs', when the union leadership broke with the Labour Government over employment policy in the 1931 crisis. This break has remained as a major psychological element in trade union political thought. Faced with massive unemployment, the General Council demanded the use of general funds for relief, a programme of public works, and, if necessary, the Government's acquisition and operation of privately owned plants. When Prime Minister Ramsay MacDonald decided, instead, on further deflation, the TUC, seeing its vital interests threatened, broke with him. MacDonald and Snowden, the Chancellor, supported by the employers and the City, proceeded to form a National Government with the Conservatives.[3]

For many veteran union executives the 1931 events remain as a mandate for continued vigilance over 'intellectuals' in the Party, and a justification for pressing for manualist representation within the Parliamentary Party. Indeed, when asked in 1965 about present

[1] B. C. Roberts, *The Trades Union Congress, 1868–1921* (London, Allen and Unwin, 1958), pp. 65–7.

[2] Cited in R. McKenzie, *British Political Parties*, revised edn (London, Mercury, 1963), p. 505; cf. G. D. H. Cole, *A History of the Labour Party from 1914* (London, Routledge, 1948), pp. 189–91.

[3] Alan Bullock, *The Life and Times of Ernest Bevin* (London, Heinemann, 1960), Vol. 1, pp. 470–93.

trade union purpose at Westminster, Mr Victor Feather, then the Assistant and later the General Secretary of the TUC, sternly replied:

We kept the Party on the rails. Bevin, Citrine and the General Council told MacDonald they wouldn't go for his policies. The entire group of the union men in the House took their lead, and showed their loyalty. In fact, more of the intellectuals would have gone over to MacDonald and Snowden if we hadn't stayed firm. The trade union group was the sheet anchor then. The trade union leaders determined they would keep a watch on policies.[1]

Table II. *Trade Union Sponsored Members of Parliamentary Labour Party, 1964, 1966*

Name of Union	1964	1966
Amalgamated Engineering Union	17	17
Transport & General Workers' Union	21	27
National Union of Mineworkers	28	27
National Union of Railwaymen	6	7
National Union of General & Municipal Workers	9	10
Transport Salaried Staffs' Association	7	5
Union of Shop, Distributive & Allied Workers	10	8
Draughtsmen's and Allied Technicians Association	1	2
[a]Amalgamated Society of Woodworkers	1	1
Clerical & Administrative Workers' Union	3	4
United Textile Factory Workers Association	1	1
British Iron, Steel & Kindred Trades Association	1	1
Union of Post Office Workers	2	4
National Union of Agricultural Workers	1	1
Electrical Trades Union	1	1
National Union of Public Employees	2	5
Associated Society of Locomotive Engineers & Firemen	1	1
National Graphical Association	1	2
Fire Brigades' Union	1	1
Association of Supervisory Staffs, Executives & Technicians	1	2
National Union of Vehicle Builders	1	1
Amalgamated Union of Building Trade Workers	1	1
Other	4	3
TOTAL	121	132
TOTAL, ALL LABOUR MPs	317	363

Source: For 1964, LPCR *Report*, p. 6; for 1966 letter from National Agent of Labour Party (6 May 1966).

[a] Omitted from Labour Party data; added after interview with Mr Eric Heffer, MP, sponsored by ASW (House of Commons, 8 December 1964).

[1] Interview (12 April 1965). See also LPCR *Report* (1931), p. 5.

Feather and veteran unionists in Parliament remain aware, moreover, that in the 'smash-up' of the 1931 General Election, Labour was reduced to forty-six seats; that no less than 36 or 78 per cent of these were trade unionists. It is well known that these Labour stalwarts showed little leadership in the domestic and foreign crises of 1931–8. They formed the nucleus of the 1945 revival, but for reasons already indicated the unions were not then a predominant influence in the Parliamentary Labour Party. Lord Francis-Williams may be correct that 'never in the history of any parliament had the Government benches provided a more completely representative cross-section of British Society. . . '.[1] Yet only 120 of the 393 Labour Members, or 31 per cent were then union-sponsored. Forty-five of the 120 were miners. The embourgeoisement of the Party, which so plainly worried the group leaders, was already clear. 'Into the House', Harrison has written, 'came a flood of middle-class Members, often straight from the services, with little experience of the trade union movement. Throughout the 1945 Parliament, the influence of the trade union MPs steadily declined, although they still included most of the veterans.'[2]

We have seen from our empirical model that there really was no great interest in parliamentary activity. The AEU, and the union movement in general, had achieved a new high status during the Second World War—a status that owed little to political action or political connections, but rested instead largely on labour's production function in the economy. Yet the Trade Union Group has continued to grow in size, and has held on to its symbolic value. When the AEU in later years decided to enlarge its group it widened the representation of skilled trades, especially after the 1964 General Election. With the 1966 General Election the group again increased in size and became perhaps more representative of the labour force because of the higher proportion of white-collar people sponsored. Table II shows the distribution by unions in both years. The group in 1966 had 132 out of 363 or 36 per cent in the PLP as compared to the 1964 totals of 121 and 317 respectively. The two successive elections thus reveal somewhat greater union strength than in 1945.

While numerically impressive, the recent inputs have not yielded the blue-collar content apparently desired by group leaders, or the model envisaged by the Party's founders. Commenting on the sixty-five Labour newcomers in the 1966 Parliament, *The Times* estimated that no more than four or five were manual workers: 'The bulk are in some kind of professional work.'[3] The paradox is partly accounted

[1] Williams, op. cit., pp. 358–9.
[2] M. Harrison, *Trade Unions and the Labour Party* (London, Allen and Unwin, 1960), pp. 264–7.   [3] *The Times* (19 April 1966).

for by changes in the labour force, and the changing trade union structure: the shrinking of the Miners' and Textile unions, the rise of the general-type unions, and the rapid growth of the non-manual labour force and their unions. To a large degree, however, the nostalgia and fear of the Party's changing composition expressed by Pannell and others was due to the type of men sponsored by the two general unions. These are increasingly, of late, professional men with only a marginal background in the union movement. Thus as the two general unions won a substantially increased number of such MPs in the 1964 General Election, the Secretary of the AEU Group, George Pargiter, MP, made this slightly veiled invidious comparison: 'After all, ours are genuine trade union members drawn from the ranks of our established membership.'[1]

The 27-men Parliamentary Group of the Transport and General Workers' Union created labour history by equalling the Miners in 1966. Its recent acquisitions, however, were primarily professionals. The 600,000-strong National Union of General and Municipal Workers (NUGMW), Britain's second largest general union, which in the past had many of its own working class officers in Parliament, had nine MPs in the 1964 House: from *The Times' The House of Commons 1964* autobiographies it appears that *all* of them were management-professional in background.

The occupational trend in the Parliamentary Party, then, has been clearly away from the former dominance by manual workers. Yet the 'cloth cap' clearly remains of significance in the movement: first, 'working class' MPs are a living recognition of the huge financial contribution made by the still dominantly manual trade unions; second, they help maintain the representative character of a 'Labour Party' which was not merely founded largely by manual unions but which still must win the support of 'labour' in a country where the organized and unorganized manual working class accounts for so huge a proportion of the population. These practical and sentimental factors combined to keep the group under predominantly blue-collar leadership throughout the period even as the Party and the group itself shifted away from manualism. So much for composition. What about function?

Many leading scholars, the Labour Party, and the unions, continue to speak of trade union MPs as representing 'the interests of labour'. Both Beer and McKenzie speak of this function, the former adding 'the ideals of socialism' to the traditional 'interests of labour' as the purpose of union sponsorship.[2] The 'interests of labour' are

[1] 'Beneath Big Ben', *Journal* (November 1964), p. 395.
[2] S. H. Beer, *British Politics in the Collectivist Age* (New York, Knopf, 1966), p. 336; McKenzie, op. cit., p. 417.

transmitted to Parliament by the Trades Union Congress. To obtain a picture of the group's actual contemporary function, accordingly, one must return to the political attitudes, philosophy and methods of the TUC and its General Council during the period. In a formal sense, as has been pointed out above, the TUC remains committed to vast social change, from 'public ownership and control of natural resources and of services', to legal regulation of weekly hours of work and a legal minimum wage.[1] Moreover, the bulk of TUC membership belongs to unions affiliated with the Labour Party, which is committed to planning and social transformation. These formal union goals would indicate a quest for legislative support and, in the British context, a Labour Government. Having achieved a Labour Government, the existence of a Trade Union Group in the Parliamentary Labour Party would suggest that the group is needed to help formulate union policy and to serve as a prod to the leadership of a Party which has come to embrace a broader constituency than trade union membership.

In practice, the TUC General Council had determinedly resisted either political partisanship or legislative initiative. Through their stands on the leadership conflicts in the Party in 1950–63 the predominant leaders of the Council enunciated a firm philosophy of *status quo;* that philosophy also came to dominate the Trade Union Group. The Council's conservatism was based on a combination of union achievement and anxiety. The achievement is well known. The unions' legal status was firm, in contrast with the American movement. The British Labour movement, already the oldest, had become by the end of World War II the most unified in the Western world; and by conventional standards, in its external relationships, it was powerful and secure. But there was considerable insecurity within the movement.

What was the cause of the insecurity? We have indicated that at the top as well as the bottom of the structure, there was weakness. At the top, powerful national unions did not yield to the Trades Union Congress authority to make the adjustments in structure and policy that the mixed economy and the long-run interests of the membership now demanded. While the TUC accepted the social reform measures and the nationalization steps taken by the 1945 Attlee Labour Government, it was not ready to offer further political or legislative initiative. The General Council went along with some Conservative Government initiatives, such as the Contracts of Employment Bill in 1963—until they saw the traditional bargaining system threatened by it. They accepted, but sought to limit

[1] W. Milne-Bailey (ed.), *Trade Union Documents* (London, Bell, 1929), 'Objects of the Trades Union Congress' (adopted, 1928), p. 66.

both Labour and Tory Government proposals for indicative planning.

The national union leaders in control of the General Council essentially preferred the continuance of market bargaining. They distrusted programmatic innovation because of the possible disruption to the bargaining system and to their own status in that system. The work-place bargaining had not been absorbed administratively by the national centres, and there was considerable anxiety that a Left-influenced Labour Party leadership might take steps towards recognizing this new 'parallel' and unofficial system of bargaining. Lacking the old incentives for political action—challenges to legality and heavy unemployment—the General Council opted for political passivity or stand-patism.

Arthur Deakin and Political Aloofness

In the person of Arthur Deakin, during the early part of the period the dominant figure in the General Council and General Secretary of the T & G, the union movement's political philosophy comes into focus. Perhaps because of his greater security in his own union, where he enjoyed not only a life-time appointment but also the authority of his famous predecessor, Ernest Bevin, Deakin shunned the familiar socialist rhetoric; he articulated and fought openly within the TUC, the Labour Party, and within the Trade Union Group *against* political activism. His candour was illustrated by a reply to Jack Tanner during a 1953 Party Conference discussion of the already perennial *Plan for Engineering*. Continuing the AEU's shadow-boxing on this *Plan*, the AEU President had seconded the Foundry Workers' motion for Conference approval. Tanner was now TUC President as well as AEU President. Deakin, however, refused to go along with the charade. He expressed what became the majority decision of the Conference by dismissing the motion, with some metaphorical strain, as '. . . the worst abortion ever conceived in the mind of man. I am amazed that the President of the TUC could come and second a resolution of this kind.'[1]

Arthur Deakin's influence and power in the Labour Movement is documented in numerous studies. However, his utilization of the Trade Union Group as a channel for implementing the General Council's views on political purpose in general, and the Party Leadership in particular, seems to have been overlooked. In an authorized biography, V. L. Allen carefully develops Deakin's changing attitudes towards political action. Deakin's rejection of post-war manpower planning is interpreted as stemming from a

[1] *LPCR* (1953), p. 125.

conviction that 'primarily . . . the intervention of Parliament would undermine the authority of trade unions'. Deakin was persuaded that the well-being of workers depended fundamentally on the prosperity of industry rather than on a political system. We are told that while he maintained a strong attachment to Labour, he believed that the danger to the movement 'lay with men preoccupied with party politics'. So, 'like Bevin before him, Deakin was only a labourer in politics, interested in political issues but not much concerned about political methods'. As evidence of this above-the-battle position, Allen asserts that Deakin 'viewed with concern the efforts to revitalize the [Trade Union] Group in 1954 because he thought it might cause further division in the Labour Movement'.[1]

Our later chapter on the T & G will abundantly support Allen's conclusion that in this institution (as in the AEU) politics, as conventionally understood, were muted; that during the Deakin regime the union found little political function for the MPs it sponsored. There is also some evidence from contemporary colleagues of Deakin's interviewed by the present writer, that he was indeed ambivalent about the group's revival in 1954. However, the historic significance of Deakin's role in the history of the Labour Party during the period is that he did enter into 'party politics' and that he did so not to advance 'political issues' but to maintain *status quo*; and that as part of that strategy he also helped the revival of the Trade Union Group—whatever his initial concern about that development.

As early as 1952, Deakin had entered into the leadership struggles of the Party, then the most crucial phase of 'party politics'. Speaking as the fraternal delegate of the TUC to the 1952 Party Conference, he warned that the trade union movement wanted no political moves that might endanger 'the well-established machinery of negotiations within a mixed economy'.[2] Many union leaders now considered that the danger to the bargaining came from the Labour Left, who, attacking the Labour policy of 'drift', were joining Aneurin Bevan in seeking to distinguish Labour's domestic and foreign policies from those of the Tories. Such polarization required an activist Party programme and an activist Leader. The General Council, Deakin now told the Party, saw in such policies and in such alternative leadership, a danger transcending any particular issue. After briefly alluding to the then division over rearmament, he declared 'the great struggle for leadership' to be Council's underlying concern: 'There are few people, today, who believe that the

---

[1] V. L. Allen, *Trade Union Leadership* (Cambridge, Harvard University Press, 1957), pp. 146 ff.
[2] *LPCR* (1952), pp. 125–6.

difference in policy on rearmament is the real issue within this Party. . . . What most people are thinking is—that there is a great struggle for leadership going on.'[1]

This leadership struggle, then, and *not* the particular issues, brought Deakin into the arena of factional fighting within the Party.

General Council Views

While Aneurin Bevan had become for the long-unhappy Left the magnetic leader they thought might replace the ageing Attlee, the union chiefs had backed Hugh Gaitskell who, as Chancellor in the Labour Government, had framed a budget which increased military expenditures and introduced Health Service charges. Bevan, along with Harold Wilson and John Freeman, resigned from the Government in protest.[2]

Clearly, the question of the manual workers versus the intellectual was of no operative significance in the leadership fight or in the General Council's behaviour. Though Gaitskell was a public school and Oxford product, a son of an Indian Civil Service official, while Bevan was a sponsored coal miner, Deakin and the General Council leadership had decided that the former was a man with whom they could work but the latter was dangerous.[3]

The Left had advanced the notion that defeat of the Churchill Tory Government could be accomplished by demanding more nationalization and a change in defence policy. On both issues the Left had the initiative, winning support from all parts of the movement. Such old stalwarts as Herbert Morrison and Hugh Dalton had been eliminated in 1952 from the National Executive Committee of the Party, and six out of seven of the constituency seats were held by the Left. All six were again elected in 1953 and then again in 1954.[4] It was quite conceivable that a new, left-wing Labour Government might be returned, with unpredictable consequences for the economy and for the bargaining system. Council leaders knew that the Labour Party was no longer merely an ineffectual political wing of the union movement; the Party had shown it could provide, and manage, an alternative Government.

---

[1] *LPCR* (1952), p. 127.

[2] Ralph Miliband, *Parliamentary Socialism* (London, Merlin Press, 1964), p. 314.

[3] 'Deakin, Williamson, Lawther and most of the trade union leaders of their generation were practical idealists in the mould of Ernie Bevin. They supported Gaitskell as Bevin had supported Attlee, not to keep out intellectuals—Gaitskell himself, with his background of Winchester and Oxford, was an intellectual of no mean calibre—but to keep out theorists who, in their view, were dangerous to the Party' (Lord George-Brown, *In My Way* (London, Gollancz, 1971), p. 80).

[4] Miliband, op. cit., pp. 326–7.

While Bevan's record in the 1945-51 Government hardly supported the notion that he would revive a socialist *sturm und Drang* by seizing 'the commanding heights', the Council leaders nonetheless feared that political changes might upset economic recovery in the existing mixed economy and—by say, state intervention in bargaining—the leadership's influence over the collective bargaining system itself. In defence against this threat, the prevailing theme in a number of public statements issued by Deakin and others on the General Council was that the trade unions might once again have to step in, as they did in 1931, to save the Party from the 'political comrades'. As our record of the group's post-1954 activities will indicate, Brown and Pannell, its leaders, assumed precisely such a role in the new crisis, and of course won informal support from the General Council. Unlike the 1931 crisis, however, the unions themselves now were as divided as the 'political comrades'—as our AEU model clearly indicated. The predominant thought among the Council leadership was that in these post-World War II years, unlike the post-World War I and depression years, the unions could carry on with traditional, job-orientated, business unionism, because of both labour market conditions and the atmosphere of political liberalism. The General Council's views were aptly summarized by the ex-Miners' agent, Mr Bryn Roberts, who served as General Secretary of the National Union of Public Employees (NUPE) from 1934 to 1962:

> They [Council leaders] are more conservative than the Tories. To these trade union leaders the past is heroic, and while the present bewilders them the future frightens them. . . . The social furniture is now nicely arranged and anyone seeking to disturb it is a disruptionist or an irresponsible militant and should be sternly disciplined.[1]

George Brown (*Later Lord George-Brown*) and Moderation

It is surely one of the more ironic twists of post-war union political history that George Brown, who after 1954 came to symbolize for some unionists as well as for the general public the manual worker-MP, was never quite accepted by his peers in the union movement as 'authentic' working-class, despite his origins as a son of a lorry driver who had been prominent in the T & G in London. His lack of a manual work experience, his elegant attire for some years before 1954, and his association with the 'press lord', Cecil King and the

---

[1] B. Roberts, *The Price of TUC Leadership* (London, Allen and Unwin, 1961), pp. 53–4.

Mirror—roughly in that order—appear to have been the main factors in their evaluation.[1]

It is useful to begin with his entry into politics and trace his sponsorship in order to show (1) the essential irrelevance of the 'cloth cap' as an operative concept; and (2) how he developed his ties with Deakin and utilized the group on behalf of the right-wing campaign to secure a moderate leader.

Brown's Labour Party experience pre-dates by some years his association with unionism; in this respect his pathway to Parliament is distinctly different from that taken by most AEU-MPs and other manualists in Parliament. As is true of most of the middle-class leaders of the Party who began their careers in the 1930s, Brown started on the Left—as a nationally known speaker and writer for Labour's League of Youth. His first extended paid work experience before becoming associated with the T & GWU (his sponsor) was as a fur salesman—appropriately attired in striped trousers and black jacket—for the John Lewis Department store in London.[2] This trade was abruptly terminated when one of his customers recognized him on a League outdoor platform and complained to the Lewis management. By virtue of his father's job as a T & GWU leader, he was then able to obtain through Ernest Bevin, the T & G's General Secretary, a position as ledger clerk in the North London Regional office of that union. He later won a position as organizer, and then obtained union sponsorship and adoption. In the 1945 General Election, at age thirty-one, he entered Parliament to represent Belper.[3]

Before winning election from the trade union MPs as Chairman of the Group, his talents had been recognized by the Party leaders,

[1] In 1951, having lost his salary as Minister of Works, Brown contemplated quitting the House of Commons. From the modest MP salary and the supplementary but minor funds from the T & G he felt that he could not support his family without additional funds. He was able to remain, however, because Cecil King of the *Mirror* began to pay him a retainer. King, he writes, 'thought it important for me to remain in politics' (George-Brown, op. cit., pp. 60–3).

Even more interesting in the light of Brown's role as a sponsored MP during the period is his observation that: 'The whole idea of trade unions having their own tied members in Parliament is out of date, and I think it is bound to wither away' (op. cit., p. 90). This autobiography, unfortunately, is silent about the circumstances surrounding Brown's accession to the Chairmanship of the Trade Union Group and his role therein, beyond a bitter reference to the fact that despite his having been Chairman and still 'an official of the Transport Workers Union seconded for parliamentary duties', many trade union MPs voted for Harold Wilson as leader in the Wilson-Brown contest of 1963 (ibid., p. 88).

[2] Sir William Connor ('Cassandra'), *George Brown: A Profile and Pictorial Biography* (London, Pergamon, 1964), p. 14. Brown refers to 'Cassandra' as 'the best friend I made at the *Mirror*' (George Brown, op. cit., p. 63).

[3] Ibid, Chap. 2; cf, George-Brown, op. cit., Chaps 1 and 2.

but his specialties had been agriculture and defence. In 1954, when elected by the group, he was opposition Defence spokesman; indeed, that continued to be his major interest for some years. Within a few months after he became Group Chairman however, Brown showed an ability to publicly synthesize the two principal concerns of Arthur Deakin and other leaders of the union movement: the threat of a left-wing Leader in the Party; and the related danger that unofficial movements might be encouraged by left 'intellectuals'. As will be seen by our later analysis of its minutes and reports, the Group as such does not seem to have discussed at that time the unofficial dockers' strike of 1954, which had evoked expressions of sympathy from Barbara Castle, Richard Crossman, and Harold Wilson in the Labour Left Journal, *Tribune*. Brown's own response to the sympathizers violated the T & G tradition that its MPs remain outside the industrial activities of the union. However, Brown very clearly expressed the anxiety of Deakin at the moment of the Group's creation, and presaged the function that Brown and Pannell would assume within the Parliamentary Party. We reproduce below in its entirety the *Guardian's* account of that response:

Referring apparently to an article in 'Tribune', Mr Brown said, 'Our colleagues who regard themselves as on the Left of the Labour movement' had chosen to intervene in the dock strike and to attack Mr Arthur Deakin and the T. and G.W.U. He commented: 'The trade union movement has won after much struggle a great position of responsibility and power. This had brought immense rewards to our people. We are not going to permit a handful of ex-presidents of the Oxford Union Debating Society to destroy it for us.'[1]

George Brown's purpose in shifting both his image and much of his energies to the trade union scene is beyond the scope of this study. It is, however, of some importance for any study of trade union political purpose that Brown not only altered his own political style, but soon succeeded in obtaining the aid of Arthur Deakin and the General Council in changing the functions of the heretofore ceremonial body.[2]

[1] *Manchester Guardian* (30 October 1954).

[2] In discussing his decision to quit the Commons in 1970, Brown implies that a major reason for his decision was his refusal to be 'vetted' by both the Regional Committee and the National Executive of the T & G about his 'adherence or non-adherence to the policy decisions laid down by the union's biennial delegate conference' (George-Brown, op. cit., p. 88). However, the officials in charge of the T & G Panel advised this writer that when Brown had begun his pursuit of a renewed sponsorship in 1970, he was told at the Regional Committee level that he had been two years in arrears in his contributions to his branch, and therefore

On their part, neither Deakin nor the Council were converted to a use of Parliament for advancing 'the interests of labour'. They would soon show to the group and to the union world that they still opposed an activist-type political policy, and that they were primarily determined to keep the industrial relations system free of political influences.

Charles Pannell and Traditional Collective Bargaining

Brown's dynamic role in the group helped bring him to the very top levels of Government and of the Party leadership. Pannell's sojourn in the corridors of power was less conspicuous and of shorter duration. Yet, his organizing activity—as reflected in group minutes—is equally important for the ten-year period in which the group assumed an aggressive role in the Party leadership struggles. In his case there is no question either of his working-class credentials or his close ties to his own union.

Pannell's closeness to his union Executive, and their common hostility to Bevanism led to Pannell's running as a stalking horse candidate on behalf of Gaitskell, and against Bevan, in the 1955 Party Treasurer's contest. At first glance this tie might appear to contradict a major point in the study, namely that the MP's tie to his union is tenuous. But, as will be seen from our analysis of this contest and Pannell's subsequent activities, the very closeness of the Pannell-AEU relationship confirms the principal theme of this book, which is that the British trade union movement was not seeking either economic or social goals in its political activity in the period. The fact that this manoeuvre took place in the highly democratic AEU merely emphasized the central importance which the trade union leadership generally attached to the Bevan threat. The Pannell campaign will be seen as only one part of a pattern of direct union intervention. The 1954 change in the functions of the Trade Union Group (described in Chapter VIII) was part of the shift from rhetoric and threats to the field of organization and action. Thus, in 1954 the two general unions, as part of their commitment to the leadership struggle, increased their *per capita* payments to the Labour Party, effective as of 1955. The T & G's political director, writing in 1964, when a new General Secretary of that union, Frank Cousins, had replaced Deakin, and was casting the huge block vote for the Left-Wing rather than for the Right-Wing, alluded rather delicately to

was ineligible. This was a 'work to rule' decision; one may assume it might not have been invoked had not Brown displeased the T & G by a number of ideological and practical moves in conflict with the union leaders' views, especially by their perception of the damage to the 'main principles' of the union by his espousal of statutory incomes policies (see Chap. XIII, below).

the origin of the increased levy payments: 'The number of members on which unions affiliate (theoretically the number who pay the political levy) appears to be somewhat arbitrary. Thus the T & GWU affiliation in 1955 increased in one jump from 835,000 members to 1,000,000 where it has since remained.'[1]

The NUGMW—whose Sir Tom Williamson was closely identified with Deakin's views—increased its affiliation at the same time, and by about the same amount. The increases, which raised the Party Conference block vote of the two general unions proportionately, came only after some years of their refusing the Party's insistent call for more funds. There were widespread suspicions, Harrison notes, in view of the uncertainty of the AEU block vote, that it was Bevan's candidacy for Treasurer, rather than Party need, that motivated the increase.[2]

Pannell's career was dependent on, and reflected the views of the conservative wing of the industrial movement. His advance from shop ranks to MP and then to a Ministerial position in the 1964 Labour Government began with important assistance from his own Executive Council. He had been an apprenticed fitter and a shop steward before he was chosen by the Executive Council for the Parliamentary panel shortly after the Rule change in 1947 gave control to the EC. However, he was placed on that panel only after his own Bevanite District Committee (London, South), above, refused to nominate him, considering him as too Right Wing. He was placed on the panel, anyhow, through the rarely invoked authority of the Executive Council. Once on the panel, his own close friendship with C. W. Hallett, then General Secretary, below, proved helpful in winning adoption by the safe constituency of West Leeds and election in 1949.

Pannell sensed that both status and material gains accrued for labour during the post-war years largely as a result of full employment, rather than through parliamentary activity. He drew from this, as did the predominant union leadership, a *laissez-faire* philosophy consistent with the Perlman model. While seeing a shortage of labour as the most effective guarantee for at least retaining labour's share, he avoided advancing either socialist proposals or economic reform. In the course of a 1961 speech in defence of the bank clerks' long fight for employer recognition, he declared from the House of Commons benches that '. . . the biggest contribution to good industrial relations is undoubtedly full employment. All good

[1] Unsigned pamphlet prepared by Tony Corfield, 'The Trade Unions and Politics', p. 3, distributed as 'background notes', along with reprints of articles from the *Record*, op. cit., by the T & GWU Political Department (mimeographed).

[2] Harrison, op. cit., pp. 148–9.

industrial relations and all the advances which have been made since 1945 have sprung from full employment. The ideal is a state of mild inflation in which employers are chasing men instead of men chasing jobs.'[1]

We have seen that although the TUC had accepted the 1948–50 voluntary incomes policy proposals of the Labour Government it was fully in accord with such a conventional market bargaining philosophy, and its essential resistance to economic planning, either for a mixed economy *or* for socialist advance, was voiced by Pannell during the debate on the previously described Contracts of Employment Bill in 1963. After expressing the group's neutrality on that measure, he gave what he called the 'philosophical' views of the unions. The struggle over public ownership had then been resolved with agreement to retain Clause IV in the Party constitution, but Pannell questioned whether the Attlee Government should have undertaken nationalization of enterprises, and whether the 'imminent' Labour Government should concern itself with 'economic issues' at all:

> The Labour Party brought 20 per cent of the economy under public ownership between 1945 and 1951, and I wonder whether we had our priorities right. We concentrated on economic issues, and many social relationships were left unresolved . . . I also believe that a future Labour Government could devote all their time over five years to social relationships, and still justify themselves— dealing with the public schools system and all sorts of things like that, the divorce laws. . .[2]

Clearly, Pannell was willing to 'do good'. But it is equally clear that he was really emphasizing the over-riding importance of traditional bargaining. When Pannell was asked in 1964: 'What do you see as the purpose of trade union MPs?,' his initial response was, as indicated, that the composition of the Parliamentary Party was becoming unbalanced. While the new statistics were not yet published Pannell was aware of the surge of lawyers and other professionals then entering the Labour side. He made no reference in the previously cited interview to his group's legislative purpose. After expressing his strong feelings about the occupational function, he volunteered at length his own informal *intra*-Party factional function. In doing so he described his close friendship with the General Secretary of the AEU, Mr Hallett, and their combined efforts to defeat the Left in the industrial and political wings of the movement, by building 'IRIS cells'. By IRIS he meant the Industrial

[1] *Hansard*, Vol. 671, c. 1540–1550.   [2] Ibid., c. 1545.

Research and Information Service, Ltd, founded in 1956 by 'a group of trade unionists' to safeguard their unions' constitutions and to protect them from the insidious encroachments of Communists and 'fellow travellers'.[1] It operated mainly as a caucus of the Right Wing in trade unions. The work he and Hallett performed through IRIS cells, Pannell felt, did 'more than any single thing to reverse the direction of the AEU, the pivotal union, when the Left Wing was about to throw Hugh Gaitskell to the wolves'. Conceding the importance of the Campaign for Democratic Socialism (CDS) and the Catholic groups in leading the conflict against the Left Wing, Pannell seemed to feel that both he and Hallett, as well as the Trade Union Group, had not been given enough recognition for Gaitskell's victory in the great Labour crisis of 1959–61.[2]

IRIS was but one weapon in the arsenal used by Pannell and Brown within the Trade Union Group, and it is by no means clear from the evidence in the documents what was accomplished by it in the leadership crisis. Yet the IRIS involvement will illustrate some of the organizational methods by which the Trade Union Group and *its* leaders helped to carry out the political purposes of the predominant trade union leadership. The manner in which the Trade Union Group functioned as a faction, or caucus, to limit Labour's political initiatives, the types of issues it formally handled and the interaction between the leaders of the General Council, the Party and the group are considered in the following chapter.

---

[1] Industrial Research and Information Service Ltd, *The Communist Solar System* (London, Hollis and Carter, undated), with a Foreword by Rt Hon. Herbert Morrison, CH, MP, dated April 1957. Back cover contains the above quotation as to purpose.

[2] For the CDS's role, cf. McKenzie, op. cit., p. 623; Beer, op. cit., pp. 226–7; Lord Windlesham, *Communication and Political Power* (London, Cape, 1966), p. 109.

Chapter VIII

Functioning of the Trade Union Group, 1954–1966

Though Brown and Pannell came into leadership of the group in 1954 with distinctly different occupational backgrounds, union ties, and political aspirations, they both shared with the General Council one basic goal: to maintain a Labour Party leadership that would resist new political initiatives. Through the Trade Union Group they were able to play a significant role in the outcome of the leadership struggles that extended until 1963, when Harold Wilson became leader. The main focus in the present chapter is on the nine-year period from 1954 to 1963. After that date the group returned to its ceremonial role. There will be a brief discussion of the period 1963–5 for purposes of contrast.

The empirical evidence is largely derived from mimeographed reports of each meeting of the group and from annual reports—both prepared by Pannell. Although these reports are even less structured than the AEU Parliamentary Group 'minutes' they do provide the basis for a comparable, rough quantitative analysis, which we supplement by interviews and references to published sources.

1954 Change: Trades Union Congress's Role

At the first meeting of the Trade Union Group under George Brown's Chairmanship, on 16 March 1954, the guest speaker was the most important trade union figure of the day, Arthur Deakin. The talk, off the record, aroused some speculation in the press, but it was agreed in the group to 'appeal for reticence and loyalty' to prevent any leaks. A *Daily Herald* inquiry elicited the official response of the group, via Pannell: 'We have no knowledge of such a meeting.' The group's report to Members on Deakin's appearance, couched in language reminiscent of some Eastern European diplomatic meetings, is hardly illuminating: 'A free, frank and not unfriendly discussion took place.'

The press had good reason to sense a newsworthy event in this meeting. Participation by Deakin, and shortly by the General Council, supervened upon a long-established hands-off policy towards the group. After Deakin's appearance there followed some

146

concrete unpublicized organizational steps expressive of TUC's interest. Thus, within a week of his first membership meeting Brown reported to the Executive Council of the group that he and Pannell had negotiated a 'more satisfactory liaison between the Trade Union Group and the TUC'. The negotiators on the TUC side had been Deakin and Mr (later Sir) Vincent Tewson, then the full-time General Secretary of the TUC. The TUC designated Assistant General Secretary Victor Feather as liaison representative, and he was to attend all Executive Council meetings. A reported agreement for seven General Council representatives to meet with an equal number from the group was approved but apparently never implemented.

Quantitative Analysis of Group Activities

Brown's report of his and Pannell's success in winning such high level liaison with the very top command of the trade union movement no doubt gave a sense of legitimacy to many of the frustrated union MPs. Whatever the political voltage generated by this association, it was clearly not meant to be utilized for legislative or pressure purposes. The first recorded action, prototypical of most of the reported activity, was geared directly to defence of the Right Wing in the now high-pitched leadership conflict in the Party. It was agreed that Brown 'should meet with the Chairman of the Co-operative party as a result of criticism of "Challenge to Britain" [the 1953 policy statement of the Labour Party] by the Co-operative [*sic*] party'. Although the twenty-odd MPs sponsored by the Co-operative Movement were not part of the group, they acted as part of the Parliamentary Party and would therefore vote on policy and on the choice of leader. These Co-op MPs, traditionally pacifist, were now troubled especially by the Leader's support of German rearmament, which was as divisive an issue in the PLP, as it had been at Conference.

We assume for quantitative analysis that Brown's Co-op assignment was primarily a Party conflict item. The frequency distribution in Table III is based on all subject entries in the group reports— including 'educational' and other discussions, as well as particular decisions or actions. 'Party Conflict', in which we include the leadership conflict, ranks third, behind 'Group Status' and 'Union Problems'. A certain amount of arbitrariness is necessarily involved in these classifications because of inadequate information, and because there is some overlapping. Moreover, although this quantitative listing of the 'minutes' suggests the scope of work, it is not meant to convey the actual priorities. A few additional examples may clarify the data and also point to the limitations.

Table III. *Subjects Treated in Reports of Trade Union Group Meetings*

Subject	1954–63[a]	1963–4[b]	1964–6[c]	Total
Legislation	6	3	3	12
Union Problems	26	—	—	26
Group Status	14	2	4	20
Party Conflict	13	1	1	15
Social Occasions	9	2	3	14
Education Programmes	13	—	7	20
Meetings with Leader	9	2	1	12
Miscellaneous	7	—	2	9
Total	97	10	21	128

Source: Reports of Trade Union Group (unpublished).

[a] Before selection of new leader in 1963
[b] After selection of new leader in 1963 and before General Election
[c] After General Election (1964)

We have no evidence of group discussion of unofficial or unconstitutional strikes until the 1959–60 Parliamentary Session, when Victor Feather 'provided facts and figures in relation to unofficial strikes'. Yet it is hardly likely that so controversial and vital a union problem was avoided during the original Deakin-Tewson arrangements with Brown and Pannell. The dockers' unofficial strikes, it should be recalled, already had brought a public denunciation from Brown. While the subject was indeed a vital interest for General Council and for some group leaders, and while Deakin and Tewson might have discussed the question with Brown and Pannell, we know, *a posteriori*, that the primary topic of their abovementioned agreement was Deakin's perception of proper Party leadership. Accordingly, we have placed that agreement under 'Party Conflict'.

Some 'Party Conflict' entries are more clear-cut. For example, the 'abusive personal attack upon the Leader', reportedly made by Mr K. Zilliacus, a left-wing MP, at a 1960 Newcastle Party meeting, led to a formal vote to bring the matter to the notice of the PLP. Both Brown and Pannell, of course, voiced frequent public criticisms of Bevan and the Left outside the group but these individual expressions are not included in the tabulation.[1]

Union Problems

The standard variety of pressure action on behalf of unions played only a minor role in group work. Indeed, we find the group debating

[1] See for example, *The Times* (8 May 1954).

the problem it faced because the TUC was ignoring the group—for union legislation! This complaint relates to 'Union Problems' but, given the British legislative process, it seemed logical to assign it to 'Group Status' because it was one of many discussions that pointed up the groups' continued isolation from the TUC and its groping for a recognized legislative role, even after the assignment of Victor Feather.

The group sedulously intervened in union problems, as suggested by the total of twenty-six entries in Table III under 'Union Problems', but these include some events that will be seen as having directly impinged on the Party conflict.

Some of the reported union discussions exhibit a traditional pressure function on behalf of trade unions—the original purpose for creating such a group in the House of Commons. For reasons that will emerge presently, such a service was never claimed by the group, and was in any case of relatively minor importance. Nevertheless, the above category of 'Union Problems' does include group discussion of *official* strikes (six items) and union recognition problems (five items). These phenomena involved chiefly the relatively weaker non-manual unions, who elicited help from the MPs. For example, the officers of the National Union of Bank Employees (NUBE), having a difficult time winning recognition in that industry, appeared before the group in 1960 to seek help in breaking a deadlock with a banking firm. The MPs expressed sympathy and also voted to approach the Minister of Labour to request his intervention. During another 1960 white-collar union problem, one Member reported the resistance of an insurance firm to recognition, and Pannell offered to apply pressure by convening a 'meeting of the Labour Members of Parliament who are Vice-Presidents of Municipal Corporations, with the directors of the Company, and if necessary, with the Minister of Labour'. (Pannell, like many other sponsored and un-sponsored Members, had been Mayor of his town before entering the House.)

An additional four items concerned union jurisdiction, or demarcation. Thus, in 1959, the group agreed to arrange a meeting between representatives of the Confederation of Shipbuilding and Engineering Unions and the Railway Unions, to offer its services for solution of the problem. (There were several important stoppages in 1955, according to Turner, that were essentially inter-union disputes but the Trade Union Group does not seem to have entered into any one of them.)[1] It is normal practice for such problems to be settled without TUC or outside intervention. However, since the Confedera-

---

[1] H. A. Turner, *Trade Union Growth, Structure and Policy*, (London, George Allen and Unwin, 1962), p. 250.

tion rules do not provide for any arbitration or demarcation questions,[1] the group could possibly have found a useful role in this particular dispute. If it did—and the record does not indicate whether in fact a meeting was arranged—then it would have been a distinctly unique function. And one may assume that the TUC would consider such a parliamentary function as a usurpation, even if the parties involved were willing to submit their difficulty to the MPs.

In another 1959 meeting the group assumed a pressure role within the Parliamentary Party on a matter of government action that affected members of various unions affiliated with the Confederation. For example, Fred Lee brought up the proposed denationalization of a steel firm to the Executive Committee, citing telegrams from branches and from the Confederation itself, protesting the move. The group carefully avoided taking a stand for or against nationalization at this point. It was decided merely to 'keep the issue alive on the Order Paper of the House of Commons and that it could be also stated to C. Johnson, the Secretary of the Labour Party that it was the desire of the Trade Union Executive that this should be kept alive by the Parliamentary Labour Party'. Another example was a plea to the group by the Association of Supervisory Staffs, Executives and Technicians (ASSET) for legislation that would aid that union in organizing.

Thus, the TUG did function—contrary to a later disclaimer—as a pressure group for the unions, and showed some potential in this field of activity. The evidence suggests also that the new officers raised the general level of group activity. But they steadily diminished both the legislative and pressure aspects of its work, and gave priority to a *sheet anchor*[2] assignment—within both wings of the movement—until the leadership conflict was settled.

Factional Function in Leadership Contest

Despite some considerable attention given to matters affecting the direct interests of union people, the greatest emphasis was placed on activities designed to retain and restore loyalty to the incumbent moderate Leader. The marginal interest of Brown and Pannell in law-making, or pressure on ministers, is suggested by two items discussed at a 1955 meeting, as officially reported by Mr Pannell and then supplemented by him in the more mellowed perspective of the 1964 interview. His minutes report a meeting of the entire group with the Parliamentary Party's Health Services Committee on the

---

[1] TUC, *Trade Unionism*, op. cit., p. 168.
[2] The phrase used by Feather to describe the more dynamic role of the unions in the 1931 Leadership crisis.

question of 'Industrial Health', a lively perennial at TUC meetings. At the same meeting it was decided to invite as a speaker for the entire group Mr Irving Brown, of the United States. While there is no report on a follow-up of the industrial health discussion, the minutes do make reference to an 'outstanding address' subsequently given by Brown.

While neither the substance of the address nor the later discussion is recorded, Mr Pannell told this writer in 1964 that Irving Brown's work was valuable in 'fighting the Communist conspiracy'. He considered it comparable with the work of the 'IRIS' cells, to which we return. Irving Brown was apparently highly qualified for consultation on union factionalism and the association of the unions with politics. According to Thomas W. Braden, former Deputy Director of the U.S. Central Intelligence Agency (CIA), Irving Brown had been in Western Europe since the 1940s, paid, first by an American trade union, and then by the CIA, 'to defeat Communists in the labour movement and in the political area generally'.[1]

Treasurer's Race: Pannell-AEU Gambit

Pannell's previously mentioned role in the 1956 contest for the Party Treasuryship was part of the industrial leaders' organized efforts in the Party leadership struggle. The AEU National Committee had already in 1955 voted to support Bevan for Treasurer. The lay delegates, constituting a majority of the entire AEU delegation to the Party Conference, had voted to cast the block vote for 'Nye'. But the AEU's Executive Council, claiming that it alone had the right to decide on how to cast the block of votes, refused to accept the majority's preference. An Appeal Court decision backed the majority. In 1956 George Brown was the right-wing candidate against Bevan. Aware that they could not win support for Brown, the Executive Council came before the National Committee with an idea for running Charles Pannell as a 'favourite son' candidate for the Treasurer's position. The Committee voted against the idea, and at Conference the union's lay delegates again voted to cast the entire AEU block vote for Bevan. But the Executive, despite the 1955 Appeal Court ruling, defied the majority, this time casting the vote for Pannell. Bevan won in any case: the T & G had now switched, under Cousins' leadership, below, to the Left Wing.[2]

Soon after his election as Treasurer Bevan made his peace with Gaitskell but the threat to the Leader remained. Frank Cousins, associated with the 'New Left' and swinging the nation's largest

---

[1] *New York Times* (8 May 1967). See Chap. XI, below.

[2] M. Harrison, *Trade Unions and the Labour Party* (London, Allen and Unwin, 1960), pp. 147–8.

union for a generally left-wing line at Congress and at Conference, posed, perhaps, a more serious challenge to orthodox leadership than had Bevan.

The well-known Right-Left differences on domestic and foreign policy are not reflected in the group's business; indeed, a striking feature of the reports is the absence of substantive discussion of an economic or political nature, either on issues of concern to the union movement or to the Party. This absence may be partly a function of the procedure in the Parliamentary Labour Party, which does not officially allow for the existence of a Trade Union Group for legislative purposes. As the Leadership crisis grew in the late 1950s, however, the Parliamentary Party leaders as well as Brown and Pannell devised a legislative façade for the group.

In 1958, Pannell announced to all Members in the group the issuance of a 'Constitution . . . after much heart-searching and discussion with the Deputy Whip and the Deputy Leader'. The PLP leaders would, according to the release, 'ask the Parliamentary Committee to pass on to this group legislative or statutory orders likely to touch trade union interests or matters of labour relations'.

Procedurally it was stipulated, first, that it was 'impossible' for the group 'to mandate its Members' and second, that no press notices should be issued. Pannell subsequently issued an undated 'interpretation' that the group now had the status of 'a specialist Group of the Party'. As already noted, he occasionally spoke on the floor of the House as Secretary of the group. Several industrial matters of interest to the Party were formally funnelled through the group, with the understanding that the matters would be given to either Robens, or Lee, both TUG members, but acting on such matters as official front bench Party spokesmen. Commenting to this writer on the purpose of such apparent sleight of hand, one front bench member of the group said: 'The Party leaders threw them [the group leaders] a bone so they could claim to be important.'

If the Members of the group were impressed with the original 1954 liaison, which did provide a real organizational tie with the TUC (albeit a non-legislative one), few of them could have had illusions about the substantive value of the Parliamentary Party recognition. Indeed, less than a year elapsed before Mr Roy Mason, a Miners' MP, wrote that the Members of the Trade Union Group were 'gagged' and in 'revolt'. The fact that Mason was young, respected, an authentic manualist, and of the Right Wing, might have compounded what he later called the 'furore' created inside the group by his article. The National Union of Mineworkers was brought into the fracas, possibly because Mason had also written that the unions were using their safe seats for elderly men whom they wanted to retire, rather than sending their young men with 'vision'. Called 'on the carpet' by Chairman George Brown, and asked to apologize, he refused; but upon receiving from Ernest Jones, the Yorkshire President of the NUM 'a letter of stricture', he did accede to a face-saving release by the group which said that Mason had admitted his charge was 'inaccurate'.[1]

The continuing lack of either legislative authority or substantive political purpose is suggested by authoritative texts on parliamentary procedure. In his *Government and Parliament*, the former Deputy Labour Party leader, Herbert Morrison, mentions the 'friendly relationship between the General Council and the Trade Union Group of the Parliamentary Party'. Although published in 1954, and revised in 1958 and in 1965, this study does not go beyond the brief fraternal nod mentioned: one finds no mention of the group (or of Brown or Pannell) in the extensive index.[2] Jennings' classic *Parliament* (1957 edition) also omits any reference to the TUG.[3]

It is not without irony that the union-MPs' irrelevance for substantive trade union political activities has been recorded by Victor Feather! Feather's *Essence of Trade Unionism*, written in 1963 for a general audience after he had served some nine years as the TUC liaison with the Trade Union Group, contains his considered ideas on the Labour Party, on legislative goals and methods, and on government. Since he later became General Secretary of the TUC, his views are clearly of value for this phase of the analysis and for the broader issue of contemporary union political purpose.

Feather was himself a Labour Party activist. As Assistant General Secretary of the TUC he was involved in some of the General Council's work with the central and lesser NEDDIES. Yet his book echoes the essentially *laissez-faire* philosophy enunciated by Charles Pannell in the 1963 speech previously cited. In his more deliberately and more carefully reasoned interpretation of contemporary trade union political purpose, the Perlman model again comes to life. Both the idea of initiating social change, as well as the allegedly socialist beliefs of the unions that founded the Labour Party are carefully exorcised by this analysis:

> If history and economic circumstances had been different the Labour Party, as such, might never have come into being, and instead, there might have been a small academic Socialist Party without a mass membership still striving to win popular support. . . .

[1] The *People* (22 November 1959); interviews with Mason (October 1964).

[2] The Rt Hon. Lord Morrison of Lambeth, *Government and Parliament: A Survey from the Inside*, 3rd edn (London, Oxford University Press, 1964).

[3] Sir Ivor Jennings, *Parliament*, 2nd edn (Cambridge, Cambridge University Press, 1957).

> The job of a trade union leader is to look after the interests of his members, not to serve the purposes of other groups or individuals who see in the unions a pathway to political power. . . . Every political situation should be judged on its merits, and only from the standpoint of the members' interest.[1]

Feather summarizes the constitutional developments that have guided the TUC in its dealings with governments; in this analysis there is no room—and indeed, they aren't even mentioned in his book—for sponsored MPs for the trade union movement in contemporary Britain: 'Trade unionists claim the right to make their representations direct to whatever government may be in authority.' That right, however, after so many years of functioning in a mixed economy, is limited by the continued faith in pure and simple unionism!

Changes in government, from Labour to Conservative and vice versa, are viewed by Feather with an Olympian detachment based on the economic rather than the political position of the unions:

> The system of Wage-fixing in Britain in general does not involve the government. The agreements reached are between employers and trade unions. Consequently, a change of government does not mean a change in the agreements which have been made within an industry. This continuing relationship in industry makes for stability and reduces the area of tension and excitement about the effects of changes which an election is bound to engender.[2]

Clearly Feather was not chosen to liaise with the group because of his faith in parliamentary politics for either the short range or long range needs of unions.

Crisis of 1959–60

In the event the nominal specialist designation of 1958 was discarded by the group's officers in 1959 as a direct result of a new leadership 'crisis'. Indeed, all the non-factional functions that the group had been cultivating since 1954 were discarded. The officers decided also that events in the outside political world and in the trade union field required a freer hand for the group's spokesmen. Without formal change, Brown and Pannell seem to have unilaterally decided to operate in a broader field than specified in the earlier 'recognition' agreement, and to remove the restraint on publicity.

[1] Victor Feather, *The Essence of Trade Unionism*, 3rd edn (London, The Bodley Head, 1964), pp. 38–9.
[2] Ibid., pp. 79–80. See Chap. XIII, below, for the TUC's and Feather's more recent views.

A new 'crisis' function was announced by Pannell in his signed 'report of the Parliamentary Session, 1959–60'—in overtones suggesting the 1931 showdown:

> We come together again at a moment of crisis. The Party Conference, by a small majority finds itself at variance with the overwhelming majority of the Parliamentary Party and the decision of the Trades Union Congress. Our tradition in the past has been to assert that we are not a pressure group and so we have concentrated our energies on industrial matters. In the new and strained situation of today . . . we, as the trustees of those who founded this Party and for whom it particularly exists, must now consider whether we should widen the scope of our discussions so that with colleagues of like mind we may ensure the effective electoral continuance of our Movement.

Pannell followed up his annual *Report* with a special undated memorandum to Members that announced the Executive Committee's agreement with the above 'sentiments' regarding the group's proprietary claim and trusteeship, and announced a simple new 'procedure': the Chairman was to speak in the name of the ninety-odd Members, throughout the country—for the duration of the 'emergency'.

What was the 'crisis' which evoked this proprietary claim to the Party, and abandonment of the formal industrial function won only about a year earlier? There were two immediate issues, each crucial to the Leadership: first, the hoary doctrinal one of nationalization and, second, the problem of defence policy, particularly unilateralism.

Nationalization: Clause IV

Immediately following the Party's defeat in 1959, Gaitskell proposed to an abbreviated Party Conference that removal of Clause IV (public ownership and workers' control) from the objectives of the Party Constitution might help the Party's electoral future. Conference took no vote on this revision, although Frank Cousins there took the occasion to voice the view that 'we cannot have socialism without nationalization'.[1] A majority of the NEC nevertheless decided to incorporate the amendment in the programme for the forthcoming Scarborough Conference. Inside the group, there was *no* discussion reported on the issue *per se*. On the other hand, Table III includes several entries under Party Conflict (such as the Zilliacus incident, above) which indicate that the *Leadership* implications

---

[1] *LPCR* (1959), pp. 112 ff.

were fully recognized, and discussed with passion and purpose. For example, on 30 March 1960 a formal motion was introduced and apparently passed (votes were never recorded) deploring the 'recurring breaches of loyalty within the Parliamentary Labour Party' by unnamed colleagues who had offered notions 'upon the Order Paper that are in conflict with the Party's official policy'. The motion denounced such a move as a 'serious breach of loyalty', and a 'defiance of political democracy'.

The spuriousness of the nationalization debate, as well as its relevance for the Leadership struggle have been deftly defined by Denis Healey, MP, a prominent revisionist and a principal in later decision-making for the choice of a Leader to succeed Gaitskell: 'Hugh Gaitskell chose to raise the issue of Clause IV (most people hadn't *heard* of Clause IV) and the battle was on. This wasn't necessary. Lots of people are prepared to commit adultery who would fight to the death against changing the Ten Commandments.'[1]

As is well known, the 1960 Conference restored public ownership as part of the Party's objects. The ritualistic nature of that act for the unions is suggested by Pannell's 1963 speech, above. The passion for public ownership had been so spent that Pannell, speaking as group secretary in the House of Commons, could casually dismiss it as a present goal, and question whether the Party should have taken it up in the past, or should concern itself with it in the future. Mr Wilson himself, after he became the Leader in 1963 and launched the Party's General Election campaign, was passionate on the subject of technology but left Clause IV unsullied but securely shelved.

Unilateralism

While the public ownership problem was again settled, the conflict had illustrated that the Left Wing had sufficient power in the unions and in the constituencies to seriously bid for the Leadership. The thrust by the New Left, rallied under the banner of the Campaign for Nuclear Disarmament (CND), created the real 'crisis' role of the group—as it did for other segments of the Movement. Not only was Frank Cousins participating personally in the Aldermaston marches to press unilateral nuclear disarmament by Britain, but even 'one of the staunchest pillars of orthodoxy', the National Union of

---

[1] 'The Mind of Denis Healey', *Sunday Times* (30 January 1966). Mr Healey was then Defence Minister. George Brown, ironically, after having climbed to power with the help of the cloth cap image, came to see this struggle as essentially part of Gaitskell's attempt to 'lead Labour away from the cloth-capped image of the past, to modernize and refashion the Party as an instrument of reform and humane Government to appeal to all sections of society' (London, Gollancz, 1971), (*In My Way*, George-Brown, pp. 80–1).

General and Municipal Workers, had resolved at its 1959 conference that the next Labour Government should take unilateral action in ceasing to manufacture nuclear weapons and in barring such weapons from British territories.[1]

The new confrontation was around a joint statement on 'Foreign Policy and Defence' drafted by the NEC and the General Council for the 1960 national meetings. Central to the official defence policy was support of the North Atlantic Treaty Organization (NATO), which the Conservative Government had endorsed, along with appropriate defence funds and provision for British training areas for the German Federal Republic army. At Congress in 1960, one key NATO feature was voted down: by an overwhelming majority delegates rejected General Council advice and accepted a T & G resolution to oppose nuclear arms and to disallow the use of British territory for the German army.[2] In the same year, at the Party Conference, T & GWU's resolution called for an end to nuclear arms testing and manufacturing by Britain, and demanded that the next 'Labour Government should take a series of positive steps toward co-existence and disarmament'. This was narrowly carried even after Gaitskell said it would be interpreted as a vote for neutralism and for withdrawal from NATO. The Engineers' 'unilateralist' resolution for 'unilateral renunciation of the testing, manufacture, stock-piling and basing of all nuclear weapons in Great Britain' was also passed over the objections of Gaitskell, Brown and many leaders of the industrial and political wings. In addition, the Executive's Defence policy—the joint statement of TUC and NEC—was narrowly rejected.[3]

Despite this challenge to Gaitskell's leadership at Scarborough, the Trades Union Congress did *not* endorse unilateralism. While Congress did vote for a T & G motion similar to the one passed by Conference it also voted to endorse the joint NEC-General Council position, above.[4] This contradiction arose from the famous flip-flop of the AEU at Congress, where John Boyd announced a reversal of its prior Conference vote for the unilateralists. The fact that TUC opposed the position taken by the Party Conference

---

[1] R. Miliband, *Parliamentary Socialism* (London, Merlin Press, 1964), p. 342.

[2] Congress *Report* (1960), pp. 393 ff.

[3] Ibid., pp. 176–202.

[4] Ibid., pp. 396–410. Indicative of the vital concern of the conflict to the trade union movement was the unusual action taken by twenty members of the General Council, who in a public statement entered the contest on Gaitskell's side. George Woodcock, on the other hand, interpreted TUC policy as supporting two policies or none, whichever way you look at it'. Lord Windlesham, *Communication and Political Power* (London, Cape, 1966), p. 109.

gave Brown and Pannell their *casus belli* for their direct and indirect pressure on the unions. They now set about switching enough votes so that the unilateralist stand taken by the 1960 Conference could be reversed at the 1961 Conference.

This strange development in trade union representation at Westminster, with the official organization of union-sponsored MPs organizing to pressure the unions instead of carrying out their historic and presumed contemporary role of speaking 'in the interests of labour'— is illustrated by three separate events: The Biennial Delegate Conference (BDC) of the Transport Workers; the scandal in the Electrical Trades Union (ETU); and a group arrangement with IRIS at Westminster.

Transport & General Conference 1961

George Brown had enough audacity to try personally to reverse the largest block of union votes, assembled at the 1961 Biennial Delegate Conference of his own union, the T & G. For this unprecedented MP function he first had to rent a hall directly opposite the meeting, having been refused permission to address the BDC. In T & G, as in many unions, the rules do not permit MPs to speak at policy conferences. While the AEU officers had occasionally bent their rules to bring in an MP, in the T & G not only the rules but a strong tradition had kept them out. Brown could contemplate this bold encounter at the perimeter of the Conference because his new status in the Movement—while to a large degree determined by his union (T & G) credentials—clearly transcended his T & G sponsorship. Writing about Brown in 1962, Sampson, in *Anatomy of Britain*, said '. . . he is sometimes considered unpredictable and temperamental. But in the past year he has worked closely with Gaitskell, and their alliance is the linchpin which keeps the party wheel in place.'[1]

For this union confrontation Brown could hardly resort, as he had during the Deakin incumbency, to the appeal of trade union loyalty: now it was the incumbent, Cousins, who was being challenged. Instead, Brown's attack was reminiscent of Bevan's old charge against Deakin *et al.*, namely, that the block vote of T & G, as cast by the General Secretary at Scarborough, was not representative of 'Labour folk' thinking. Brown, of course had abundant reason to question—as did much of the press—whether the million-odd membership of the T & G had really turned so completely and so soon from the posture they had assumed under Arthur Deakin's direction. Not surprisingly, however—in view of the power of the General Secretary—the BDC decided to back unilateralism.

[1] Anthony Sampson, *Anatomy of Britain* (New York, Harper, 1962), pp. 101–2.

Electrical Trades Union (ETU)

The sensational trial of some ETU Communist leaders for stealing a union election provided the group with its most sustained trade union involvement of the entire 1954–1960 period; or, for that matter, in the years to follow. This scandal accounts for no less than *five* entries under the heading 'Union Problems' in Table III. It also led Charles Pannell, as he told the Party Conference in 1961, to sit in the High Court hearing the case, for 'many, many days at the request of my colleagues of the trade union group of the Parliamentary Party'.[1] This scrutiny by Pannell, and his reporting of it to the Conference, suggests the general political interest in the outcome of the trial. The group officers, however, greatly inflated the general political significance of the issue. Again, this involvement must be seen in the context of the group's new factional role, rather than as a sign that either the Government or the trade union movement as a whole was moving away from the tradition of legal abstention.

The case had had an industrial background dating back to 1958, when the TUC had begun a formal investigation of publicized allegations of irregularities in ETU elections. The TUC's formal investigation was still in progress when the High Court in 1961 upheld a complaint from Mr John Byrne that the incumbent President and General Secretary had fraudulently prevented his election as General Secretary. The 1961 Congress voted to expel the union.[2]

Within the Party, the ETU was one of the 'big six' union targets for the campaign launched by Gaitskell, the Campaign for Democratic Socialism (CDS) and Parliamentary Party leaders, to reverse the 1960 Party Conference vote. Each of these large unions had cast their block votes against the Executive. Gaitskell had called on the Parliamentary Party to refuse to accept the Conference decision because it was a 'suicidal path' for the Party and the country. George Brown, Denis Healey and others had backed Gaitskell. On the other hand, Harold Wilson had announced himself a 'unity' candidate against Gaitskell, largely on account of the latter's refusal to accept the Party Conference's defence position.[3] Thus, the ETU scandal was an integral part of the Party Leadership contest. Pannell himself made the point clear in an article written for the AEU *Journal* in 1961, where he included the ETU with other details of his efforts on behalf of 'the Gaitskell lines' of Party policy.[4]

[1] *LPCR* (1961), pp. 92–3.
[2] Congress *Report*, pp. 311–12; cf. Henry Pelling, *A History of British Trade Unionism* (Harmondsworth, Penguin, 1967), pp. 250–3.
[3] R. McKenzie, *British Political Parties*, revised edn (London, Mercury, 1963), pp. 616–22.
[4] 'Away from Big Ben', *Journal* (September 1961), pp. 280–1.

The NEC of the Party, in advance of the 1961 Conference, disaffiliated the ETU. (It was re-admitted—with new officers—in 1962.) Citing that part of the High Court judgement which declared that the union was 'a Communist-controlled organization', it ruled the ETU ineligible under the Party Constitution.[1] Conference upheld the NEC.

Altogether the group held five formal recorded meetings at Westminster on the ETU matter, apart from the visit of Pannell to the Court. First, Feather is reported to have spoken to the Members of the group before the verdict. After the verdict, Pannell, using his new authority on publicity, issued a release announcing to *all* MPs that an open group meeting would consider 'the implication of the ETU Court Judgment . . . bearing in mind that the Parliamentary Party might be forced to give a political answer to what should be considered an industrial question'.

At this second of the meetings, the newly designated (or properly elected) officers of the ETU appeared; there followed a third meeting to hear the TUC's General Secretary, George Woodcock; the fourth meeting was one for private group discussion; the fifth was addressed by Lord Citrine, the long-retired Secretary of the TUC and once assistant Secretary of the ETU.

As might have been predicted, neither the Government nor the Trades Union Congress was prepared to seek the 'political' solutions about which Pannell had warned. The General Council decided, as did the Ministry of Labour, to leave to each national union the problem of how to 'prevent breaches of their election rules'.[2]

IRIS at Westminster

We have already discussed Pannell's perception of IRIS' work within the AEU on behalf of the Gaitskell cause. However, that organization, significantly enough, was also brought into the Houses of Parliament by the Trade Union Group during the period—shortly after the Trades Union Congress had censured IRIS for its factional work within the industrial wing of the movement.

IRIS' attempts to influence the outcome of union electoral contests was brought to light at the 1960 Congress by two leading left-wing non-manual unions affiliated to the Confederation of Shipbuilding and Engineering Unions—the Draughtsmen, and ASSET. After the spokesmen for both of these associations described IRIS' attempts to defeat left-wing candidates in their respective organizations and to elect in their place right-wing people, Congress voted a censure motion. Sir Vincent Tewson, the then General Secretary of the TUC,

[1] *LPCR* (1961), p. 23.   [2] *Congress Report* (1962), p. 284.

indicated both the polarization and the predominant leadership's preference when he announced that the General Council accepted the motion as being consistent with TUC's previous position against outside interference in the unions, but added that there was other 'far more insidious propaganda which comes from other bodies'.[1]

Despite the 1960 TUC censure vote, a special meeting was staged at the House of Commons in June 1961 by IRIS on the invitation of the Trade Union Group. Guests were described by Pannell as sixty-five 'comrades from the captive nations of Europe—Poles, Yugoslavs, Albanians, Hungarians, Germans and ex-Soviet citizens—all people who chose freedom and who were all trade unionists'. Brown as chairman of the group addressed them and they then 'resolved the meeting into a Brains Trust', with Pannell and three other MPs sitting in on an (undisclosed) discussion. In January 1962, upon IRIS's initiative, Brown authorized Pannell to arrange another meeting and 'recruit such Members as are felt necessary'. There is no record of this having been arranged.

The effort of George Brown at the T & G's Delegate Conference; the group's intense concern with the ETU scandal; the associations with IRIS—all these organizational activities of the group leaders had made them an intimate part of the broader Leadership struggle. Summarily, the group broadly reflected the basic political purpose of the predominant elite in Congress—*status quo* for both the industrial and political wings of the movement.

The Party as a whole achieved substantial unity after Scarborough for the anticipated General Election; and Gaitskell's Leadership seemed secure. Some large unions, including not only the ETU, but also the more pivotal AEU, had switched away from the CND position, enabling Gaitskell to win a reversal of the 1960 position on defence before the 1961 Conference.

The group's 1960–61 Report, signed by Pannell, exulted over the defeat of the 'unilateralist cause' and claimed credit for that defeat, but is wholly silent on either the immediate or long range strategic decisions affecting trade unions in Britain. 'This is a much more agreeable report to write than that of a year ago,' Pannell said in opening that *Report*, adding:

Then the party seemed to be facing ruin and the leadership about to be repudiated. Now we say the Party is on its way back. . . . Electorally the unilateralist cause has done badly and the Annual Conferences of the Unions have rallied to reverse the decisions of a year ago. . . . The political climate has changed beyond belief in

---

[1] Congress *Report* (1960), pp. 485–6.

one year. . . . For all the progress made in this last year—the Trade Union Group can take its fair share of the credit.

Whatever the factional and indirect electoral contribution the group made, Pannell's account suggests no attempt to reclaim the 'industrial' role which had been shelved for the 'emergency'.

1963 Settlement of Leadership

The death of Hugh Gaitskell a few months after the 1962 Party Conference threw the Leadership open; the stages and details of Brown's own contest with Harold Wilson and James Callaghan for the succession are well known.[1] Professor McKenzie noted that Deputy Leader Brown failed to become Leader because he 'had a reputation for impulsiveness, truculence, and insensitivity which more than offset his greater reputation for loyalty to the parliamentary leadership . . .'; that Wilson won because he was 'incomparably the ablest parliamentary performer'; and, prophetically, that Wilson's accession represented no swing to the Left by Labour.[2] In any event, after Wilson became Leader, a solid front was restored for the 1963–4 General Election campaign. Brown, still Deputy Leader, was very much the number two man in the Party, and, later, in the Labour Government.

The vacuum of purpose within the Trade Union Group and, indirectly, the political vacuum in the sponsoring unions themselves, became apparent once more after the Leadership struggle abated. While the meetings continued they were now so infrequent that James Griffiths, a vice-president, queried Brown about the change of pace. Evidently other MPs were also upset, for Pannell gave the following revealing account in the *Report* of the 1963–4 Session of Brown's reply: 'The Parliamentary atmosphere had been so peaceful, the unity so strong and without controversy, there has arisen no urgent necessity for further meetings.'

Along with this ingenuous epitaph for the factional function, the Secretary unconsciously revealed how marginal all the 'Legislation' and 'Trade Union Problems' had been in relation to the TUC's limited political purposes. With not a word about the General Council's assignment of Feather, he wrote in the same *Report*—his last one: 'A novel feature of the year was a deputation from the TUC to discuss the Trade Union Amalgamation Bill, the *first official delegation from that body that this Group had received in a period of at least eleven years*.' (Emphasis supplied.)

[1] Anthony Howard and Richard West, *The Making of the Prime Minister* (London, Cape, 1965), *passim*.
[2] McKenzie, op. cit., p. 630.

Labour Rule (1964–6)

Brown and Pannell, as well as Lee, all entered the Government. Pannell's farewell statement to the union-sponsored MPs is not exultant. After a quite brief reference to the electoral victory, he gives a wistful, if rather vague expression of purpose for the future of the group: 'The spirit, as well as the activities of the group were never more necessary than now.' He had perceived that the 1964 victory had brought another influx into the Party of middle-class members; he was upset, despite his personal success, about the 'bloody lawyers' possibly dominating the Labour Party. Pannell had had no programmatic policy in mind for the bearers of the cloth cap. And under his successors the group's 'spirit and activities', clearly, were not legislative.

The three legislative items shown in Table III for this new phase merely establish the group's rather desperate clinging to a TUC-tie, and incidently reflect the essentially defensive nature of TUC plans even under Labour. The first deals with the legislative remedy sought by the TUC to remedy the Rookes-Barnard judgement, which was considered a threat to the right to strike. This was quickly won from Labour, without participation by the group. Having tried and failed to get Woodcock to talk to them about the proposed legislation, they asked 'that General Council actions would be conveyed to the Trade Union Group through the Secretary [Mr Neil McBride]'.

We have previously discussed at some length the second 'legislative' item, the Contracts of Employment Act which the MPs discussed in the light of the Rookes-Barnard judgement.

George Woodcock did address the group in 1965 on a third problem, incomes policy, three months after the issuance of the 1964 'Joint Statement of Intent on Productivity, Prices and Incomes'. By the time of Woodcock's appearance, the Government had already published a White Paper, 'Machinery of Prices and Incomes Policy', and warned that if the voluntary method did not prove effective, statutory controls would be needed to halt 'pay increases which are inflationary in effect'.[1] However there is no indication in the minutes of this meeting with Woodcock, or of later meetings, that the fast-changing political approaches—establishment of a Prices and Incomes Board, a norm for annual wage increases, and the references to the Board of price and wage increases—were ever formally or

---

[1] *Prices and Incomes Policy*, Cmnd 2639. For Brown's account of Labour's economic policies see his *In My Way* (London, Gollancz, 1971), Chap. 5. Here the incomes policy is described as but one feature of the Department of Economic Affairs, which Brown considers a 'social revolution that failed'. We discuss incomes policy shifts and trade union attitudes during the 1967–70 period in Chap. XIII, below.

163

informally debated by the union MPs. Instead, it is well known that when the Government decided to put its 'early warning' system on a formal statutory footing, the former Chairman of the Trade Union Group, now the Hon. George Brown, First Secretary of State, and Minister for Economic Affairs, instead of consulting with his trade union peers in the PLP, proceeded to a meeting with the General Council of the TUC, assembled at Brighton in the autumn of 1965. Only after Council approved did the Minister bring the matter, personally, before the annual Trades Union Congress for action by the delegates, and when the legislation was ready, Brown met with the Economic Committee of the General Council to win their approval. The matter was then formally brought before the House of Commons by the Government. The group was by-passed.

McBride, in 1965, did not claim a legislative pressure function for the Trade Union Group. 'We try to do a little educational work, that's our main job,' said Mr McBride to this writer.[1] Thus the group, while retaining its symbolic importance, was resigned to a largely passive and ceremonial function under the Wilson Government—reverting to the role it had played in the Attlee Government.

To sum up: the evidence from the group's own accounts of its activities in the 1954–66 period confirms the trade union MPs' irrelevance for TUC political goals. Paradoxically, it also establishes that for the purpose of resisting political activism within the Labour Party the group was a valued ally of both the TUC General Council and the Parliamentary Party Leadership. Again, in this broader canvass, as in the portrait of the AEU, oligarchic tendencies in the movement were strengthened rather than weakened as part of this process of combatting Bevanites and others who sought to utilize political action for affirmative economic or ideological goals.

Pannell early perceived the value of full employment for the status and material gains of the workers. George Brown later became identified with an incomes policy and governmental planning. But during the focal period 1954–63 the entire Trade Union Group in Parliament mirrored the union movement's distrust of dissent and innovation and real planning. Like the AEU, it did not significantly part from *laissez-faire* unionism.

[1] Interviews (1965). It should be added, however, that following the issuance of a 1967 White Paper announcing plans for more stringent wage controls, the Trade Union Group became more directly involved. The Prime Minister is said to have appeared before these MPs seeking support, and the Miners claimed that his plans were moderated as a result of pressure by Union MPs, 'particularly by the Miners' Group, and by this [NUM] Trade Union' (Lawrence Daly, in *Scottish Miner* (January 1968), p. 4).

Chapter IX

The Transport and General Workers' Union (T & GWU)

The central importance of the Transport and General Workers' Union for a study of post-war political purpose has already been clearly indicated from previous discussion. Each of the T & G's famous General Secretaries—Bevin, Deakin, Cousins and Jones have been at the centre of the political stage. We have seen Bevin's decisive intervention against the Labour Government in 1931. We have also depicted Deakin hammering for the Right Wing in the early 1950s, and Cousins for the Left Wing in the late 1950s and early 1960s. Cousins' successor has continued the identification of the T & G with left-wing Labour politics.

In exploring more thoroughly in this chapter the operative meaning of these labels it is helpful to keep in mind the relationship that exists between structure and labour market conditions on the one hand, and leadership stands on political questions on the other hand. Ever since Ernest Bevin amalgamated several dock and transport societies to form the T & GWU in early 1920s, the outstanding structural feature of this union has been the authority of its General Secretary. The casual nature of the labour market, the high rate of membership turnover, the absence of a tradition of organization, and the relative lack of education and experience of most T & G members, all favoured the growth of a strong central leadership.

The exceptionally tight labour market (on the whole and until 1966), however, favoured a shift towards work-place bargaining by shop stewards. We have seen this general tendency grow more pronounced during the period. Paradoxically, the fact that the T & G had centred so much power in the hands of its General Secretary may have permitted Deakin's successors to make a more deliberate institutional adaptation to local bargaining than was true of the less centralized and possibly more democratic Engineers'. The combination of Frank Cousins' and his successor's resistance to the Labour Government's incomes policies and the acceptance by the same leaders of work-place bargaining, has created a general image of the modern T & G as a politically-inspired trade union seeking ideological goals. However, the central argument of the present analysis is that the union made no significant shift towards reliance on political techniques for achieving its fundamental economic goals; that the political confrontations between the T & G and the Labour Government in the latter years of the period arose not over ideological questions but primarily because of the constraint imposed by the Government on all bargaining through statutory incomes policies. The incomes programmes, in turn, provided additional incentives for shifting to work-place agreements. And in shifting its own emphasis towards the work-place, the contemporary union consciously and deliberately retreated from parliamentary techniques—even though it had steadily expanded its Parliamentary Group. While it did indeed utilize its political and economic power to challenge the Wilson Labour Government's economic policies, the empirical evidence suggests that this union nevertheless conforms well to the Perlman model.

Structure

The T & G's continuing success in a highly competitive union system, and in a changing economy, owes much to Bevin's ingenious method of combining a centralized national office with autonomy for 'trade groups'. This had continued to attract into amalgamation unions unable to maintain a viable independent existence. The General Secretary, however, continues to be the voice of the national organization, enjoying prestige and great authority inside the union and—as head of the largest union—inside the entire movement.

The General Executive Committee (GEC) is functionally and structurally dissimilar to the Executive Council of the AEU and other unions that evolved out of skilled societies. This GEC does not consist of full-time officials who meet weekly and determine policy. Instead it meets infrequently and generally merely approves policy decisions made by the General Secretary. The formal policy-making body, the Biennial Delegate Conference (BDC), reflects the power which the professional elite retains in the institution. Unlike the 52-man AEU National Committee, this BDC consists of 800–900 delegates. Instead of a yearly meeting, they meet every other year and crowd their business into four days as compared to the two weeks of the AEU's conference. The Conference's debates are free and often heated. The General Secretary's interventions, however, are generally decisive, and he is rarely reversed on political or economic policies. Yet, in an important sense, the Biennial Conference of this union, like the AEU's smaller conference, has also evolved into a forum for political activists. At the 1961 BDC, which was the scene of George Brown's foray on behalf of Gaitskell's defence position, no less than eighty-eight speakers addressed themselves to the subject.[1] It is 'natural' for BDC to be political, said Mr Harry Nicholas, Acting General Secretary in 1965, because constitutional matters are reserved for Rules Revision Conferences, and 'trade issues' are kept for the trade groups and area groups.[2] The operational results of the BDC's political dialogues have been minimal.

Political Department

The T & G Political Department reflects not only the centralization but the professionalism characteristic of the union structure. During Cousins's rule it also reflected, in some degree, his ideology. The Department, during 1956–67, was managed by Mr Tony Corfield, an Oxford graduate and a left-wing Labour activist. He and his assistant, a trained young researcher, were responsible for and performed virtually all the parliamentary and formal political work of the Department.

During Cousins's incumbency Harry Nicholas served on the National Executive of the Labour Party as the union's representative, and was also for some years Treasurer of the Party. He took over the position of Acting General Secretary of the T & G in 1964 to allow Mr Cousins to take leave and enter Parliament and the Cabinet under the Labour Government.

Despite these commitments by officers at the top the direction of political activity for the substructure is left largely to the Labour Party machinery by T & G. There was no information available at headquarters regarding the extent of affiliation at the local or regional levels. We have already indicated that precise information on contracting-out is not generally available, and this writer could obtain no estimates from the main T & G office. Few, however, go to the trouble of withholding the levy. As of 1954, the T & G had only 84 per cent of its members as political contributors, while the National Union of General and Municipal Workers (NUGMW), which had a compounded contribution system—a system which facilitates collection of the levy by merging it with the regular contribution—had a 99 per cent rate. When the T & G switched in 1957 to a compound contribution, its proportion of paying members went up to 96 per cent—even though the levy was doubled at the same time to 2s.[3]

By 1964–5 the rate of payment had climbed to 98·1 per cent.

[1] Biennial Delegate Conference (BDC), unpublished *Proceedings*, pp. 445–8.

[2] At time of writing Sir Harry Nicholas, General Secretary of the Labour Party. Interview (2 December 1965).

[3] M. Harrison, *Trade Unions and the Labour Party* (London, Allen and Unwin, 1960) p. 103; Allen Flanders, *Trade Unions* (London, Hutchinson, 1968 edn.), p. 153.

Despite the T & G's clear Rule-book explanation to the contrary most members make no distinction between regular and political contributions. From interviews with members and officials it is clear that the *combined* payment is viewed, generally, as simply part of joining up and remaining a union member in good standing.

It will be recalled that the AEU's accumulation of political funds prior to 1962 was, in itself, a significant factor in expanding that union's parliamentary plan. Cousins, before he entered Parliament and the Government, greatly enlarged the MP group sponsored by T & G. However, when Nicholas and Jones, as caretaker leaders, were interviewed in 1965, while Cousins was on leave for his Government post, they were both uncertain even about the number of MPs needed for the direct political work of the T & G. *Both agreed that the growth in the number of MPs, which was then still continuing from Cousins' thrust, was determined largely by the amount of money available in the fund.*[1]

Affiliations

The grass roots activity in the Labour Party under Cousins, as measured by affiliations to local and regional parties, hardly supports the notion of a politically radical organization carrying the torch for social transformation. The union made no pretence of being directly concerned with the numerous Constituencies in which it had a high membership, but only with those represented by Members of its parliamentary group; financial and other 'useful' reports were received regularly from these Constituency agents. The more general question of Labour Party affiliation appeared in occasional articles in the union's journal and in planning notes for the union's schools, where Mr Corfield for several years made the question of Party affiliation and political activity a major topic of discussion. Apart from the foregoing, and discussions injected by delegates to the BDC, there were no regular efforts by the national office to open political channels with the branches and regions.

A survey of the T & G regions to determine the affiliation of branches to local parties and to the regional party organizations was made in 1966 by the union at the request of this writer. Of the thirteen regions, eleven sent back returns. In five there was a blanket affiliation by the region of each branch to the appropriate local party, or parties. In six the branches appear to have made their own decisions. As in the AEU, even where a branch decided on its own to affiliate, the affiliation *per se* may range from a nominal tie to real involvement. In the case of blanket affiliation, the affiliation

[1] Interviews (19 December 1965).

may be merely a means of making a financial contribution. Although it is no more accurate as an index of commitment and activity than the levy there was considerable interest indicated. For the five regions of the T & G that reported a blanket affiliation to local parties, the number of members affiliated ranged from under 20 per cent to slightly more than 50 per cent of the total eligible. In regions where the branches appear to have decided on their own whether or not to affiliate, about 50 per cent affiliated, with an average of about 50 per cent of their membership.[1]

One may speculate, on the basis of the limited information available, that the more favourable showing of affiliation to Labour, compared to the AEU 1963 data, is due to the stronger tradition of political action present in the general unions—dating back to their origins under socialist leadership—and perhaps the continued need in many 'trades' for legislative assistance (explained below). The quality of the returns, probably due to the higher authority enjoyed by the national centre in the regions, as well as the greater proportion of paid staff employed by T & G in the field, show somewhat more internal consistency and care. Yet, here, as in the AEU survey, several regional secretaries suggest in their report that they regard such information about political activity as beyond their competence or interest. In effect the T & G has largely delegated the political work to the Labour Party, and has made no serious effort to concern itself with how its own branches and regions are pursuing their Party work. The available information does suggest that on the basis of affiliations and regional reports, the T & G may have a greater formal commitment to the Labour Party than has the AEU. In the absence of controlled research procedures on affiliation, and given the previously discussed limitations on national levy payments as a guide, we are unable to quantify further the T & G's commitment to the Labour Party. The sponsored MP data are more useful.

Choosing MPs

One of the more interesting aspects of political power distribution in the movement is that the orthodox Mr Deakin's arrangement of 1954 for liaison between the TUC and the Brown-Pannell Group continued long after the left-wing Mr Cousins assumed command at T & G. Possibly this was because he was a 'new boy' on the General Council and did not inherit Deakin's immense authority in both the Council and the Party.

Cousins, however, was able to alter the make-up of the T & G Group he inherited from the Bevin-Deakin regimes after the deaths

[1] Survey, unpublished, by T & G Chief Office (1966).

of some Members and the retirement of others. He replaced these, and also added a substantial number to the total. As early as 1957, one year after he took office, Cousins indicated to the Executive of the Party that his union was determined to increase its share in the total of sponsored Members of Parliament.[1] Then from within the T & G, in 1962, 'Brother Cousins emphasized the need for young, lively trade unionists to go forward to Parliament, seized with the necessity of adopting a Socialist programme'.[2]

The latter may have been merely a *pro forma* gesture however. From the course of action taken with respect to T & G sponsorship it appears that Cousins doubted he could find among the regular T & G members people who could win adoption, reflect the line he was pursuing within the Labour Party, and also perform adequately at Westminster. In the event the T & G's new group contained a conspicuous number of people from outside the regular membership, many of them already in the House of Commons when given sponsorship, and generally in the centre or on the left on controversial issues.

The formal T & G procedure for selecting Panelists is not unlike that of AEU: after branch approval, the aspirant appears before the Regional Committee, and if approved there, the GEC's Finance and General Purposes Committee makes the final decision. This procedure takes place between General Elections, whenever the head office announces the Panel is open for revision. The Regional Secretaries are permitted some latitude in the decision-making, apparently accounting for at least one strongly pro-Gaitskell man among the 1966 crop of MPs.

The new T & G Group created Labour history by catching up in 1966 with the Miners' total. The 27-strong contingent then comprised a large number of articulate, well-educated MPs with professional backgrounds. For purposes of union membership they are included among the great variety of Labour and T & G staff; professionals; businessmen—and divers other white-collar people who belong to London branch 1/128 of the T & G's white-collar group.[3] Such distinguished names as Peter Shore, former Head of the Research Department of the Labour Party; Dr Jeremy W. Bray, a management official and statistician; Anthony Greenwood, an

[1] Memorandum of NEC of Labour Party, 'Observations from Trade Unions' (27 February 1957) (mimeographed).

[2] 'Problems and Progress', T & GWU *Record* (May 1962), p. 44.

[3] The valuable study by Bain traces the structural or 'trade group' adaptation by the T & G for white-collar recruiting and servicing. He also makes the point that 'the vast majority' of those who contract out of the political fund in T & G are white-collar workers, but gives no direct proof on that point. George Sayers Bain, *The Growth of White-Collar Unionism* (London, Oxford University Press, 1970), pp. 105–7, 118.

ex-journalist; Trevor Park, a university lecturer; John Silkin, a solicitor—these and others with mainly professional backgrounds, all came into the group during the late 1950s and early 1960s. Some were given sponsorship only after they had already been adopted by their constituency parties, but before the election; others were given sponsorship, and their constituency parties allocated funds, only after they had taken their seats in the House.

Limitations and Functions of Group

Although the new crop of MPs altered the image of the T & G Group on the ideological—and social—spectra, it was not until 1967, when the union considered its 'main principles' challenged by the statutory incomes proposals of the Wilson Labour Government that the leaders began to be directly and seriously concerned with its MPs' political stands. Prior to that date the group may have increased Cousins' influence in the Labour Party and the Labour Government, but as a group they had not been more successful than the Deakin-group had been in their search for a closer identification with the union. Nor did the leaders attempt to exploit the new talents for strategic policy decisions affecting trade unions in general, or the T & G in particular.

In his initial appearance as General Secretary before the group in 1956, Cousins 'expressed his desire to see close relationships with all members of the group, and to arrange in all ways possible for the views of the union to be put forward in the House when legislation affecting the membership was under discussion'.[1] But in practice, according to one of his aides, 'Frank was an isolationist as far as MPs were concerned'. Cousins kept them at arm's length, specifically turning down a group request for attendance at BDC meetings with the rather disingenuous explanation that the Parliamentary Group 'forms an integral part of the [Political] Department, and that the Department Secretary attended Conference in that capacity'.[2]

The union machinery nominally provided to channel political policies or 'philosophies' continued to operate within carefully drawn restrictions, as it did under the Deakin regime. Not only were the MPs denied access to the Delegate Conferences but union policy conveyed to the group was carefully restricted to narrowly defined 'trade' problems. The group minutes, prepared by the Political Secretary, generally were limited to such issues as cab regulation, road haulage laws, public market and fishing regulations. According to Nicholas 'only on trade matters do we expect them to follow our policy'. Both Nicholas and Jones agreed that neither 'industrial' nor

[1] Minutes of Parliamentary Group (1 July 1956), p. 3.
[2] Minutes (12 May 1959).

'broader political questions' are within the group's purview; the former was reserved for the union, the latter was delegated to the Party.[1]

But the complexity of the union's responses to the Labour Government's initiatives permit no such simple classifications. To illustrate the nature of the T & G's political policy under the 1964 and 1966 Labour Governments, it is useful to focus on the union's point of view on three significant events: the Party debate on Commonwealth immigration; the entrance into, and the resignation from the Wilson Cabinet of Frank Cousins; and the incomes policy stand and Royal Commission testimony of the union under the Wilson Government.

Commonwealth Immigration

The stand taken by the T & G against the Labour Government's Commonwealth immigration policy suggests that on some 'broader' issues this union, like the AEU, was willing to waive the general limitation on the scope of the MPs' work. Immigration for the T & G was both an industrial and political question. As an open union it had organized many 'coloured' immigrants from the former Commonwealth countries—Pakistan, India and the Caribbean islands. On the other hand, many members, and especially the vocal and powerful dockers were now 'closed' in their outlook towards new entrants in general and coloured workers in particular. The officers were no doubt sympathetic towards the immigrants threatened by the new restrictionist policy of the Government. Yet the position of the T & G was presented not by a general officer, but by 'the sponsored MP, Dr J. Bray, MP, who spoke to the 1965 Party Conference against the Government's (and the NEC's) policy. The Left Wing in general was in opposition, but even the T & G staff was not of one mind on either the bill or administrative policies that should be followed within the union. Thus, the issue was perhaps too touchy for the officers to take a public stand. This writer, from the visitor's balcony, witnessed Bray's impassioned, reasoned plea for open immigration and the instant and loud applause from the Left. But the T & G delegation (made up largely of lay, elected delegates as well as the full-time officers) was visibly unenthusiastic.

Such rare use of a sponsored MP to plead a 'broader issue' may have had some value in the political debate. For the union, however, it was at least a partial substitute for the very tough administrative actions that effective integration of immigrants at the work-place would have demanded from the national bureaucracy.

[1] Interviews (17 December 1965).

Cousins in Parliament

Cousins's own isolation from T & G parliamentary activity was apparently dramatically changed in 1964, when he entered the House of Commons through the safe seat of Nuneaton, and then became a member of the Labour Government. His understanding with his own Executive Council and with the Prime Minister was that he reserved the future right to return to the union. The precedent for such action had been set by Bevin, who entered the Cabinet during World War II for the critical job of Minister of Labour and National Service. While Bevin's move was part of the union movement's response to national crisis, this clearly was not the case with Cousins. His colleagues at Transport House were by no means in agreement as to his personal motivation. Yet Cousins himself told the members, as he prepared to leave, that he was taking the Cabinet position to fulfil the union's desire for 'an increasing share of an increasing cake'.[1] This hardly suggested a break with traditional pure and simple trade unionism.

Whatever the union's or Cousins' own purpose, the move was directly related to the T & G's economic concerns. Cousins, as Minister of Technology, would, of course, concern himself with productivity—a subject that had been stressed by him before the 1964 General Election. His union, shortly, would make a significant reorganization of staff, and by other actions show that productivity bargaining was its alternative to governmental plans for incomes controls. It is quite clear, nevertheless, that neither the Minister nor the union were now 'seized with the necessity of adopting a Socialist programme' to raise productivity or to achieve social change.

Thus, although both Cousins and the T & G had been identified with the standard public ownership demands, the former had already focused on narrower goals. He told his membership in 1964: 'Efficiency and fairness—these are the big issues of the General Election'.[2] When the AEU MPs, Stanley Orme and Norman Atkinson, both of whom were leaders in the pursuit of 'socialist' alternatives to incomes policies, called on the Minister early in 1965 to suggest public ownership and operation of some machine tools plants—for experimental purposes, as a means of stimulating productivity—Cousins responded by stressing voluntary co-operation with the existing owners, and pleaded with them not to take up their idea with the Parliamentary Party.[3]

Cousins's resignation from the Cabinet in July 1966 had very

---

[1] *Guardian* (9 November 1964).
[2] *Record* (*General Election Number*) (October 1964), p. 14.
[3] Interview with Atkinson (2 June 1965).

little to do either with ideological issues or with technology *per se*. His letter of resignation to the Prime Minister dealt solely with the Wilson-Brown decision to push a Prices and Incomes Bill that provided for legal enforcement of 'early warning' notification of proposals for wage increases, and fines for union strikes or other actions 'to implement an award or settlement' in defiance of then-current incomes policy.[1] Subsequently, the Government won 'reluctant acquiescence' from the 1966 TUC Congress for its statutory freeze—but only by a narrow vote, and over Frank Cousins' objection that the 'entire concept was a threat to the activity of a free trade union movement'. To head off statutory control, Cousins had already in 1966 startled some traditionalists by calling for greater power for the General Council to vet wage claims voluntarily. He also later led the 1967 Congress move to reject the Government's statutory plan and to approve instead the TUC's voluntary plan.[2]

This much is clear: neither nationalization nor defence policy—the two great ideological testing points of the period—were factors in Cousins' resignation. It is significant that while he was in the forefront of the CND, he, like the Labour Left in general, consistently avoided criticism of NATO, the keystone of British foreign policy under both Labour and Tory Governments. Indeed, the bahaviour of the T & GWU under his long and dramatic leadership was consistent with Professor Hugh Clegg's observation about the NUGMW, the second largest of the general unions: 'Business unionism is an American expression, but it is a fair description of a great deal of the work of the NUGMW.' He quotes an officer of that general union: 'It is the business of the union to sell labour and to get as good a price as it can.'[3]

As we have suggested, the political stance of unions almost always merely implements its labour market objectives. The favourable market for labour was seen to be a determining factor in the two general unions' decision to abjure activist Labour policies in the early 1950s. Full employment strengthened the bargaining ability of the general unions as it did that of the AEU, but this favourable market development combined with full legality gave encouragement also to work-place bargaining, which could bring about more rapid upward adjustment to market conditions than the centralized bargaining that had been characteristic of the T & G's approach.

---

[1] 'Can Wilson Keep Labour Together?' The *Observer* (10 July 1966).

[2] Margaret Stewart, *Frank Cousins: A Study* (London, Hutchinson, 1968), pp. 167–75.

[3] Hugh Clegg, *General Union* (Oxford, Blackwell, 1954), Part 5.

Incomes Policy Adaptation and Royal Commission Testimony

T & G's comprehensive 1966 testimony for the Royal Commission on Trade Unions and Employers' Associations constituted a structural and functional shift to take into account the shift in economic power and to *de-emphasize* parliamentary forms of political action. The basic objective appears to have been the maximization of earnings within the limits of the Government's incomes policies. It has been seen that this union had been the centre of opposition to the 1965 proposal for statutory powers for the National Board for Prices and Incomes—to check on prices and wage claims to assure conformity with national incomes policy. However—perhaps out of a sense of discipline or out of fear of more direct action by the Government—the T & G went along with the TUC 'vetting' plan. Indeed it re-organized its central staff so that the union could better conform to this phase of incomes policy, and even boasted of sending more claims to Congress House than any other affiliate. To win more money for its members, the Department and the top officers gave priority to incentive or productivity bargaining schemes that were negotiated at the work-place. Then, having taken this tack, the union pursued it forthrightly and aggressively: it found no significant blocks at Congress House.

In the process, this largest of all Labour affiliates deliberately downgraded political action and set about to take advantage of the opportunities afforded by market bargaining within the guidelines of the Government's policies. The structural change was clear: as late as 1964, the reports issued by Corfield had been on behalf of a combined *Political, Research, Education and International Department*. Out of this the union now created a *Research and Production Department* (RPD). The RPD was placed under Miss Ellen McCullough, who had performed the combined political and research tasks for Bevin and Deakin, and had in the interim worked for the TUC Educational Department; from the latter position she had returned to take the new Research and Production job. The portrait of the contemporary union which this veteran civil servant of the union movement prepared for the Commission was unmistakeably drawn to de-emphasize politics.

The main thesis of the T & G brief is quite in accord with the Perlman model, a classic defence of 'economism' or business unionism: voluntary collective bargaining, it asserts, 'is itself a powerful means of achieving a measure of social equality without which no real social advance can be made. . . .' The T & G approach is not in any way in conflict with that of the TUC's brief which was also essentially non-political. It differs, however, in making the

175

retreat from politics quite explicit: 'The Union's political activities are always consequent upon and subsequent to their trade union work.' To underscore the point, the political and legislative programme is relegated to a brief appendix of the 60,000-odd word brief! And this, in turn, is merely a reprint of an old Corfield report, consisting of MP Panel changes and some of the trade chores performed by various sponsored Members.[1]

Thus, while the T & G had accumulated more MPs, and may have developed more extensive ties at the local Labour Party level than did the AEU, it also made a more deliberate retreat from reliance on political allies and techniques. There was little pretence that the MPs served an affirmative function. On the other hand, the T & G found it necessary to resort to negative political techniques. For example, it moved against those MPs, notably George Brown, who were supporting the statutory incomes policies of the Labour Government. Until 1967 it was assumed that incumbents would not be subject to re-examination at the end of each Parliament. At the 1967 BDC, however, a motion 'was accepted in broad general principle' to the effect that all 'Existing members of the Parliamentary panel should be permitted to apply for enrolment on a newly constituted panel. . . .' In explaining the motion later, Harry Nicholas, then Assistant General Secretary of T & G, reiterated the principle 'that an MP's responsibility is to his constituents,' adding, however, 'obviously there would be no point in a person being a member of our Parliamentary Panel *if he were opposed to our main principles*'. According to Nicholas, the motion was inspired by the fact that certain unnamed MPs were opposed to the union's incomes policy.[2]

---

[1] *Written Evidence Submitted to the Royal Commission on Trade Unions and Employers' Associations* (January 1966), p. 7.

[2] Letter from Nicholas to writer (5 December 1967). Emphasis added. By 1969, the language was more direct and the meaning much more plain than in 1967. The BDC then decided that each region would consider whether to forward the nomination of incumbents and new aspirants alike, and the Executive would vote on each name. Frank Cousins, having returned to T & G from Parliament, announced a new hard line, based on both incomes policy and the attitudes towards Labour's 1969 trade union reform proposal, *In Place of Strife*: 'In future only members who fight for Union policies and have a proven record of Union work should be supported' ('Frank's Farewell', *Record*, Conference Special (1969), undated, p. 3).

As indicated in an earlier footnote (Chap. VII, p. 141) George Brown expressed his resentment about such a procedure and indicated that he decided to avoid the indignity and give up his sponsorship, whereas the T & G officials questioned about the matter asserted that he was found to be in arrears and therefore ineligible. In 1970, Jack Jones, Cousins's successor, reiterated the new policy in even stronger terms (*Report and Balance Sheet*, p. 12).

For measuring real rather than nominal political interests one can usefully

In 1966, J. L. Jones, soon to become General Secretary, developed what he called a 'Socialist approach' to wages. This was widely hailed in the left-wing press as an alternative to the Government's wage control scheme, but it envisaged no immediate political change or direct political pressure. Its major significance was that it represented an attempt at a structural and functional adaptation of aggressive national union leadership to the realities of the labour market within the constraints of a public concern over wage cost inflation. Whatever the ultimate political implications, the immediate thrust was away from Parliamentary politics.

In an extended 1966 article for *Tribune*, the Left-Wing Labour weekly, Jones stressed the need to expand the scope of *work-place bargaining*. While this became for many a model of industrial militancy it was not in conflict with the Perlman model. Jones demanded access to the books, as well as shop steward representation on management boards, and an extension of the power of the 'workers' representatives' (i.e. the joint shop stewards) over hiring and firing and safety enforcement. For national expansion of the union, he repeated T & G's standing invitation for further amalgamations. Jones recognized the bargaining vacuum created at the top by the resistance of unions and firms to central bargaining, and proposed that the TUC and the Confederation of British Industries engage in national centralized negotiations to replace the 'frantic "scramble" of the fragmented national negotiations'. But the major weapon in his counter attack against Governmental wage restraint was 'production or efficiency bargaining locally'.[1]

focus on the T & G's recent changing attitude towards sponsoring George Brown and the related problem of incomes policy with which he was identified. It was widely known that Brown had been able to win a more lucrative form of sponsorship from the *Mirror* in the early 1950s than that paid by T & G. While both were continued, there is no record of the T & G raising the question of conflict of interest—either under Deakin's leadership, when the arrangement with the publishing firm began, or under Cousins', during which it continued. Brown's revelation in 1970 of the sums involved by the *Mirror* arrangement—beginning with £500 per annum and going up to £1,250, plus fees for articles—were apparently published to answer 'some pretty wild rumours' outside the union itself (George Brown *In My Way* (London, Gollancz, 1971), p. 61). Yet this arrangement appears to have had no influence on the withdrawal of sponsorship by the T & G. Brown's pre-eminent role—supported by many other T & G MPs—in the statutory incomes policies appears to have been the main cause of the shift in union attitudes towards incumbent sponsored MPs in general and Brown in particular.

[1] 'The Unions in 1967', *Tribune* (23 December 1966), p. 7. Of course this was not altogether inconsistent with Government policy as long as the latter continued to emphasize continued expansion of production. Cf. National Board for Prices and Incomes, Report No. 36, *Productivity Agreements* (1967). For more recent aspects of T & G philosophy, see Chap. XIII, Epilogue.

M   177

Given the still favourable market for labour, Jones saw in productivity bargaining the means for higher wages and counted on working out agreements of mutual benefit with profit-maximizing employers, without the assistance of the Government. Thus, the left-wing T & G echoed the bargaining philosophy of the model, the AEU, as expressed to the Royal Commission in 1965, but whereas the AEU leadership still saw the shop steward movement as a threat, the T & G national leaders moved to close the gap and overcome the crisis of isolation that had threatened the AEU and the earlier T & G leadership.

The union did not continue to inflate the importance of the MPs, as the AEU had done. However, it did not reduce the Labour commitment. Indeed, the new General Secretary assumed a position on the *Tribune* editorial board. While such an act would normally imply a more politicized stand, in Jones' case we see the medium used for a conscious retreat from the cherished concept of government planning in favour of more industrial militancy. This was in harmony with the shop steward hierarchies' tendency to be apolitical. Expressing fear that a Labour 'Government-imposed closed shop' would be traded off by union leaders who might then join the Government in curbing work-place bargaining, he warned that this trade-off might be part of a 'planning' trap:

> Even on the Left, this concept has its fellow-travellers; those whose desire to see social planning is so great that they see the Emperor as clothed, when he is naked of the vestments of economic control. Over-estimating this, they under-estimate the importance of the great tradition of independent working class power of which the trade unions are still the greatest source and symbol.[1]

He anticipated and approved the 'wage drift' which might result from productivity bargaining. Although Jones brought in, somewhat tangentially, 'a determination to achieve Clause IV of the party's constitution', he appears to have come full circle to an explicitly non-political unionism. Again, one sees a faith in non-revolutionary syndicalism and a continuation of pure and simple unionism.

To summarize: the professional leadership of the Transport and General Workers' Union swung from an unequivocally stand-pat political posture under Deakin to a seemingly radical activism under Cousins and his successor, Jones. The Parliamentary Group was altered and greatly increased in size. Harry Nicholas served as Treasurer of the Labour Party. Frank Cousins entered the Cabinet. The Political Secretary, Tony Corfield, advanced a comprehensive socialist ideology. The T & G possibly influenced many formal policy

[1] Ibid.

decisions made by 'the Movement'—on Clause IV, defence and other intensely debated political issues. Yet, the impressive MP group continued to be carefully restricted to a narrow field of 'trade' work. The resignation of Cousins from the Cabinet over the incomes policy of the Government was a sign that the T & G, the largest single affiliate of the Party, was unable to exercise decisive political influence on a vital interest. This resignation and the actions against some incumbent MPs constituted a defensive form of political action. Clearly, such action was not inconsistent with Gompers' philosophy of MORE. The T & G had now put forth an aggressive programme for straightforward business unionism. Along with its *de facto* retreat from parliamentary politics, there was an accompanying concentration—with appropriate structural change—on market bargaining as an alternative to participation in the running of the mixed economy. 'Productivity bargaining' meant, even when conducted by socialists, an acceptance of the employers' increasing their profits as a precondition for the workers' increase in gross earnings. Whatever the public claims made, this represented a reinforcement of the *status quo* within the existing social order. It was consistent with Perlman's *laissez-faire* model.

Chapter X

Association of Supervisory Staffs, Executives and Technicians (ASSET)[1]

White-collar unionism in Britain has been growing rapidly, although not nearly as fast as white-collar employment. As we have seen from attempts of some non-manual associations to elicit help from the Trade Union Group, many of these unions were still striving during the period for the elementary organizational objectives that the major manual unions long ago achieved. Their behaviour, including their political behaviour, was essentially designed to provide MORE for white collar union members. The present analysis of one major national non-manual union will serve a chiefly heuristic function.

The Association of Supervisory Staffs, Executives and Technicians (ASSET—as it was called at the time of this study) was a TUC and Labour affiliate. It *needed* political aid during the period primarily for the purpose of pursuing pure and simple business unionism. Accordingly, it made extensive use of serious political pressure working largely through its own Parliamentary Committee—a committee that, significantly enough, *had no connection with the Trade Union Group*. The Association's General Secretary, Clive Jenkins, offered this form of Parliamentary union activity to contemporary white collar TUC affiliates as a model of political work, the purpose of which was quite parochial: '. . . [we should] concentrate on trade union and industrial issues which affect our [white collar union] members'.[2] Why was genuine political activity needed?

History and Scope

Originating in the engineering industry in 1917 as the National

[1] Changed to Association of Scientific, Technical and Managerial Staffs (ASTMS) by merger in 1967 of ASSET, with some 58,000 members, with the Association of Scientific Workers (ASW) which had about 28,000. The General Secretary of ASSET, Clive Jenkins, remained as General Secretary of the merged association. It claimed over 200,000 members in 1970. ASTMS *Journal* (1970), Issue 6, page 1.

[2] Clive Jenkins, 'The Labour Party and the Non-Manual Worker' (19 January 1961), typed memorandum for Labour Party Conference of Non-Manual Unions.

Foremen's Association, this now predominantly white-collar organization has lately extended its coverage horizontally and vertically. It is affiliated with the Confederation of Shipbuilding and Engineering Unions (CSEU), but has recently staked out a seemingly open-ended jurisdiction among 'technicians' in a wide range of industries. In 1966, for the Royal Commission on Trade Unions and Employers' Associations, ASSET listed a large variety of occupations it represented in 'five main fields: engineering, transport, chemicals, metals, and the gas industry'. Even this broad field was not considered adequate to define ASSET's potential membership: the brief asserts a conception of occupational change that suggests a 'general union' approach to the entire 'technical' field: 'ASSET realizes, however, the nomenclature is constantly changing with the introduction of new techniques, and we therefore organize these new technical grades, irrespective of title'.[1]

While going on record for rather sweeping organizational goals, ASSET made the central theme of its testimony the relative weakness of the trade union movement—particularly the non-manual sector. The awareness of ASSET's own weakness in relation to the employers (and its rivals among other unions) led it to adopt two of the features that distinguished the early general unions: first, an emphasis on political techniques (which, we have seen, the two general unions have since minimized); second, a highly centralized, professional leadership (which the general unions have retained).

A significant factor in ASSET's growth and in its parliamentary activity is the large number of people who came under the 'Executives' and 'Supervisory' classifications—for political and/or social reasons. Among its members in 1964–6, none of whom had a perceptible economic reason for joining, were: a chartered accountant; a television producer; an owner of a large publishing company; several owners of small businesses; the General Secretary of the Communist Party of Great Britain; the manager of the London

---

[1] *A Hundred Years On—And How Much Progress for the Unions?* (February 1966), p. 21. Jenkins, writing for ASTMS in 1971, argued for 'organizing allied and linked workers' in an enterprise. While concentrating his analysis on scientists, foremen and inspectors, his main point is that 'narrowly based unions—in the end—disappear, or become totally ineffective except in very narrow areas'. Although the 'lesson' is that the union must seek 'the development of the company and public industry contract' the jurisdictional area of the union is not defined. ASTMS, *Journal* (1971), Issue One/Two, p. 8. As this is being written, the advertisements of ASTMS in newspapers and billboards indicate a willingness to accept managerial levels as well as an unlimited range of technical *and* white collar occupational groups in all industries. In 1971 it merged with the Union of Insurance Staffs and apparently was thereby embarked on a rivalry with the National Union of Bank Employees for recruitment of both bank and insurance staff (*Tribune* (3 July 1971)).

branch of the Narodny Bank of Moscow; several barristers and solicitors; also university dons and former university dons (including the then Prime Minister).

A cross-section of these people—excluding Communists, of course —made up the 1964–6 ASSET Parliamentary Committee, its principal vehicle for political activity. A long-time member of ASSET'S NEC, and of the National Executive of the Labour Party, Mr Ian Mikardo, MP, joined the union in 1942, when he was an industrial consultant. Entering the House of Commons in 1945, he began to recruit Labour MPs. The Parliamentary Committee was formed from among these MPs. As of 1966, no less than twenty-six MPs and five Labour Peers were members of the Committee.

Government and Structure

The General Secretary, who is appointed for life as are other full-time officers, assumed a highly centralized authority. The National Executive Committee (NEC), made up of lay members, was officially 'the chief authority in the Association' and an Annual Delegate Conference by rule, 'shall, with the NEC, formulate the policy'. The General Secretary, however, acted rather like a general manager for the Association. The incumbent during the 1960s, Mr Clive Jenkins, was perhaps a model of the 'meritocracy', an eloquent career trade unionist shaped by, and in turn shaping, the trade union movement. The son of a union miner in Wales, he went to work at fourteen, educated himself in night school as a metallurgist, and became a foreman at nineteen. At the age of twenty, he was appointed as a full-time ASSET Divisional Officer, becoming General Secretary in 1961 (after a year as Acting General Secretary) at the age of thirty-four.

Political Activity

Close observation by this writer of Mr Jenkins's work over the period indicated that a major and perhaps preponderant share of his time and energies—on and off his job—was devoted to political operations designed to enhance ASSET's bargaining position as well as Jenkins' prestige and authority. In a variety of political activities, Jenkins had the reputation of being a left-winger; in his ASSET Parliamentary Committee role, however, he was distinctly eclectic and opportunistic. He limited himself largely to strategies that would yield organizing and bargaining increments. While these narrow goals may not have been appealing to some ideologues and political careerists holding ASSET membership cards, there can be no doubt that the Association's operative policy was to synchronize political

182

techniques with the bread and butter purposes of the union. Yet, while the Association leaders were sold, either because of ideological predisposition, or because of practical gains, on the extensive use of political techniques, they had difficulty collecting adequate political funds from the members. The probable reason for this is that white collar workers in general resist the Labour Party and its candidacies. Thus, most ASSET members either formally contracted out, or simply withheld payment of the levy.[1]

Unlike our manual model, the AEU, where an accumulation of enormous political funds was in itself a factor in its spurious political behaviour, ASSET reached out for greater funds than the levy provided for its genuine pressure activity. First, the political fund was enlarged by calling in branch shares of that fund. Second, general funds were allocated to, and some outside funds were secured for, legislative phases of the political programme. There was also very close co-ordination of the electoral and legislative phases— as one generally finds to be the case in any effective pressure group.

The branches formally had access to one-third of the levy. For the 1964 campaign, however, they were informed that because of urgent need in some important constituency elections, each branch share would be 'impounded' and put into the central fund, unless objection should be voiced within seven days of receipt of the letter. It appears that none objected.

In 1964, the focal activity of the entire full-time staff in the General Election was on behalf of 'Brother Wilson', the Party Leader and potential Prime Minister. Because of his potential importance to ASSET, Wilson's Huyton CLP also received a significantly higher allocation of funds than most, even though the membership density did not warrant the move. Jenkins, in reporting to his Executive after the General Election, included Wilson among the 'thirty-eight ASSET members [who] stood as Labour Candidates. All the members of ASSET Parliamentary Committees were returned, and eight new members were elected. In all the constituencies, ASSET made some financial contribution; in the marginal seats, the contributions were in some cases quite substantial.' The Party Leader was not in a marginal but in a safe seat; still the largest pre-election cash contribution (£315.0.0) and some office equipment was allocated to his Huyton CLP.[2]

ASSET gave only token contributions to the general election fund of the Labour Party, because, in the words of one executive, 'we've got to put it where it counts for us'. That decision, judging from the

[1] A relatively high 15 pence per month.
[2] Memorandum on General Election, Clive Jenkins (26 October 1964), mimeo.

financial data cited here, as well as numerous conversations with Jenkins and others, was based on the perception of the Association that friendship with a Labour Prime Minister could offer both general and concrete pay-offs for the organizational and economic objectives of the union.

The open use of general funds for political purposes is rare in Britain. The fact that ASSET used staff for campaigning and allocated such funds for pressure work can be taken as a measure of the priority accorded to political techniques for the fundamental objectives of its members. The pressure phase of their political programme hinged on work with the Parliamentary Committee. Each month, the officers of the union had a luncheon meeting with these Members of Parliament in a House of Commons dining-room. This luncheon, it had been decided by the Association, was not merely political, but was part of the organizational and *educational* programme. Hence it was considered legitimate to finance such activity out of general funds.[1]

(During the period a part of the cost for the luncheon was met by the Draughtsmen's and Allied Technicians' Association (DATA), a regular participant in the meetings.)[2]

Parliamentary Committee: Size and Functions

When the 1966 Parliament opened, though ASSET had twenty-six MPs and five Lords in its Parliamentary Committee, only two of the MPs were formally sponsored[3] and therefore considered officially part of the Trade Union Group, and listed accordingly with other union-sponsored MPs. Neither of these two bothered to attend the Group meetings, but they did function as part of the heterogeneous professional-business ASSET Committee, despite the fact that it *had no official standing* with either the Labour Party or the Parliamentary Labour Party. Unlike MPs sponsored by the AEU and the T & G, ASSET Committee Members were regularly invited to the Annual Delegate Conferences, and often featured as speakers. The importance attached to these Parliamentary Committee meetings by the union is suggested not only by their frequency (monthly), the attendance of all major officers, and the allocation of funds, but also by the nature of the agenda prepared for the Chairman of the Committee by Jenkins.

Although Jenkins (and ASSET) generally were found on the Left in TUC and Labour debates, neither the perennial *Plan for*

---

[1] Interviews with Clive Jenkins (1965–6). It will be seen from our American analysis that political expenditures were also often classified as educational.

[2] As indicated in Chap. I, DATA was combined with the Engineers in 1970.

[3] Increased to four as a result of 1970 General Election.

Engineering, which Jenkins co-authored above stage, nor other ideological issues, were brought before the committee. The most persistent problem to which committee attention was directed was one which this union shared with other white collar unions, namely, the difficulty of bargaining with a resistant management.

Clive Jenkins's extensive writings have shown an acute awareness of the inadequacy of contemporary trade union structure to encompass the needs of a changing labour force, and to cope with the problems of a mixed economy. Moreover, he has been perhaps the only contemporary national union leader to publicly admit that the lower-paid worker (particularly one with dependents) could be helped more by 'specific social security measures', than by 'the collective bargaining relationship'.[1] On the other hand Jenkins was probably the most persistent public critic among union leaders of every phase of Labour's incomes policies, seeing even the voluntary stage as possibly narrowing the traditional differentials between manual and those non-manual workers he sought to represent.[2]

While the Association made significant use of genuine political weaponry it did not part from the Perlman model of trade union political action that is entirely consistent with pure and simple business unionism, i.e., political action that implements and reinforces collective bargaining for better conditions for the membership.

The job-directed objectives of its work at Westminster are illustrated by two major legislative campaigns: *for* severance pay, and, more importantly, *against* employer-sponsored or 'company' unionism.

Severance Pay and the Contracts of Employment Act

We have already observed that the union movement has been slow to demand severance pay for workers dismissed on account of redundancy, as evidenced by the benevolent neutrality with which the Trade Union Group and the TUC greeted the Contracts of Employment Act. ASSET, on the other hand, through union channels and through its Parliamentary Committee, denounced the Bill and then launched a major campaign to win passage of a law requiring severance pay. Thus, Mr J. Rankin, MP, a committee member, condemned the Contracts of Employment Bill—he had first received from Jenkins a legal analysis—as 'anti-union legislation

---

[1] From 'TREND', a column written for *Tribune* by Clive Jenkins (6 January 1967).

[2] *Congress Report* (1968), pp. 356–7; cf. George S. Bain, 'The Growth of White-Collar Unionism in Britain', *British Journal of Industrial Relations* (November 1966); and Loveridge, *Technicians and Their Institutions* (*op. cit.*).

brought in by a back door method'.[1] At a later date Jenkins would suggest repeal of that measure, but at this time the major thrust was clearly towards affirmative action for severance pay as a legal obligation of employers. Each Member was presented by him with an elegantly printed analysis, *The Gold-Plated Handshake*, which stressed the employers' unilateral power over dismissals, and pleaded for legislation.

Mr John Diamond, a highly respected MP and a Gaitskellite, was chosen to introduce a Severance Bill in 1962. He was joined by no less than eight other ASSET MPs. Jenkins arranged a press conference for the occasion and several articles bearing Diamond's signature appeared in widely circulated publications. All of this was no doubt appreciated by the Committee Members, to whom Jenkins reported it in detail. The Bill itself failed—as was to be expected under opposition sponsorship.

On 14 February 1964, Mr J. Silverman, MP, after clearing with the committee, took advantage of a private member's Bill to introduce the measure again. Again it failed. Later, however, when the Queen's 1964 speech to Parliament indicated that the Labour Government would enact severance pay legislation, the Committee 'Noted with pleasure', and went on to boast that ASSET's Committee 'had led the campaign for severance pay when this had not been thought [by the rest of the Labour Movement] to be generally acceptable'.[2]

Foremen and Staffs Mutual Benefit Society (F & SMBS)

The *main* legislative campaign of ASSET arose directly out of its perceived need for political help to combat a 'company union', the Foremen and Staff Mutual Benefit Society (F & SMBS). The latter was organized by the employers in engineering companies in 1899, shortly after the formation of the first external Foremen's and Technicians' Friendly Societies. Since that time the staff Society has paid about half of the cost of pensions, life assurances and sickness benefits to foremen and technicians as well as other comparable white collar grades who become members. However, its constitution prohibits its members from belonging to a union; moreover, it requires those who do join a union after being accepted into the F & SMBS to forfeit the employers' contribution to the benefits fund.[3]

---

[1] Hansard, Vol. 671, c. 1594–1595. In this speech he also backed the Severance Pay Bill introduced by John Diamond, below, on behalf of ASSET.

[2] *Minutes* of meeting between ASSET National Executive Committee and ASSET Parliamentary Committee, House of Commons (11 November 1964).

[3] Loveridge, op. cit.

The severe threat of the employer-dominated Society to the existence and growth of ASSET was clearly reflected in the latter's testimony for the Royal Commission: 'union rights are too limited and should be enhanced while the arbitrary authority of employers is too great and should be diminished'. Unlike the TUC, AEU and T & G briefs to the same Commission, ASSET urged specific legislation to help unions organize and bargain. It also urged legal enactment to combat 'house and staff associations directly supported by employers with the object of frustrating the growth of genuine trade unionism, amongst their staff'. ASSET proposed to the Commission that implementation by legislation of International Labour Office Convention 87 was needed for union protection in general; and that for the specific obstacle posed by F & SMBS the ILO Convention 98, which protects non-manual employees' rights, should be enacted into law.[1] (In 1956, Ian Mikardo, as an MP, had approached the Trade Union Group to sponsor legislation outlawing the Society's 'anti-union' rule, but the group had rejected the request. This refusal was probably due to the TUC's own general resistance to such legislation, as well as the resistance of the manual unions to ASSET's possible poaching on their territories.)

At a November 1963 meeting which discussed the legislative aspects of this problem, the Committee, on Jenkins' suggestion agreed[1] that Brother Julius Silverman, MP, should draft a motion in general terms, and should seek, with the help of other members of the Committee, to get as many signatures to it as possible to put it on the order paper, and members of the Committee should seek to get into the ballot for private members' Bills; in default of this, consideration should be given to putting down a suitable amendment to the Finance Bill at the appropriate time.[1]

In June 1964, Mr Diamond, soon to become Chief Secretary of the Treasury in the Wilson Government, introduced a Bill 'to invalidate rules of friendly societies discriminating against membership of trade unions'. Again, eight committee colleagues joined Diamond on the Bill.[2] Other committee members helped frame

---

[1] *A Hundred Years On* (February 1966), p. 13. R. Loveridge, has observed that the attention paid by ASSET and its successor, ASTMS, to the Mutual Benefit Society 'is an indication of the wide measure of success which the latter has enjoyed'. Loveridge notes that in its Report the Royal (Donovan) Commission gave it as their view that 'it is quite foreign to the purpose of a Friendly Society that it should prescribe in its rules that no one can be a member and draw benefit if he is a trade unionist'; and that the Commission accordingly recommended that no Friendly Society should have such a rule. He notes further that ASTMS subsequently arranged for introduction of a private Bill to carry into effect the Commission's recommendation (mimeo, 1971).

[2] Bill 153 (3 June 1964), House of Commons.

questions to be asked of Conservative ministers and submitted memoranda to Labour shadow ministers.

The election of a Labour Government did not ease, but rather increased ASSET's pressure for what it perceived to be its needs in Parliament. At a December 1964 Committee luncheon, the Prime Minister, 'Brother Harold Wilson . . . sent a message that he would come to the meeting before its conclusion'. He did not appear, but the Parliamentary Secretary to the Ministry of Labour, Mr E. Thornton, was present and heard the members raise the F & SMBS problem as well as the problem of 'trade union recognition and collective bargaining facilities' for non-manual workers. In addition, it was agreed that Jenkins (who had by this time established a close personal relationship with Mr Wilson) would write directly to the Prime Minister expressing the Committee's interest.

We have thus far seen that partly because the TUC was maintaining a policy of abstention, and partly because of more general difficulties in pursuing its fundamental goals, ASSET found it necessary to seek legislative assistance. The severance pay and F & SMBS campaigns were cited as examples of specific legislation. For similar reasons, this Association also found it useful to resort to its Parliamentary Committee for pressure on Whitehall. This writer was present in Jenkins' office the morning after ASSET in March 1965 called a strike against a private airline in London. His first calls that morning, after he ascertained from the branch officers the state of the picket line preparations, were directed to key members of his parliamentary Committee—asking them to call the Minister of Aviation for the purpose of cancelling the struck firm's Government contracts.

In sum, ASSET's exceptionally active role in genuine trade union pressure politics arose from a combination of personal and institutional interests and needs. The personal reward for the Labour candidate for Parliament—and some sitting Members as well—was that ASSET offered to many of them the most feasible union connection open to people of their professional or business ties. And, of course, such a union membership remains vital for winning the nod from Labour Party selection conferences. For at least some Members active in the committee in 1965–6, the choice of ASSET, and the ASSET Committee, was based on the congeniality of the Members, plus the smooth and effective publicity assistance available through Jenkins. Also, the creation of the ASSET Committee by Ian Mikardo, plus the exceptional managerial and public relations talents and ambitions of Clive Jenkins, added to the personal elements in the set of causes in this particular union's activity.

The basic reason for the genuine commitment of this union to parliamentary techniques, however, was simply that as a fledgling union fighting resistant employers, as well as some TUC rivals, it needed political allies to legitimize and strengthen its bargaining role in the many heterogeneous and fragmented labour markets encompassed by the area of organization it had staked out for itself. The highly intelligent leadership and membership were quite aware of the value of full employment for the advancement of living standards and the improvement of the status of the salariat and other sections of the labour force. However, the association resisted enlarging the economic function of the TUC, and fought the incomes policies of the Labour Government because in the first instance it had not established its own legitimacy in the manual-dominated TUC, and, in the second instance because it depended on maintaining and widening wage differentials as a key to its own growth.

Chapter XI

The American Unions' Political Purpose and Methodology

In this brief and necessarily incomplete account of the main objectives of trade union political action in the United States, we will focus on national legislative and electoral activities, in order to provide a basis for comparison between the United States and the United Kingdom. We will avoid the numerous differences and similarities which one can list for a comparative anatomy. Experience shows that national differences in historical context produce significant structural and behavioural differences. Aside from some differences in context, however, comparison of the two trade union movements reinforces the British thesis.

Workers in both of these democratic, advanced capitalistic societies, have evolved broadly similar institutions and philosophies to protect and advance their interests. The British movement during the period, having achieved its main political ambitions—legalization and government support for full employment—was satisfied with the *status quo*.

Central Thesis

The American unions, like their British colleagues, have not sought far-reaching socio-political change; the movement has not acted out a social conscience role, despite appearances to the contrary. The central thesis of this chapter is that the American trade union movement was nonetheless very purposefully engaged in political action during the post-war years. The activity originated and grew primarily out of the unions' perceptions that their various traditional bargaining systems were menaced by legal attacks. The main objective was to ward off, and then to repeal or amend 'anti-labor' laws. Only by such means could bargaining goals be realized. For this purpose the individual national unions as well as the central American Federation of Labor-Congress of Industrial Organizations (AFL-CIO) steadily enlarged allocations of money and manpower for legislative and electoral activities, particularly at the federal level.

The central argument is in no sense inconsistent with the argument developed in the British analysis, and is indeed designed to throw additional light on the present interpretation of British experience. The underlying purposes of different national unions and groupings of unions varied, but the overriding objective was to establish or maintain, and where necessary, re-establish a traditional collective bargaining system characteristic of pure and simple unionism.

The generalizations contained in this statement of the thesis will be modified as required in the discussion of the empirical models below.

Historical Context

A brief discussion of the structural, legal and socio-economic context will illuminate the American thesis as well as some behavioural differences with the British during the period. The main features of the historical setting were as follows: (1) Although the American unions have origins extending back into the eighteenth century, they have faced continuous threats to their legality. During the period they had less recognition, a lower proportion of eligible members organized, both in the economy as a whole and in most sectors, and had to cope with generally higher rates of unemployment than did the British. (2) Structurally, there is a skeletal similarity with the British movement. There exists a central federation with its local (and state) federations; and a series of autonomous national unions, each with its own substructure. But a distinctive feature of great significance in the political behaviour of the Americans is that the predominantly closed, craft unions organized and sustained the American Federation of Labor as the only centre until the mid-1930s. For some fifty years, the craft structures continued to follow the closed union, anti-socialist philosophy of Samuel Gompers and other founders. They systematically excluded non-whites and the unskilled, accepted *laissez-faire* and resisted social legislation. The older federation often associated itself with open and virulent forms of racism and jingoism.[1] (3) Craft unionism failed to organize the mass production industries. It was only in 1935 that some dissident AFL leaders, mainly from the handful of industrial unions—notably John L. Lewis of the Mineworkers and Sidney Hillman of the Clothing Workers—formed the *Committee*, and soon, the Congress of Industrial Organizations (CIO) to bring union protection to the American workers in mass production industries, which meant also millions of unskilled. The New Deal and the Democratic Party, and particularly the National Labor Relations (Wagner) Act, were the major, and probably decisive factors in the success of the CIO. And

[1] Marc Karson, *American Labor Unions and Politics 1900–1918*, (Boston, Beacon, 1965), pp. 132–47, and *passim*.

191

the CIO unions, in turn, beginning in mid-1930s, became the major propaganda and organizational apparatus of the Democrats for national elections. (4) The New Deal-CIO political alliance was based on a web of mutual interests, mainly the Democrats' need for a broader constituency, and the CIO's need for legal protection, legitimacy and social legislation. (5) The AFL created Labor's League for Political Education, its own national electoral machinery, in 1947, as a direct result of the passage of the Labor Management Relations (Taft-Hartley) Act. This act created the impetus for joint AFL and CIO political activity and their merger in 1955 into the present AFL-CIO. (6) The CIO recruited and integrated the largely unskilled black workers into their open unions and also helped make the black community part of the coalition with the Democratic Party. By the time of the merger, the CIO's interest in the black workers had generally waned. At about the same time, however, the 'Black Revolt', which originated outside the union movement, focused national attention on the second class status forced on Negroes by all major American institutions, including unions in general, but particularly the craft unions that not only remained closed, but were still the backbone of the now combined labour movement, the AFL-CIO.

The Perlman Model: Building Trades Local Union

In his American analysis Perlman sought to establish that 'economism' or 'pure and simple' unionism was not only the choice of Samuel Gompers and his AFL colleagues but 'fitted' both the external environment and 'the American workman's psychology'. By 'external environment' he meant that the very structure and functioning of the American *laissez-faire* political system precluded significant 'economic reform'. This was deemed an advantage, since it would prevent the illusions fostered by social democracy in Europe:

> However, the American situation has at least this merit, from the point of view of labor, that it does not disguise the weakness of government, in contrast with Europe, where labor, deluded by the theoretical 'omni-competence' of the state over industry, centered on capturing that instrument, but found it wanting in actual use.

Perlman derived his conclusion about American workers' 'psychology' largely from observation of the skilled workmen or 'mechanics' (the term which they still prefer) who were then the predominant influence in the American Federation of Labor. These men were members of his preferred model, the local of the Building Trades group of national AFL-affiliated unions. By their locally based bargaining these workmen had attained an 'equilibrium' in an environment that was hostile to wider forms of unionism or union activity. 'Labor is in a minority', Perlman wrote, and the 'fragility' of even the existing unions, he believed, would be endangered by moves for larger scale organization.[1]

The Empirical Models

The AFL-CIO nominally speaks for the entire movement on political matters. However a striking feature of political methods and objectives of the affiliated national unions in the contemporary setting is the fragmentation of political effort. Any choice of models is therefore certain to present an incomplete picture. We have chosen two polar types that together formed about one-third of the entire AFL-CIO membership during the period: (1) the Building and Construction Trades Department (BCTD), a confederation of seventeen national, predominantly closed, craft unions which has functioned continuously since 1908, with an aggregate membership of some 3·5 million; (2) the United Auto Workers (UAW), above, the 1·5 million-strong, largest open union affiliate of the CIO, and later of the AFL-CIO, which has operated largely in national labour markets. The 'Building Trades' function through their 3,500-odd locals, largely in local labour markets, and remain predominantly closed.

Individual locals as well as city, county and state Building and Constructions Trades Councils are known to be engaged in pressure politics at the local level. Their significant recent role in federal politics, and their influence on AFL-CIO policy has been generally ignored or under-estimated. Even in the AFL era they were deeply involved in the struggle for legality in the early years of the present century. As far back as 1931, with AFL backing, the BCTD won the passage of the Davis-Bacon Act, which has been an important means of sustaining high wage rates in all local areas, by requiring the payment of prevailing wage rates (usually union rates) on all federally-financed construction.

Taft-Hartley

The Building Trades had established themselves long before the National Labor Relations (Wagner) Act was passed in 1935.

---

[1] S. Perlman, *A Theory of the Labor Movement* (New York, Macmillan, 1928), Chap. 5.

Although they soon became concerned about maintaining craft separation for National Labor Relations Board elections, neither the Act nor the Board were primary concerns for them until passage of the Labor-Management Relations (Taft-Hartley) Act of 1947 directly threatened their way of bargaining. Vast changes in both the quality and quantity of AFL and Building Trades political activity followed in the wake of Taft-Hartley. That Act empowered the National Labor Relations Board to police the practices of unions as well as those of management. It specified many limitations on the scope of bargaining, the right to strike and picket, the categories of employees who could be unionized, the types of contracts to be signed, and many other routine union activities, including a bar on direct union expenditures for federal elections.

While the law itself is far too complex to be discussed in detail here, scrutiny of two of its features may help illuminate the political purpose of the AFL, the merged AFL-CIO, and in particular the roles of the Building Trades and the Auto Workers. The two features to be discussed are the non-communist affidavit and the series of provisions on union security and compulsory unionism.

The non-communist affidavit was the first Taft-Hartley problem that had to be solved. In Section 9(h) (since repealed) the law made it a condition for use of NLRB procedures certifying union elections and for hearing charges of unfair labour practices that union officers at all affected levels must file *each year* an affidavit stating that they were neither members nor supporters of the Communist Party and that they neither advocated nor supported the violent overthrow of the government. While the initial union reaction of a few AFL and all top CIO leaders to Section 9(h) was violent opposition, George Meany, then the AFL Secretary-Treasurer, persuaded the 1947 Convention to accept the affidavit requirement, despite John L. Lewis' dramatic appeal to make this section the focus of all resistance to the entire Act.[1] The CIO also decided to comply, signalling a purge of its Left Wing and facilitating joint action with the AFL.

There was universal agreement among the closed and open unions on the danger of Section 14(b), the 'right to work' section, which yielded to the states the authority to outlaw some of the most basic forms of union security, such as maintenance of membership, as well as the more traditional forms of compulsory unionism, including the union shop and closed shop. And, as predicted, the states passed

[1] Philip Taft, *Economics and Problems of Labor* (New York, Stackpole and Heck, 1948 edn), pp. 459 f. (Lewis had brought his United Mineworkers out of the CIO and back into the AFL after his personal split with Roosevelt in 1940. The miners withdrew from the AFL after his stand on the affidavit-signing was rejected, and have remained independent ever since.)

such laws with alacrity. Throughout the 1950s and early 1960s, campaigns to defeat or nullify these state laws or to repeal Section 14(b), were a top priority at the state levels and in Washington. By 1966, such laws had been defeated or repealed in twenty-nine states, but nineteen states (mainly rural) had them still in force.[1]

The Taft-Hartley requirements directed against the union shop (Section 8(b) (3) are numerous. But the main restriction, which required that a majority of those eligible to vote in union elections must approve contract clauses requiring workers to join the union (after thirty days, with a special provision of only seven days in the construction industry), was not for long a serious issue. The Act's authors had evidently believed that workers might object if given the chance to vote, but 'Partly in consternation that the clause had produced the "wrong" result and partly because the [NLRB] faced over 5,000 building-trades elections where the result was a foregone conclusion,' Congress repealed the provision in 1951.[2]

Whereas the union shop was the standard form of union security in the mass-production industries, where hiring was out of the hands of the union, the closed shop, in which only union members could be hired in the first place, had been the traditional form of job control by the craft unions. In the eyes of the construction crafts, secondary picketing (sometimes called 'secondary boycott') had been for years an essential tool for enforcing the closed shop. Without such picketing organized plumbers say, might be forced to share work on a large contract with a sub-contractor's non-union carpenters. Neither the plumbers nor the carpenters would be able to picket the general site to announce the fact to other crafts that the carpentry work was being done by 'scabs'.[3]

Section 8(b) (4) states a union can be guilty of an unfair practice if it pickets or otherwise attempts to cause neutral employers to stop doing business with an employer engaged in a dispute with a union. Under such conditions, the NLRB is required to seek an injunction. The NLRB soon ruled that picketing at a general construction site in order to pressure one particular sub-contractor to hire union men was a violation of Section 8(b) (4). The ruling was upheld by the Supreme Court in *NLRB v. Denver Building Council*, known as 'the *Denver* case'. The effective ban on secondary boycotts had been a

[1] Gerald J. Skibbins and Caroline S. Weymar, 'The "Right to Work" Controversy', in *Harvard Business Review* (July–August 1966), reprint from National Right to Work Committee, Washington, D.C.

[2] Alfred Kuhn, *Labor: Institutions and Economics* (New York, Harbrace, 1967 edn), pp. 229 ff.

[3] The Act banned the closed shop but this proved ineffective in construction and other trades dependent on the union for recruiting labour.

major concern of the AFL in fighting Taft-Hartley, but the CIO had not been particularly interested. As will be seen, the Denver case soon became a matter of central importance for the Building Trades, and then for the AFL-CIO.

This source of division was not permitted to intrude on the merger of the two central bodies in 1955. However, the official wedding picture, with President George Meany of the AFL and CIO President Walter Reuther happily joining hands around an oversized gavel, signified a unity that simply never existed between the conflicting philosophies of open and closed unionism, at least in the political arena. The AFL won the two top offices because they brought nearly 11 million members to the new federation; the CIO contributed less than half that. Meany, a plumber by trade and a Building Tradesman by conviction, became president and principal spokesman of the AFL-CIO, while the better-known Reuther, a former socialist of broad civic vision, was chosen as one of many vice-presidents and as the head of a new Industrial Union Department. The Secretary-Treasurer's, or number two, job also went to the AFL.

The political arms of the two union groups, Labor's League for Political Education and the CIO Political Action Committee, were also merged, forming the Committee on Political Education (COPE). The new AFL-CIO's official declaration of political purpose, the COPE enabling resolutions, was entirely consistent with the traditional *laissez-faire* policy of the AFL. It was silent about the social and economic policies, including the welfare-state policies that had been a hallmark of the CIO's pioneering political efforts.[1] The document confined itself to a defensive attack on Taft-Hartley, calling for total repeal but concentrating on the right to work provisions of the law. There was no mention of the Building Trades' special picketing problem. This surprisingly defensive and distinctly sectional document did not represent unity, but heterogenous and often conflicting tendencies, with unresolved differences that were soon reflected in a proliferation of separate electoral and political pressure campaigns.

The conflicting goals of the various affiliates can best be illustrated by reference to the declining share of COPE money in years following the merger, and the divergent legislative and political paths followed by the closed Building Trades and the UAW.

Although it is generally assumed that COPE directs AFL-CIO electoral activity, we see from Table IV that COPE's share of funds has gone down from roughly 38 per cent of total expenditures in 1958 to *less than 15 per cent* in 1968.

[1] Constitutional Convention, American Federation of Labor and Congress of Industrial Organizations, *Proceedings* (1955), pp. 158–9.

Table IV. *Trade Union Expenditures for Federal Elections*

Year	Cope	Total
		(Including COPE)
	$	$
1958	709,803·00	1,828,778·00
1960	795,140·00	2,450,944·00
1962	761,468·00	2,305,331·00
1964	941,947·00	3,816,242·00
1966	906,166·00	4,289,055·00
1968	1,206,736·00	7,631,868·00

Source: Congressional Quarterly, *Weekly Report.* It should be noted that above figures do not include COPE or individual union expenditures on *registration*, which is regarded by unions and by COPE as 'educational' and is financed by general funds.

BCTD Campaign

Beginning in 1955 and continuing to the present, the Building and Construction Trades Department has been engaged in a national pressure campaign which has probably exceeded—in terms of persistence, numbers of people involved, and sums expended—any other single union campaign in the United States or Great Britain since 1945. This campaign, to prevent the federal government from interfering with their long established bargaining system and their control of the supply of labour, has had a top rank in AFL-CIO priorities (although unofficial at first) from the time of the merger.

This extraordinary effort did not follow the bureaucratic model established by the British unions as well as most national unions in the United States. As is well known, the national union bureaucracies generally discourage their affiliates from sending large numbers to Westminster and to Capitol Hill. Indeed, even during the Taft-Hartley debates, the AFL and the CIO each discouraged mass activity. Yet, the crafts each year produced, from the local unions and councils, a flood of lobbyists who were welcomed by and received assistance from AFL-CIO executives and the Legislative Department. Their device was the Annual Legislative Conference. The first Conference was attended by about 2,000 delegates; the average attendance has been around 3,000. To indicate the seriousness of purpose behind the conferences, most of these delegates have been elected local Business Agents (BAs), the administrators of local unions, chosen for their skill as negotiators.

The cost of this week-long lobbying effort is largely unreported, but some educated guesses can be made. In 1966, BA's were paid an average of about $20,000 annually for salary and fixed expenses.

For 3,000 man-weeks, the salaries paid for lobbying manpower would come to about $1·2 million, plus an extremely conservative estimate of $0·5 million more for lodgings, meals, travel and incidental costs of running the conference itself. By contrast, the total cost for the more diversified work of the year-round seven-man Legislative Department of the AFL-CIO in 1966–7 was $294,108.[1]

The first BCTD Legislative Conference was held in Washington 7–11 March 1955, nine months before the scheduled AFL-CIO merger, and was devoted to defining the specific legislative objectives of the crafts. On the advice of their own Executive Council, they decided to seek extension of Davis-Bacon to uncovered federal construction programmes such as roads, to extend the 8-hour law, and to tighten enforcement of both laws.[2] These demands were eventually won. As for Taft-Hartley, whereas the new AFL-CIO would repeat the familiar cry for total repeal, the Building Trades decided their purposes could be achieved merely by removing those 'defects' which interfered with their traditional forms of bargaining. This conference, accordingly, gave its primary attention to the problems created by the *Denver* case, as it did in all subsequent conferences.

The Building Trades sought to override the *Denver* decision with the *Situs* Picketing Bill, which exempted picketing on construction sites from the provisions of Section 8(b) (4). The craft unions were not especially strike-prone. While the main public argument for the bill was that it would restore equity among unions since the picketing weapon remained available for strikers in industry generally, the Building Trades now were mobilizing their power so that they could restore the legal right—in the words of the main legal analysis given the delegates—'to throw the scabs off the job'.

As of 1955, however, there was no longer a simple dichotomy of scab versus union man. The competition from District 50, United Mine Workers (an industrial union founded by John L. Lewis to function as an open union in construction, and a consistent opponent of the *Situs Bill*), as well as the clamour for entrance into the skilled trades by Negroes, were threatening the 'exclusive jurisdiction' given the Building Trades by the AFL in 1908, and which they alone of all affiliates managed to retain after the merger. In sum, the *Situs* picketing right was a key weapon for continued control of the job: to keep out not only non-unionists but members of rival unions.

It was apparently this problem that motivated the President of the International Plumbers' and Pipe-fitters', Martin P. Durkin, one

[1] Report of the AFL–CIO Executive Council, Seventh Convention, p. 21. BCTD cost estimates calculated by writer based on interviews with staff.

[2] *Proceedings* First National Legislative Conference (1955), pp. 2–3.

of the top Building Trades leaders, to accept appointment as Secretary of Labor under Eisenhower in 1953 (at a fraction of his Union salary-expense arrangement). Durkin quit the same year, because, according to Meany, the Republican President had 'repudiated the proposals for revision of the Taft-Hartley Act which the President had promised Mr Durkin to support', and instead 'offered new anti-labor provisions'.[1]

Non-partisanship was to be a central feature of the BCTD's pressure campaign. It was also a feature of its little known federal electoral activity. Perhaps because they had reason to believe for some years that the *Situs* bill would pass, the BCTD entered the latter activity rather late, in 1962, and even then the sums collected and spent were small, as shown in Table V. The method of collection of funds for backing candidates, according to one official, was for 'the delegates [to] just dig down into their pockets and come up with a ten or a twenty dollar bill'. Reports filed by the BCTD with the Clerk of the House of Representatives for 1968 indicate that an average of $500 was donated to each of 80-odd Congressional candidates with no apparent discrimination made between Republicans and Democrats, whether liberal or reactionary.

Table V. *Receipts and Expenditures for Federal Elections by* BCTD

		$
1962	received	38,625
	spent	31,225
1964	received	27,191
	spent	33,280
1966	received	25,312
	spent	49,625
1968	received	47,999
	spent	63,970

Source: Congressional Quarterly, *Weekly Report,* for 1962–6; for 1968, direct examination by writer of BCTD reports filed with Clerk of House of Representatives.

These itemized reports suggest not only a continuation of Building Trades neutralism, but an ability to draw on the movement for financial assistance. For the 1968 elections, the delegates themselves chipped in $27,299; the additional sum of $20,700 that accounts for the total shown as having been received in 1968 was provided from the political funds of two major national BCTD affiliated unions— the Carpenters and the Electrical Workers—and by COPE itself.

[1] Constitutional Convention, op. cit., pp. 158–9.

Such open support for the narrow goals of the craft unions by either the AFL-CIO or by COPE had not been possible at the time of the merger, when the CIO unions were so vigorously behind the Democratic Party, and when there was also bitter rivalry between the Building Trades craftsmen and the skilled men in the CIO unions. Yet the AFL men won informal approval from George Meany, president designate of the AFL-CIO, at the first Conference and more open approval for their goals and their strategies in later years.[1] Meany legitimized the programme in 1955 by voicing his confidence in the BCTD leadership that called the Conference, by re-affirming the crafts' historic autonomy, and by stressing the importance of their retaining the closed shop. On the other hand in 1955 Meany found it expedient to avoid an explicit endorsement of the central feature of the conference, the *Situs* Bill.[2]

On-the-job picketing was not mentioned in the COPE enabling resolution either. Under normal trade union mutual support arrangements, one would have expected endorsement from the entire AFL-CIO, and certainly from Meany, as the issue was of such overriding importance to so powerful a sector of the movement. The silence on *Situs* may have resulted from prudent recognition of two unresolved problems: the clash of job interests between the industrial and craft sectors, and the problem of racial discrimination.

In the early 1950s the skilled sectors of the industrial unions and the Building Trades were often on the verge of violence over jurisdiction of work by carpenters, electricians, plumbers, etc., on the maintenance and repair of buildings and grounds of manufacturing firms. The craft unions wanted such work done by outside contractors and their employees (chosen by the Building Trades locals), whereas the industrial unions felt that their members, employed directly by the manufacturer, should do the work. This competitive problem was not resolved by the architects of the merger and was referred to

[1] For the first time since 1955 the 1972 Conference was cancelled. It appears that the Executive Council of the BCTD did so in order to avoid the necessity of giving a forum to Sen. George S. McGovern and the Black Congresswoman, Rep. Shirley Chisholm, at the time the two most liberal candidates for the Presidency on the Democratic ticket (*Washington Post* 10 Feb. 1972). Not surprisingly, in view of the preponderant power of the Building Trades in the Federation in 1972, the Executive Council of the AFL–CIO voted to remain neutral in the Presidential election rather than endorse McGovern. The AFL–CIO was part of the 'Old Guard' coalition that had attempted to defeat McGovern at the Democratic Convention in July. Like other conservative sectors at that Convention the union leaders had decided that with McGovern as his opponent 'the country could get through four more years of Nixon pretty well, better perhaps than if this untried South Dakotan should win'. (Jude Wanniski, 'Is Nixon So Bad? Some Democrats Ask', *Wall Street Journal*, 14 July 1972.)

[2] Proceedings, op. cit. pp. 8–9.

a permanent joint committee of the BCTD and the IUD for 'adjustment of any conflict of interest that may presently exist or arise in the future . . .'.[1]

The second factor favouring silence in 1955 was union discrimination against black workers. The Negro protest movement and the 1954 desegregation decision of the United States Supreme Court had made the issue of *civil rights* the central domestic issue. The founding convention of the AFL-CIO endorsed the principle of racial equality without getting into any unpleasant debate on the more delicate issue of discrimination by unions against Negroes, which had been a feature of CIO propaganda against the AFL in earlier days. Non-whites were still barred by constitutional policy from the ranks of several major unions of skilled workers. Also many CIO local unions were practising or countenancing various forms of racial discrimination. Finally, craft job control, in conjunction with systematic discrimination in apprenticeship tests, had continued as major means of virtually excluding Negroes from skilled work in the construction industry. In short, the silence on *Situs* avoided debate which would have sorely embarrassed AFL and CIO alike.

Even with the prior approval of Meany, the BCTD's carefully prepared political plan was given no formal sanction. Yet it would nonetheless assume commanding importance in the AFL-CIO. The priority given to the *Situs* Bill and to other BCTD interests by the AFL-CIO will be seen in our analysis of the 1967 Legislative Conference, but the achievement of this priority will be clearer if we turn to a brief view of the autonomous political path followed by the UAW both before and after the merger.

The United Auto Workers of America

Perlman had not anticipated in his *Theory* the successful organization of open, industrial unions, partly because of his perception of the role of government in the *laissez-faire* era. The advent of the recovery plans of the New Deal of course altered Perlman's conception of the role of the federal government. In his popular 1933 lectures at the University of Wisconsin, Perlman addressed himself to the demands then being voiced by certain unionists and political figures for industrial forms of organization to meet bread and butter needs of the unorganized, and to the corollary demand on the Roosevelt government to aid the effort. But, painfully aware of the failure of social democracy on the Continent and the 1932 rise of Nazism in Germany, Perlman feared that labour-led national political action, which would likely accompany industrial union

[1] Convention *Proceedings*, op. cit., p. 165.

201

organization, was doomed to failure and might well provoke fascist reaction.[1]

The factual refutation of Perlman's position (although not of his basic model) was the successful alliance of the CIO unions with the Roosevelt Administration, which in turn provided the mass base for a labour-Democratic coalition. Thus, in an important sense, one may compare the political effects of the CIO breakthrough with those of the New Union movement in Britain, which created the base for the mass Labour Party. While this breakthrough was aided by the New Deal, the CIO, in turn, as early as 1936, profoundly influenced the Roosevelt Administration by its infusion of money and manpower into the Democratic campaigns. What did the CIO seek?

The CIO's formal entry into politics dates from 1943, with the establishment of the CIO Political Action Committee, under the chairmanship of Sidney Hillman. CIO-PAC was in business within two weeks of the passage, over President Roosevelt's veto, of the War Labor Disputes (Smith-Connally) Act of 1943. Smith-Connally was only the trigger, however. The 1942 elections had frightened both the CIO and the New Dealers. Not only had a generally reactionary Congress been elected, but the Special House Committee on Un-American Affairs (the Dies Committee, as it was then known) had been strengthened. This committee under the reactionary Texas Democrat, Rep. Martin Dies, had for years made the CIO and New Deal agencies and legislation the special targets of the search for 'reds and fellow travellers'. Sidney Hillman, the leading trade unionist in the New Deal, President of the Amalgamated Clothing workers, a major figure in the CIO, as well as a Jew and strongly anti-fascist, read the results of the 1942 election and its aftermath as omens of possible defeat for Roosevelt in 1944. Smith-Connally, which not only restricted war-time strikes, but banned direct union financing of federal electoral activities, was an even clearer signal to him and to other more orthodox leaders in the CIO. Hillman quickly put together a staff of intellectuals to launch what soon became the major organizational apparatus of the National Democratic Party.

Even though the PAC staff was not particularly attractive to many conservative CIO leaders, the new organization was able to assemble a surprisingly broad coalition and to make a striking beginning in national labour politics. The national CIO unions provided nearly $500,000 in direct grants for administration of the new organization. As much again came from voluntary contributions from union members, most at the rate of a dollar apiece. Another $380,000 was

[1] Lecture notes by the writer, from Professor Perlman's classes at University of Wisconsin, 1933.

collected by the National Citizens PAC, a collection of left-wing and liberal Democrats, artists, and intellectuals, professionals, and leaders of minority racial and religious groups. The total disbursed by CIO-PAC in the 1944 elections was about $1,330,000. All the rest of American labour combined spent only $252,000.[1] A measure of PAC's success was the most quoted remark of the election, purportedly Roosevelt's view of Hillman's role: 'Clear everything with Sidney'. The AFL remained neutral.

The United Auto Workers was one of the largest contributors to PAC activities. The UAW's direct grant was $100,000. And while voluntary donations by members were small, due to haphazard administration of the 'buck for PAC' drive, further union contributions in the form of manpower and other resources were massive. In contrast with the British Engineers' rather marginal involvement in 1945, most of the UAW's officers and executive board members participated directly in the presidential campaign. The UAW also opened its first legislative office and political action department in 1943 with a staff of seven in Washington and three in Detroit with additional full- and part-time staff members in every UAW regional office.

This effort did not come about simply in response to the threat to the New Deal and the CIO. There was a factional threat to the UAW leadership as well. Walter Reuther, then a vice-president of the union, had begun an attack from the right on the UAW's centrist leadership, which was supported by left elements in the union as well. The incumbent President and Secretary-Treasurer found additional power and prestige in political activity, which they also felt provided an alternative for strikes in the war years.

All these efforts in the 1944 election were aimed largely at producing high voter turn-out and Democratic majorities. At the Congressional level, the union fought several bills restricting union legal rights. And since unemployment rates in mass production had been over 14 per cent as late as 1940, it stressed measures to assure full employment after the war. It sought to counteract the effects of the Dies Committee. Special pressure was put behind passage of bills easing voting for members of the armed forces, eliminating poll taxes, and passing a permanent Fair Employment Practices Act. These latter measures failed, but parallel efforts in the field were more successful. The UAW alone had a score of its international 'reps', or organizers, working to register not only UAW members, but low-income workers in general. The hated Martin Dies was elimi-

[1] American Federation of Labor and Congress of Industrial Organizations, 'Union Political Activity Spans 230 years of U.S. History', Publication No. 106, unnumbered twelve-page booklet (Washington, D.C., 1960).

nated in the Democratic primary by the votes of more than 50,000 newly registered Negroes, Mexican-Americans, and other poor people,[1] and the PAC was generally credited with a major share of Roosevelt's fourth term landslide victory.

The CIO's political activities did not result from an indiscriminate desire to influence events, but from a very specific apprehension that unless Roosevelt was re-elected, 'unemployment and breadlines', as Hillman put it, would follow. In addition, the CIO unions feared legal attacks on their own form of union organization and felt strongly the need for maintaining countervailing power against a generally reactionary Congress. They also found political activity to be a useful replacement for strikes and normal bargaining during wartime. Thus, we find them reaching out and organizing a national constituency that stretched far beyond the CIO's own affiliates, if not so far as the AFL unions.

With Roosevelt's death, the CIO-PAC continued, with a general consensus around the support of President Truman. This continued until the outbreak of the Cold War. By early 1947, the polarization that we have seen in the British movement was evident in more pronounced form in the CIO. The Right and Centre supported Truman's 'loyalty' programmes at home and his anti-communist policies abroad; only the Left Wing—including the bulk of the PAC staff—joined in creating the short-lived Progressive Party, with Henry Wallce as their 1948 standard bearer.

Despite the disaffection of a dozen Communist-led CIO national unions and many militants Truman was re-elected. The new Congress was also Democratic, and union support (now including the AFL) had proved vital in the election, but Taft-Hartley was not repealed. While the election results may have protected unions from new restrictions, Truman's 'loyalty' programme and his engagement in the Cold War hardly helped the climate for repeal of the 'anti-communist' Taft-Hartley Act.

Indeed, the anti-communist features of Taft-Hartley, combined with the investigative avidity of the House Un-American Activities Committee, which continued to grow in importance despite the removal of Dies, became useful to many aspiring CIO leaders. As Edwin Lahey, a knowledgeable columnist, reported some years after the fighting was over, '. . . it is no secret that anti-Communist leaders of the CIO used the Committee on Un-American Activities to help expose their own Communist caucuses in 1948 and 1949, when the CIO came to grips with its Communist problem'.[2]

[1] Sidney Hillman, speech, *Proceedings of the Ninth Convention (1944) of the United Automobile Aircraft and Agricultural Implement Workers of America* (UAW–CIO), pp. 236–43.　　　　　[2] *Miami News-Herald* (1 April 1964).

The conventional charge of 'sell-out' is too simple and pat to describe this political tactic used against Communist and other left-wing unionists. Quite apart from any of the diverse personal motivations of the major leadership, few of whom had *any* political convictions, the CIO felt threatened by the possible loss of the Presidency to the Republicans and feared further repression. The national Democratic party, in spite of its divisions and weakness, seemed the only available protection for the new unions. Many Radicals, Socialists, and Communists had already joined the Democrats as individuals. On the other hand, many union leaders (craft and industrial) who had found the Roosevelt administration too far to the Left on either domestic or foreign policy questions (or both) were happy to fall into line behind the strongly anti-Communist but 'pro-labor' Truman.

Reuther had been elected President of the UAW in 1946. However, he had been unable to win control of the International Executive Board. At the 1947 Convention Reuther's centrist opponents in the UAW, at least partly inspired by the design of the Communist Party activists for a national electoral move toward Henry Wallace and the Progressive Party, sought to condemn both major parties for their part in passing Taft-Hartley. The main question for many, however, was whether the union had sufficient economic strength to operate without the protection of the NLRB.

Reuther did not think the UAW was ready to give up this protection and urged that the affidavits be signed 'under protest' and that this be followed by an attack on the entire law with 'a vigorous, militant and unceasing drive in the political field to repeal'. In any event, the UAW convention voted with Reuther, who now emerged as undisputed leader of the pivotal CIO affiliate.[1]

CIO President Philip Murray had come to agree with Reuther and was also urging accommodation, however temporary, with Taft-Hartley.[2] His *rapprochement* with the AFL was improved as the AFL came to similar conclusions about Congressional action as the best means to deal with the law. The AFL opened its own political agency, Labor's League for Political Education (LLPE) for the 1948 election with a budget of $343,293, second only to CIO-PAC.[3] The AFL also emerged as the 'top spender' among Congressional lobbyists with a 1947 budget of $834,565.[4] While the

[1] *Proceedings* of the UAW Convention (1947), pp. 77 ff.

[2] Ibid., p. 67.

[3] Philip Taft, *Organized Labor in American History* (New York, Harper and Row, 1964), p. 615.

[4] Congressional Quarterly Service, *Congress and the Nation* (Washington, D.C., 1965), p. 1,586.

AFL still made no official endorsement for the Presidency, Joseph Keenan, first LLPE director, recalls that he personally campaigned with President Truman and the CIO-PAC leaders; these efforts stemmed from the conviction within the AFL that the unions were endangered and that only the re-election of President Truman and a Democratic Congress could bring about the repeal of Taft-Hartley, which was the most pressing danger.[1]

While accommodating to the law, the UAW continued its CIO-PAC voluntary dollar contribution, and in 1951 created its own Citizenship Fund, which operated within the limits set by Taft-Hartley. Financed by ten cents out of each member's monthly dues, half of which went to Solidarity House, UAW headquarters, and half to the locals, the fund was used for direct funding of *local and state* campaigns, for the union's Washington office, and for what the UAW called 'political education work'. By the late 1960s the Fund was spending $876,000 annually, of which some 30 per cent was spent for 'partisan political activity', according to the union, while 'the greatest share of time and money', they state, went for 'educational and civic activities encouraging maximum citizenship, responsibility and participation'.[2]

Reports filed at the Labor Department, as required by the Management-Labor Reporting and Disclosure (Landrum-Griffin) Act of 1959, did not make any distinction between 'educational' and 'political' beneficiaries of the Fund, but there were dozens of easily identifiable partisan organizations—city, county, and state Democratic committees—as well as many others that were at least quasi-Democrat, including the civil rights groups, the Americans for Democratic Action, scores of local AFL-CIO councils and the Industrial Union Department of the AFL-CIO.

Whether 'political' or 'educational', however, the UAW's Citizenship Fund was clearly following the pattern established in the 1944 election by CIO-PAC, aiding the Democratic party with both direct assistance and encouraging voting and other participation in politics among groups likely to support the Democrats.

In addition to the Citizenship Fund's automatic collections, and in addition to the UAW's massive electoral contributions of organizing manpower (discussed below), the Auto Workers managed to bring in and spend substantial voluntary contributions for *federal* elections (see Table VI).

The increase in the proportion of voluntary funds spent directly by the UAW represented a reduction in COPE support. According to

[1] Interview (2 January 1968).
[2] 'IEB Determination on Political Expenditures Pursuant to Article 16, Section 6 of UAW Constitution', *UAW Administrative Letter* (18 July 1969).

the union's political staff, the reasons for this trend were a greater desire on the part of the UAW to support some liberal Democrats who had received less than full support from COPE and disagreement with the legislative priorities of the AFL–CIO.

Table VI. *Voluntary Collections and Disbursements for Federal Elections, as Reported by UAW, 1957–1968*

Year	Received	Spent
	$	$
1957	69,094·00	16,835·00
1961	104,489·05	61,431·15
1965	261,354·00	269,212·00
1968	241,306·00	559,188·88

Source: Congressional Quarterly, *Weekly Report*, except for 1968 expenditure figure which was obtained from UAW Washington office, correcting total of $472,166·00 at CQ.

One can find little evidence to measure the members' own direct interest in the electoral activity. The local unions' commitment may be seen from the fact that they organized raffles, dances and similar fund-raising events to raise their quotas of voluntary or 'hard money'. The national union's vital interest in such activity was manifested by a 'voluntary' check-off system instituted in 1964 (and continuing to date) to collect from each of the 1,000-odd international representatives ('reps') and officers $2·00 per month for the fund.

Finally, there were the UAW's contributions of manpower, the largest and least reported union political contribution. The UAW's full-time electoral staff alone was larger than the staffs of COPE and the National Democratic Committee combined. One staff economist estimates that in 1968 the UAW provided $10 million in services to the Humphrey Presidential campaign. While this is many times greater than the reported expenditure on all federal elections ($559,188·88) it may still be a conservative estimate.

The UAW assigned in 1968 no fewer than sixty reps, each drawing about $20,000 per annum (including fixed expense allowances), to full-time political work in various UAW strongholds, an expenditure of about $1·2 million. Another 100 reps worked full-time on the Presidential campaign in its last three months, at a cost of $500,000. Moreover, beginning with the 1964 elections the entire corps of 1,000 UAW organizers was ordered to spend half its working time on political action, an additional expenditure of about $10 million. Thus, for salaries alone, the UAW spent about $11·7 million in 1968, not counting the officers' time on political activities, direct mail campaigns to the members (based on computerized breakdowns by Congressional districts), media expenses and other 'educational' efforts.

In spite of internal and external changes—the end of ideological factional fights, the growth of oligarchy, the merger of the AFL and CIO, the great changes in the American economic and political scenes—the political goals of the UAW clearly remain much the same as they were in 1944: the building of a broad-based coalition seeking social-welfare goals working to elect a friendly Democractic President and Congress. This generalized need for White House support was rooted, as in 1944, in fears of high unemployment and of harassment through the law.

As for specific goals, ever since the merger in 1955 the UAW has shown a distinct departure from the priorities of the Building Trades, and to some extent from the AFL-CIO as well. As an open union with diverse representation by age, sex, and race, it was naturally more responsive to rapid social change. Thus, the UAW's resolutions on citizenship and political action at its 1955 convention were considerably broader and more explicit than the enabling resolution on COPE which was the equivalent statement of the entire AFL-CIO. The UAW's political resolution covered the entire range of social issues, including job equality, which had been swept under the rug at the AFL-CIO convention. The UAW's own debates on the issue revealed serious racial friction within the union, especially over the barriers against the blacks' entrance into factory-based skilled trades, but the leadership clearly hoped to encourage federal legislation which might accomplish the solution that the leaders themselves were unwilling or unable to provide.[1] The UAW's underlying concern about rising unemployment in the period is reflected in all the 1955 political resolutions.

The special resolution on Taft-Hartley suggests that the UAW was ready to live with the law, provided it had a friendly NLRB. The main attack was on President Eisenhower's appointments to the Board. Significantly enough, *Situs* picketing, the central concern of the BCTD, was not mentioned.

The Taft-Hartley resolution also attacked Section 14(b) for 'protection [given] to the opening of sweatshops [in] anti-labor states'.[2] The UAW had of course helped to stop or reverse a number of state right-to-work laws, especially in states where its union shop arrangements were threatened, but in the mid-1960s, it was subordinating its efforts on the issue to the problems of civil rights and

---

[1] *Proceedings,* Fifteenth Constitutional Convention (1955), p. 248.
[2] Ibid., pp. 88–91.

full employment.[1] These two related issues, it will be seen, contributed to the UAW's decision to leave the AFL-CIO.

UAW Political Schism with AFL-CIO

There had been virtually no prior public conflict reported within the AFL-CIO or its councils when the UAW issued its sensational charges against the 'complacency' and 'status quo mentality' of the central body in December 1966. George Meany was quite credible when he gave as the only reason for the split Reuther's 'frustrated personal hopes'.[2] Certainly Reuther hoped to succeed the ageing Meany as AFL-CIO president, and must have been frustrated by the failure to do so. Yet, the policy differences between the UAW and the Federation, as we have seen, extended back to the very start of the merged organization. While they remained unpublicized, the vast changes within the movement, in the automobile industry and in national economic policy, as well as the conflict in philosophies and personalities, all combined to bring about the schism.

Paradoxically, the UAW avoided linking its policy differences with the political action programme. To have made an attack on the COPE organization would have endangered their own key role in the coalition of the unions and the Democrats, which had now become a central activity of the UAW. Nevertheless, after charging that the AFL-CIO had countenanced a stand-still in the organization of the labour force, the UAW went on to charge that the Federation had shown insufficiently deep commitment to and involvement in the 'war on poverty and equal rights'; had failed to develop sufficiently strong ties to the traditional allies of the labour movement—youth, intellectuals, and minority groups—and was following a 'narrow and negative' line on foreign policy rather than seeking to build 'bridges' with labour abroad.

These failures, it might be noted, were failures in building and maintaining the historic political coalition built by the UAW and the CIO in the late 1930s and early 1940s, but they are not convincing reasons for the UAW's withdrawal as they stand, though they are indicators of the success that the conservative AFL and Building Trades style of political involvement was having within the AFL-CIO.

Stanley Weir has suggested that the UAW leadership split away from the central body was a diversion for the 1966 Convention, where there was threatened secession of skilled tradesmen, on the one

[1] Cf. Henry M. Christman (ed.), *Walter P. Reuther: Selected Papers* (New York, Macmillan, 1961); *Technology and the American Economy*, Report (Washington, G.P.O., 1966), Vol. 1, pp. 67 ff.

[2] AFL–CIO, Transcript of Panel Discussion at Georgetown University (18 April 1967), p. 8.

hand, and a 'new radical mood and on-the-job militancy' among the rank and file on the assembly lines, on the other.[1] While these factors were both present, two specifically political factors loom as important and possibly decisive: the blacks' struggle for equal rights and labour's position in international affairs.

The UAW had always been officially dedicated to equal rights for blacks and whites, and Walter Reuther—despite some serious opposition from his own caucus and even from some of his fellow officers—had been publicly identified with many major black organizations and causes. But as of the early 1960s blacks remained outside the skilled trades[2] and had only token representation at the union's top leadership levels. By the mid-1960s Negroes were well represented on the auto assembly lines. In Detroit, where they now constituted 35 per cent of the population, they had about 50 per cent of UAW membership, if not leadership. Earlier, UAW members in an informal Black Caucus had helped form a national movement of black unionists to win greater equality in the plants and in the unions. While blacks had been part of the CIO coalition and remained important for COPE, the latter had frequently found it expedient to accommodate itself to the exclusionist and chauvinistic approaches of the Building Trades and other conservative elements both on issues and candidacies.

One of the first serious signs of black dissatisfaction with the UAW came in 1961, when Negro members of the UAW led a breakaway of the Detroit Negro community in protest against the official COPE mayorality choice. The Detroit COPE—under Reuther's control—was backing a favourite son of the Building Trades, a 'law-and-order man'. The Negro community backed an unknown candidate, James Cavanaugh, and saw him elected.[3]

By 1966 the black workers in the industry had organized predominantly black 'revolutionary' caucuses inside most major UAW plants and a 'League of Revolutionary Workers' in the Detroit metropolitan area. Just before the UAW announced its clear intention to leave the AFL-CIO, many COPE-backed candidates were defeated in the 1966 elections and lack of Negro support was considered a major factor. Nowhere was this more apparent than in Detroit, and in Michigan generally, where COPE was virtually a UAW subsidiary and where the traditional Negro-labour alliance

[1] 'Behind the Reuther-Meany Split', *New Politics*, Vol. 5 (1966), No. 3.
[2] Penetration of blacks into craftsmen's jobs in the aerospace and automobile industry in 1966 was lower than in construction (Derek C. Bok and John T. Dunlop, *Labor and The American Community* (New York, Simon and Schuster, 1970), pp. 127–8.
[3] B. J. Widick, *Labor Today* (Boston, Houghton Mifflin, 1964), pp. 136–40.

had been strongest. Thus, aside from the moral and social considerations that were so important to the UAW leadership, there were vital institutional pressures both within the UAW and on the UAW-led coalition inspiring the UAW's emphasis on civil rights and equal employment in the official breakaway document. Indeed, it is perhaps not too much to say that Reuther's pre-eminent position as the voice of liberalism in the trade union movement, as well as the very survival of the UAW in the auto capital of the world, were at stake.

Nor were the UAW's charges concerning the field of international politics any less firmly based in practical considerations. International labour politics in the post-war era is far too tangled and unfortunately shrouded in secrecy to permit close examination in this paper. Even the relationships and policies favoured by the UAW cannot be examined in any detail, but the job factor was clear. The Auto Workers stated, after the secession, that foreign policy differences had been 'even more acute' than differences on domestic policy. As the UAW pamphlet 'One World . . . But Whose' put it, these differences stemmed 'basically from the AFL-CIO leadership's insistence that cold war objectives should dominate all others and that anti-communism justifies virtually any form of intrusion by the AFL-CIO in the internal affairs of other nations'. The UAW went on to accuse the AFL-CIO of accepting as much as $50 million from the Central Intelligence Agency and other government bodies to be used for international labour 'institutes' which the UAW said were designed for 'the subversion of . . . free trade unions'.[1]

The UAW had long been accustomed to bargaining nationally. By the mid-1960s it was belatedly ready to move into international bargaining largely because of the rapid shift of world production of motor vehicles. Reuther had been president of the Automotive Division of the International Metalworkers' Federation—associated with the International Confederation of Free Trade Unions (ICFTU) —since 1956. In 1964 he announced that the UAW had raised a $1 million 'solidarity fund' for the IMF to use in its efforts. By 1966, the UAW was organizing World Auto Councils to represent workers at the plants of international auto makers—Ford, General Motors, Mercedes-Benz, Volkswagen. The union was also working with British and other unions for an international union contract covering GM plants all over the world.[2]

[1] UAW International Affairs Department, 'One World. . . . But Whose', undated pamphlet released in Spring 1969; cf. Richard Dudman, 'Agent Meany', *The New Republic* (3 May 1969), for recent data on CIA-directed activities conducted by the AFL–CIO and some national affiliates.

[2] Interview, Victor G. Reuther, Director, International Affairs Department (29 December 1966).

The political activity of the Auto Workers was thus pitched at a high trade union level—as high or higher than any major US labour organization. Nevertheless, that genuine political action conformed to the Perlman model because it was necessary action to either (1) overcome unemployment, or (2) establish and protect the legal security of its organization, or (3) survive as a union in production centres having a large black labour force contingent, or (4) to protect their own organization and domestic job standards in the face of spreading international competition.

In the meantime, the AFL-CIO was taking an entirely different approach. The AFL-CIO's preferred response to job threats from foreign and multi-national corporations was to lobby for protectionism. Nor were Meany and his associates 'bridge-builders'. Meany is personally credited with arranging and stage-managing a temporary cut-off of United States contributions to the ILO after an assistant general secretary from the Soviet Union was appointed. And, while the UAW was working with the ICFTU, the AFL-CIO was withdrawing, charging the ICFTU with departing from its founding principles of fighting communism and seeking *rapprochement* with Moscow.[1]

The view was expressed by one UAW economist assigned to the IMF work that the UAW would have found co-operation with political and non-political unions abroad, and with their political allies, extremely difficult so long as there was any association with the hard, interventionist line of the AFL-CIO. The same might be said of co-operation with its allies at home while associated with the narrow social views of the parent body. In any event, the largest COPE affiliate and the one with the greatest success at COPE-type partisan politics,[2] had now broken with the AFL-CIO on certain vital aspects of two of the central public issues of the day, racial equality and foreign policy.

AFL-CIO Sans *UAW: 1967 BCTD Conference*

With the UAW withdrawn from the AFL-CIO Executive Council, the central body showed a distinctly more conservative political posture, associated with a more open and vigorous support for the goals of the Building Trades group. This change was apparent at the Twelfth Legislative Conference of the BCTD in 1967. The exclusionist policies of the crafts had come under severe attack for

[1] AFL–CIO Eighth Constitutional Convention, *Proceedings*, Vol. 2, p. 106. For a more extended report, as seen by the TUC's negotiators on the ICFTU Executive Board, see TUC *Report* (1970), pp. 343–51.

[2] Cf. J. David Greenstone, *Labor in American Politics* (New York, Knopf, 1969), Chap. 4.

many years. Now the Government's concern with skilled labour shortages during the Vietnam war escalation and the 'Black Revolt' of the mid-1960s made the crafts particularly vulnerable. Civil rights activism could no longer be ignored but on-the-job picketing was again the political business of greatest interest.

Although the AFL-CIO had worked for passage of the Civil Rights Act of 1964, its 'backbone' unions had continued to practise *de facto* racial exclusion. While the young black workers in many cities had unemployment rates as high as 20–30 per cent, construction work was undergoing a short-run expansion. Since such work was also the most visible source of higher paying jobs—much of this work was federally sponsored and in ghetto areas—Negroes had mounted both political action and direct action of their own against their exclusion from the skilled crafts.

The Civil Rights Act had been backed the next year (1965) by an Executive Order requiring affirmative action by contractors on hiring minority workers for federal construction projects. Violation of both enactments by the crafts was so widespread, however, that in 1966, Walter Reuther and two other members of the AFL-CIO Executive Council, all members of the National Commission on Technology, Automation and Economic Progress, joined in with industry and public figures to assert:

> At present the economic opportunities of Negroes are barred by exclusive hiring practices, discriminatory promotion policies, and unreasonable and unnecessary restrictive hiring requirements. Some unions refuse to admit more than a few Negroes to membership, thereby excluding Negroes from apprenticeship programs and from many highly skilled jobs in some industries.[1]

Although Reuther and other union leaders avoided the question, the formal three to six year apprenticeship programmes—used by the crafts to control the local supply of labour and maintain their own monopoly—were coming to be considered technologically and socially obsolescent by independent observers.

The pressure from Negroes, from the federal government, from some unionists and from social developments did not lead the crafts to yield their historic bar to penetration of the trades, but rather to defend their apprenticeships and attack the civil rights movement. The Plumbers' president reportedly told an audience that the rapidity of developments on civil rights and employment 'simply transgressed all bounds of common sense and reason'.[2] Meany took a similar

[1] *Technology*, op. cit., p. 66.
[2] Thomas O'Hanlon, 'The Case Against the Unions', *Fortune* (January 1968), p. 171.

position in his remarks opening the 1967 Legislative Conference:

> We have experts in the field of social welfare and we have do-gooders of all kinds. We have politicians, even some labor leaders who are far removed from the building trades, who suddenly become experts on the problem of urban renewal and rehabilitation. . . . There is no short-cut to a journeyman's card except through apprenticeship training, programs in which the industry, contractors, and everyone affected co-operates with the trade union in the the field. There is no other way. (Applause)[1]

Whatever the long-run costs, the AFL-CIO was placing its accumulated political capital at the disposal of the exclusionist policy of the Building Trades to help them preserve their job control. President Johnson now became a key factor. Meany had already expressed his support for the President for 1968, and for the Vietnam War. Johnson replied in kind when he spoke at the 1967 BCTD Legislative Conference. The President cited his own and the AFL-CIO's dedication to the general welfare. He expressed gratitude for AFL-CIO and Building Trades support for his international policies. The Building Trades Group of unions, he observed, had sent him his 'very first organizational message' in support of the interventions into the Dominican Republic (1965) and Vietnam. He did not mention union or company violations of the laws on equal employment, nor did he mention his responsibility for enforcing these laws.[2]

The President, however, had given only implied absolution to the crafts for their resistance to the Civil Rights Act and the Executive Order on minority employment in federal construction. The direct responsibility for enforcement lay with his Secretary of Labor, W. Willard Wirtz, who was also to speak at the Legislative Conference. Wirtz's department included not only the Office for Federal Contract Compliance but also the Bureau of Apprenticeship Training, and the vast Manpower Training and Development Act activity. The year before, the NLRB, reportedly at the urging of the Secretary and the Office of Federal Contract Compliance, had initiated proceedings against the Building and Construction Trades Council of St Louis for refusing to work on a job with plumbers who were members of a largely black independent union and employed by a black sub-contractor. The NLRB Trial Examiner found this walkout to be a violation of Section 8(b) (4) of the Taft-Hartley Act, a secondary boycott in construction, a violation of the law as stated in the *Denver* case, the *bête noir* of the Building Trades.[3]

---

[1] *Proceedings*, Twelfth Annual Conference, p. 11.   [2] Ibid., pp. 49–55.
[3] *NLRB Trial Examiner's Decision in TXD–501–66; 164 NLRB No. 40.*

If the President had been implicit, Wirtz could hardly have been more explicit in his approval of the crafts' traditional and immediate political goals. He gave his support to the *Situs* Bill, which would permit on-the-job picketing. He concurred with Meany's defense of the existing exclusionist apprenticeship system, terming charges of discrimination 'totally unfair'. He gave high praise to the crafts for 'honest' and 'sincere' efforts made in removing 'a past differentiation on the basis of race' in apprenticeships and memberships, and announced a meeting with BCTD leaders to work out a voluntary 'plan' for future compliance with the Executive Order.[1] Soon afterwards the AFL-CIO and various crafts unions took some mincing steps toward integrating non-whites into some trades. They received grants under the Manpower Training and Development Act for a variety of training and educational plans, notably OUTREACH, which, with the help of some Negro organizations, sought to find and train qualified minority youths to become apprentices.

Thus, the 1967 BCTD Conference scored a defensive political victory. It ignored the repeal of Section 14(b), as well it might have. The year before the AFL-CIO had devoted great energy to fighting for repeal of 14(b) in spite of only mild interest on the part of the UAW, which was interested in broader goals. At any rate, the effort to defeat 14(b) failed. The AFL-CIO correctly labelled as the immediate reason for failure a filibuster led by Senator Everett M. Dirksen, an Illinois Republican. But the Building Trades, which got part of their political funds from COPE, were using some of those funds to support the same Senator Dirksen![2] The end of the Taft-Hartley story is that at the Legislative Conference that year, the 14(b) struggle was ignored by the BCTD, having been pronouced 'doomed to failure' by the AFL-CIO's own Director of Legislation, Andrew J. Biemiller, who indicated to the conferees that the AFL-CIO was now giving top priority to the *Situs* bill.[3]

To sum up: The structural evolution of unions in the United States prevented the emergence of political activity by a unified labour movement. The early CIO unions engaged in political action to maintain in office a friendly President, and they succeeded in using their Political Action Committee as a magnet for attracting a diverse constituency to support the social goals of the New Deal. This represented a significant departure from the AFL's traditional *laissez-faire* political philosophy. The AFL–CIO COPE continued

---

[1] *Proceedings*, op. cit., pp. 14–21.
[2] BCTD Reports to Clerk, op. cit.
[3] *Proceedings*, op. cit., pp. 9,90. See also AFL–CIO, Radio Interview of Biemiller (2 January 1968). The Executive Council's strong stand for *Situs* is shown in its 1967 *Report*, op. cit., pp. 220–1.

this *de facto* alliance with the Democratic Party and general identification with 'welfare state' programmes, but as we have seen, COPE's share of funds declined as affiliated unions turned toward their own political interests.

Job-conscious business unionism remained the dominant philosophy. With respect to political action, the entire movement, including the most politically developed, the UAW, was forced into instrumental pressure politics because of continued threats to the bargaining system, threats to union exclusiveness and to a lesser extent the presence of high unemployment in many sectors. Some unions clearly recognized that the union practices and philosophies developed in a *laissez-faire* era were no longer compatible with an economy increasingly managed by the State and with vast social changes. The AFL-CIO, itself, became known as a sort of 'Peoples' Lobby' in many quarters. The Federation did indeed become a powerful voice in Washington, with increasing authority on all political issues in Congress and before the Executive. Yet its 'social conscience' work was distinctly ancillary, and on substantive political matters it remained responsive to the narrow trade union objectives of its most powerful affiliates. Given a choice between the broad political techniques and goals of the leading open union and the narrowly defensive market-based methods and objectives of the closed sector, the AFL-CIO chose the latter. The direct costs of these policies would appear to include the loss of its largest affiliate, a continued inability to raise the percentage of the labour force in unions, and finally, the alienation of a large sector of labour's traditional political allies.

Chapter XII

Summary and Conclusions

The introduction of compulsory social insurance in cases of sickness,
or compulsory social insurance in cases of unemployment means that
the workers must be subject to . . . regulations and limitations. . . .
To that we shall not stand idly by and give our consent.

AFL President Samuel Tompers to
Conference on Social Insurance, 1916.

The involvement of trade unions in contemporary political life is so
pervasive that while some significant generalizations can be made
about their formal political activity, no simple conclusion may be
drawn about their purpose. It is helpful to recall first, the basic
function of trade unionism and second, the difficulty of sorting out
the views of the *people*—officers and members—in unions from
institutional behavioural patterns. Trade unionism as we know it
today in the United Kingdom and North America grew out of the
industrial revolution and capitalism. The workers combined (as did
the employers) in the main for the purely selfish reason of improving
their economic status. For this, they evolved organizations that were
broadly responsive to the needs of particular craftsmen; the less
skilled workmen also developed similar protective institutions.
Genuine, substantive political techniques in general have over the
long run implemented the goal of economic status improvement.

Unions have been a favourite field of activity for social reform
leaders, socialists and communists. For a period before World War II
the philosophy of revolutionary syndicalism, which viewed parliamentary politics as futile, gripped many union activists and thrust
some into national leadership of British unions. It is perhaps less
well known that trade unions have always contained significant
numbers who believed in and often worked for rightist causes.

The leadership of present-day national unions covers a wide range
of social and political thought. Yet there is little doubt that many,
perhaps most major national leaders tend to distrust innovations,
maintain 'a strong presumption in favour of the status quo', have a
strong liking for 'distinct social classes', and have other 'conservative'

217

characteristics attributed to the nineteenth-century British trade union leaders by the Webbs.

In any event, one can hardly equate the political views of the members in contemporary workplaces with the behaviour of the national institutions. The growth of oligarchy, the shift in economic power to the less political shop stewards, the frequent alienation from the job—all these factors militate against such an equation. Furthermore, any conclusions about political action must be tempered by the knowledge that even under the democratic process which generally prevails in most British unions, the members' views will be only imperfectly recognized and channelled.[1] What follows then is a set of tentative conclusions about trade union political purpose as obtained from close examination of institutional behaviour of certain representative union organizations during the period.

The central conclusion deduced from extensive study of an empirical model, the AEU, confirmed from a broader examination of the activity of the Trade Union Group in Parliament, and from the example of the Transport and General Workers' Union (the T & G), is that since 1945 the predominant section of the British movement has not sought central planning nor social change; nor has it found it necessary to engage in political action for the economic goals, or the operational requirements of the unions. On the other hand, the American unions typically reacted to threats of legal changes and unemployment during the period with heightened political activity. The exceptional and perhaps accidental case of the Association of Scientific, Technical and Managerial Staffs (ASTMS, formerly ASSET, as it was known at the time of this study) is of interest because it shows that pressure politics of the American type can be usefully adapted to the different constitutional, political, social and economic circumstances in modern Britain—given the need and the leadership skills. What comes through, then, from a comparative analysis of unions in Britain as well as in the United States is that the underlying objective of political action in the post-war years was simply the achievement, maintenance, or restoration of 'free collective bargaining'. Whenever there is a threat to the legal status of unionism or to free collective bargaining, trade unionism moves toward genuine political action to counter that threat. When legal status and traditional forms of collective bargaining are more or less assured, and when unemployment is minimized and subsidized, the political action, in Perlman's words,

---

[1] 'The Annual Delegate Conference itself is too big to do more than make a blunt appreciation of the NEC and the officers' work'. Clive Jenkins, General Secretary of ASTMS, *Journal* (1971), Issue One/Two, p. 3.

becomes '. . . reduced to merely a few measures bearing the stamp of Gladstonian liberalism . . . [and] the whole clockwork in the mechanism . . .' runs down.[1]

Although the Engineering Union was in some respects a political maverick in the post-war years, it did not significantly part from the TUC General Council's political stands. The Council fully accepted the Attlee Labour Government's reforms, most of which were directly connected with the level of living—food and transportation subsidies, national health service and old age insurance, and public housing. Private enterprise could supply none of these services. Labour's nationalization measures were also backed. However, having achieved union recognition and job improvement in the nationalized sectors, there was little interest shown by the unions in proceeding toward greater nationalization or a more equitable society.

The Tory Governments that took power in 1951 and held it until 1964, in general accepted the Labour reforms as well as the commitment to the full employment policies which had prevailed since the war. The unions, essentially, remained satisfied. The General Council intervened in Party politics in the early 1950s not to advance substantive political goals, but to prevent significant political or social change. The Council's purpose was very plainly defined by Arthur Deakin in his warning to the 1952 Party Conference that the Party leadership struggle transcended the particular issues then under debate: that the union movement was not prepared to accept a Party Leader who might threaten 'the well-established machinery of negotiations within the mixed economy'. Deakin's warning grew out of the fear that a left-wing Leader (and potential Prime Minister) might upset the collective bargaining machinery either by 'seizing the commanding heights' of the economy, or by encouraging the growing unofficial bargaining movement at the work-place or by wage control.

This was no idle declaration. There followed serious activity within the political movement by the General Council's leading figures. But it amounted to a sort of pseudo-politics—a series of bureaucratic organizational steps to implement the policy of *status quo*. This was illustrated by Deakin's assistance in reviving and legitimizing the Trade Union Group, and establishing a liaison between it and the General Council. For the ten year period 1954–63, Victor Feather, Assistant General Secretary of the TUC, served as the Council's representative inside the group. This unusual arrangement was shown to reflect the Council's spurious political purpose, namely,

[1] S. Perlman, *A Theory of the Labor Movement* (New York, Macmillan, 1928), pp. 129, 149.

219

to serve as a caucus to help assure that the Parliamentary Labour Party retained a Leader acceptable to it.

With the Government becoming increasingly involved in management of the economy, the Trade Union Group, containing about one-third of the entire Parliamentary Party membership, might have contributed to the Labour Movement's policy formation in general, and industrial policy in particular. But the TUC, largely satisfied with the functioning of the economy, was not seeking new political initiatives and, for such political work as it did do, it had achieved sufficient status to deal directly with the Government without resort to the union-sponsored MPs as intermediaries. In the event, while some of these MPs were interested in seeking genuine political co-ordination between the group and the TUC, the documentary evidence established that the General Council made no significant effort to use the group for substantive politics under either Conservative or Labour Governments.

This was the context in which the empirical model, the AEU, the second largest union in Britain, decided to expand its Labour commitment in general and its parliamentary programme in particular. Yet, throughout its history and up to the General Election of 1945, the Engineers had avoided political weaponry—except when it was necessary for legal protection of the bargaining system. As the *New Model* of national craft unions, the ASE had viewed its members' labour as a commodity which had to be sold in an impersonal market. These artisans combined, as the authors of the *Communist Manifesto* perceived, to overcome the competition in the sale of their labour power, but they fought against the notion that 'The proletariat are more and more equalized in proportion as machinery levels all distinctions of labour, and nearly everywhere reduces wages to the same low level.' Indeed, for generations the ASE viewed unskilled workers as an obstacle to their own monopolization of the better jobs rather than as class allies.

The ASE's fleeting association with Karl Marx and the 'First' International is enshrined in the official history of the union as a symbol of class solidarity and as part of a revolutionary tradition. Ironically, the most interesting feature is that the Newcastle Nine-Hour-Day strike and associated events which brought the International into the picture, merely underscored the business unionism and opportunism of the ASE and its strong aversion to either class-conscious unionism or class-conscious politics.

The Amalgamated Society of Engineers did join with other craft societies and the New Unions in founding the Labour Party. We noted that there were many internal and external factors in that development, but the main objective for the ASE, as for the older unions generally, was to remedy by parliamentary action the courts' threats against legality. After full legality was achieved by the Trades Disputes Act of 1906, the Labour alliance was retained, but that alliance was not in general exploited for the purpose of genuine political action. In order to assure survival, the Engineers gradually and unavoidably opened membership to the unskilled and semi-skilled—under the impact of technological change and competition from the general unions.

At the end of World War II, the Amalgamated Engineering Union remained a Labour affiliate and was now fully 'open'. However, the union's status was perceived by the various leaders as being due not to political connections or activity, but to its increasingly important role as producers in the economy. The President of the AEU, Jack Tanner, whose path to the top had been hacked out by years of 'unofficial' action, during the shop stewards' movement in World War I and later unofficial movements, retained a belief in syndicalism and scorned Parliamentary politics. Yet he, like other major union leaders, supported the social service reforms of the 1945 Labour Government.

Moreover, by 1950 Tanner and his colleagues not only decided that Labour could govern but—more important—that it could maintain full employment and what Charles Pannell called the 'ideal . . . of mild inflation in which employers are chasing men instead of men chasing jobs'.

Neither Tanner nor other national leaders—except for the Communist minority—were persuaded that additional Parliamentary advances were needed. The union's acceptance of an enlarged centralized Parliamentary Panel, and the subsequent innovative selection and training system, was not accompanied by a co-ordinated development of political action in the sub-structure of the institution. Nor was the growth of the AEU Parliamentary Group in the 1950s and 1960s related to legislative functions of the members, or legislative goals of the AEU or the TUC. The decision to enlarge the group arose from such basically bureaucratic non-political factors as (1) the desire to influence the outcome of the Party Leadership struggle; (2) accumulation of political funds; (3) competition with other unions, notably the Transport and General Workers; (4) prestige and status considerations. Of course the elected national spokesmen of the AEU were interested in the preservation of 'free collective bargaining', but really did not see substantive political action as necessary to that end.

T & G's behaviour during the period indicates that with full employment and strong organization even the unskilled and semi-skilled workers, who never could rely on limiting the supply of

221

labour, were also in a general retreat from substantive parliamentary politics. We know as a general proposition that the organization of the unskilled grades into general unions had required political friends, and the success of the general unions had, in turn, helped make possible a mass Labour Party. But having solidified itself under the strong central leadership of Bevin and Deakin, and survived the worst cyclical down-turns, this largest of all British unions made clear to the 1945 Labour Government and to the entire movement—through Deakin—that it was content with post-war social and economic arrangements, and would resist efforts from the Right or Left that might interfere with the traditional bargaining system.

Under Deakin's successors, the T & G's political purposes became more complex, but the basic historical direction did not change. Frank Cousins, the most important figure on Labour's Left in the period, enlarged and altered the ideological complexion of the Union's Parliamentary Group. He himself entered the Wilson Labour Cabinet, as Minister of Technology. However, the stand taken by the union during his absence, his own resignation, and the subsequent policies he pursued upon returning to the union, all pointed to a rejection by the T & G of political techniques for either its operational requirements or for more general economic or social advance. The T & G MPs under Cousins and his successors were shown to be as insulated from policy formation as they had been under Deakin. Cousin's departure from the Cabinet was not based on political demands conventionally identified with him and with the Left Wing in general— nationalization and nuclear disarmament —but was a result of his, and the T & G's opposition to the new statutory incomes policy. The union was persisting in 'free collective bargaining'. And, significantly, it did adapt its structure to pursue collective bargaining at work-place as well as company-wide and industry-wide levels. It also called for greater authority for the TUC to bargain centrally with employers and the Government. At the same time, the union publicly and explicitly subordinated both political work in general and planning in particular to market bargaining within the constraints of a statutory incomes policy.

In a limited sense, it is true, the T & G in responding to new Labour Government initiatives under the evolving managed economy engaged in very significant political activity—to oppose the Government. Yet, the organizational and political steps taken by the officers in the mid-1960s were as consistent with a non-revolutionary syndicalist philosophy and business unionism as with parliamentary strategy or socialist philosophy. (And it was no doubt not lost on the trade union movement as a whole that these steps paid off, at least *pro tem*.) Thus, the T & G's aggressive unionism was as plainly based on market bargaining as was that of its principal competitor, the AEU. To evade incomes policy, it accepted work-place or plant bargaining; this was a clear continuation of what Deakin had established as basic post-war union policy. In sum, political opposition to statutory incomes policy represented a time-honoured insistence upon private wage negotiation around the job.

With Cousins's retirement and Jones's accession, the T & G acquired a dedicated socialist who ideologically accepted 'real' planning. However, Jones, like the Left in general, rejected the kind of more or less integrated macro planning required in the mixed economy and avoided challenge to the existing social order. On the contrary, his accession saw the conscious adaptation of incentive payments systems and 'profitability bargaining', thereby reinforcing the socio-economic *status quo*.

We conclude then, that the T & G and the AEU, comprising the two largest affiliates of the TUC, and with quite distinctly different styles of leadership and structure, both substantially conformed to the Perlman *laissez-faire* model.

In the United States, by way of comparison, we saw that the structural evolution of the unions prevented the unity of purpose which is implied by many generalizations about the political activity of that 'labor movement'. The CIO had succeeded in utilizing its Political Action Committee as a magnet for attracting a diverse constituency to support the social goals of the New Deal, the survival of which was perceived by the new open unions as a pre-condition of their own survival. The AFL-CIO, through COPE, continued the forms of a 'welfare state' programme and a *de facto* alliance with the Democratic Party. But it was seen that COPE won only a minor share of union funds and that 'welfare state measures' were of declining importance to the Federation—even before the UAW breakaway in the latter part of the period.

A major turning point in trade union structural development in the U.S. case was the stopping of the CIO's organizing drive in mid-passage immediately after the war. This resulted in a void in the organization of the unskilled, especially the non-white, workers. One consequence was that at the merger in 1955 the members of the construction industries' craft unions remained the 'backbone' of the AFL-CIO, as they had been in the earlier craft-dominated Federation. This was reflected in the election of a craft union careerist, the former Plumbers' Business Agent and AFL leader, George Meany, to the powerful post of President of the AFL-CIO. Thus, the spectacle of the chief spokesman of the AFL-CIO supporting the Building Trades in their defiance of equal hiring laws in the mid-1960s was not so much an abrupt reversal of his and the

223

Federation's public position in favour of such laws, as it was a continuation of the predominant craft power within the movement.

Even genuine political action is not necessarily progressive. While the American study shows greater direct involvement of the unions in political action as compared to the professedly socialist unions in Britain, this was due first, to the absence of a Labour Party to which the political work could be delegated and second, to the different level of U.S. unionism and that movement's insecurity. As successive restrictions by Congress were enacted, the 'fragility' of unionism which Perlman described for an earlier socio-economic climate in the United States continued to retain validity. The insecurity was heightened by general job insecurity because of the substantial unemployment that prevailed during most of the period.

While the insecurity was general the various types of unions felt different kinds of threats. The construction unions' political objectives were frankly limited to the elimination of legal restrictions that had been placed against their particular and closed system of bargaining—which remained substantially unchanged from the years that Perlman had used them as models of 'job conscious' or business unionism in a *laissez-faire* era. They continued to rely on maintaining a monopoly on the supply side of the labour market to improve their security and status. To eliminate the Taft-Hartley picketing restriction which stood as an obstacle to their traditional method of job control they mounted what became the largest pressure campaign of Anglo-American post-war labour history. Yet, they remained largely outside the COPE programme, and determinedly neutralist. Notwithstanding this neutralism, they won complete backing of the Federation, even though it meant committing the Federation to political action against the wrong side of the central social movement in the United States, the black workers' demand for job equality.

Differing circumstances make it unfeasible to attempt an accurate measure of comparative political expenditures in the two countries. The principal point, perhaps, is that the Americans spent huge sums and energies for specific (and often divergent) objectives and could not delegate their political work to either their own political arm or to a political party. In Britain delegation of the political work has been achieved, and the Labour Party in general reflects trade union political philosophy as well as the philosophy of many of its allies. The British unions' passivity during the period, as compared to the North American activism, was due chiefly to the fact that the Party was viewed as symbolic, a form of protective insurance against government actions that might prove harmful to trade union interests. For the period, it served mainly bureaucratic purposes. With unemployment minimized and the legal status not under attack, the unions were content with a policy of *status quo*. Labour affiliation by the trade union branches, while by no means as extensive as the levy collections and propaganda suggest, nevertheless reflects a much deeper involvement of the unions—at least in pecuniary terms—than can be matched by American labour involvement with the Democratic Party. Thus, delegation is firmly based in Britain. And while indifference and disenchantment are widespread in union circles, there would seem to be little danger of a serious split between the unions and the Party. Barring unforeseen changes, the present arrangement provides a double defence of *status quo:* the British political system relies on unions maintaining the Labour expenditures, and, since the unions (including those on the Left) show no signs of seeking major social change, one may reasonably expect that they will continue to collect and disburse the levy for the Party.

The unions remain primarily concerned with MORE within the existing economic framework, and political action will be mainly designed to protect their power to achieve that goal, irrespective of its effects on planning and other presumed official goals. Given the continuation of present structures and governance systems in the unions, one may expect also that political action will be directed to reinforcing the existing bureaucracies.

Chapter XIII

Epilogue: Based on Events in Britain Since 1967

Of course, this involves us in politics. Indeed, issues such as legislation against unions and unemployment, are making unions more politically involved than ever before in the post-war period. It is inevitable that we shall see a greater involvement by trade unions in the affairs of the Labour Party, which can only be to the benefit of both the industrial and political wings of our Movement.

> From letter dated 18 May 1971 by Hugh Scanlon, President, Amalgamated Union of Engineering Workers (AUEW), prepared in answer to written questions submitted by author of this book.

Hugh Scanlon wrote not only about the model union, the Engineers, upon which we have concentrated our analysis, but of the British trade unions as a whole, when he asserted that 'legislation against unions and unemployment are making unions more politically involved than ever before in the post-war period'. He went on to anticipate 'even greater involvement in the affairs of the Labour Party'.

Did this predicted new involvement in political affairs indicate a change in political purpose? Scanlon was writing when a Conservative Government had taken office and was preparing to enact a far-reaching Industrial Relations Bill containing many features of the Taft-Hartley Act. The national rate of unemployment had risen in 1966 during the last years of the Wilson Labour Government and in 1970–1 was approaching American post-war highs.

The emergence of severe unemployment had been a stimulus to genuine political action in the United States. And there were abundant indications of concern among TUC leaders about the rising rate in Britain. But one remarkable feature of the post-1967 period was the negligible political reaction from the Labour movement to the increasing level of joblessness, despite certain local, and unofficial, protests in some areas. However, the reactions to the

226

successive Labour and Tory industrial relations proposals and, even before that, to the statutory incomes measures of Labour, confirm the central thesis of this study: whenever there is a threat to the legal status of unionism or to free collective bargaining, trade unionism moves towards genuine political action to counter that threat.

The TUC called together one of its rare Special Congresses in 1971 at Croydon to adopt a manifesto demanding 'Repeal of the [then anticipated] Industrial Relations Act on Labour's return to power'.[1] To observers who recall the American unions' behaviour after passage of the Taft-Hartley Act in 1947, this may arouse an overpowering sense of *déja vu*. There are of course many distinctions between the two situations. For example, it is not clear how the present Conservative Government will enforce the measure. Also while there are advocates of accommodation within the TUC, one sees greater determination among the British unions to resist than was evident at a comparable period in the American movement. The main distinction is that the British unions clearly have the ability to win repeal. Whereas the Americans were far more fragmented generally, and never had more than a strong minority status within the Democratic Party, the British unions' place in the Labour Party and in a potential Labour Government was now clearly strong enough to virtually assure action on any bill—if the TUC should decide to give it a really high priority. Indeed, union power in the Party was greater than at any time since the end of World War II.

In 1969, the union MPs, clearly reflecting the General Council's sense of political priorities and its power in the Labour Party, forced the Wilson Government to abandon its own Industrial Relations Bill. Had the Prime Minister persisted, according to Victor Feather, who succeeded Goerge Woodcock as TUC General Secretary in 1968, the General Council were prepared to 'face just as great a Labour disaster as in 1931'.[2] However, there was no repetition of the 1931 break with Prime Minister Ramsay Mac-Donald: the Right and Left of the General Council and a wide spectrum of leadership in the Parliamentary Party united to persuade Mr Wilson to withdraw the Bill.

The resultant new power and confidence of the industrial wing of the movement was widely noted following the Labour Government's surrender. It could be utilized for broader purposes than mere repeal of the Industrial Relations Act and restoration of *status quo ante*. Indeed some leaders of the movement decided that the greater involvement of the industrial wing assured swifter progress towards

[1] The Labour Party 'The Croydon Manifesto', *This Week*, No. 9 (19 March 1971), p. 1.
[2] Interview (2 August 1971).

the goal of socialism. Thus, Eric Heffer, MP, a left-wing member of the Trade Union Group, and a Front Bench Opposition spokesman against the Conservative Government's Industrial Relations Bill, described what he saw as an ascendency of trade union leadership of 'the parliamentary left'; he contrasted this with the Bevan period, when the Left consisted mostly of intellectuals (Castle, Crossman, Foot, etc.). And this new level of union involvement, he felt, would result in a renewal of 'the party's socialist faith'—symbolized for him by the singing of the 'Red Flag' by the entire Labour side in the Chamber of the House of Commons after the Tory leaders used the 'guillotine' to shut off debate on their Bill.[1]

What Direction for the Unions?

What is more likely than a resurgence of 'socialism' via greater nationalization, for example, as a result of the unions' increased role in the Party, is a growth in real union participation in the secularly expanding central planning system. Yet the continuing influence of traditional collective bargaining will undoubtedly appear and re-appear as the struggle over the union's role in national planning unfolds. These cross currents clearly appeared during the years 1967–9 in the ebb and flow of power and controversy over (1) incomes policy and the related problem of an optimum unemployment rate and (2) Labour's proposals for 'trade union reform' during the years 1967–9.

Incomes Policy Developments

Historians may see the Tory's Industrial Relations Bill as a turning point towards heightened trade union political action; but a clear signal of that turning was given in 1967, when the TUC decided that the Labour Government's statutory incomes proposals were a threat to its vital interests. To illuminate recent trade union political purpose, then, we begin by recalling the State's objectives in both incomes policy planning and 'trade union reform' and proceed to analyse trade union reaction to both. One eminent scholar and practitioner in the field of industrial relations recently observed that incomes policies have been 'by far the most important development' in the industrial policies of 'the mixed economies as a whole' since 1945.[2]

We have seen that the Wilson Government in 1964–5 introduced its own voluntary version of a Prices and Incomes plan. George

[1] 'The Left on the Left: Consensus and the Price of the Bill', *Spectator* (13 February 1971), p. 217.
[2] H. A. Turner, 'The Royal Commission's Research Papers', *British Journal of Industrial Relations*, reprint, Vol. 6 (undated), No. 3, p. 358.

Brown, the 'Deputy Prime Minister', won quick endorsement from both the TUC and from industry, for the combined goals of planning, increased productivity and control of inflation. In spite of the socialist rhetoric accompanying its presentation, the new sophistication in the organization of planning agencies, and the 'revolutionary' claims later made regarding incomes planning by George Brown, Labour's programme was neither conceived nor administered as an instrument for the more equal distribution of wages, income, wealth or power. Early in the exercise the TUC and the Government approved of the social case for special aid for those with low pay. However, no definition of low pay was evolved. This failure, according to Clegg, was due to the difficulty of reconciling it with the doctrine of 'fair comparison' as a means of pay-determination; and second, to the difficulty of preventing proportionate increases being demanded by higher-paid employees to maintain established differentials.[1] Jack Jones of the T & G claimed that in making its own significant adaptation to incomes policy his union was raising the wage levels of 'the lower-paid' through the bargaining process: 'While the advocates of incomes policy gave verbal support to the needs of the lower-paid, this Union has acted.'[2] Cousins and Jones did propose and win TUC support for 'a [target] basic national minimum wage or earning guarantee'. The TUC advanced that idea to the Confederation of British Industry in 1968 and both agreed to conduct 'an examination of the characteristics of low-paid workers'.[3] But there is no evidence that the actual effect of T & G wage claims was to raise wage levels of the lower-paid. Indeed, in each general union, and in the Engineers, the span of negotiated earnings levels provided the means by which a pattern of 'leap-frogging' or 'whip-sawing' claim and counter-claim could be established.

In 1964–6, the well established and stronger unions managed to evade wage restraint in spite of a great deal of verbal support by the TUC and others to the concept of incomes and price restraint. Given the system of payments by results (rather than the American specification of hourly rates for the contract period), full employment and the right to strike, the unions and employers continued to find means of implementing agreements for raising wages. As Donovan would later report, the 'arrangements [at the work-place] were flexible and required minimal institutional change'. Unions and management both adapted their 'formal' industry-wide and 'informal' work-place agreements to labour markets.

[1] Hugh A. Clegg, *How To Run An Incomes Policy and Why We Made Such A Mess of the Last One* (London, Heinemann, 1971), *passim.*
[2] T & GWU *Report and Balance Sheet, 1970*, p. 11.
[3] Congress *Report* (1968), pp. 357–8.

The tiny majority of the 1964 Labour Government may have inhibited that Government from new social initiatives, but the vast increase in power which it won in 1966 failed to lead to bolder policies. Nor did the trade union movement develop the necessary co-ordination and structural change that might have enabled it to offer its own alternatives for meeting Britain's apparent economic and social preference, in the latter part of the 1960s, for higher unemployment as the route to the control of inflation.

The TUC had continuously struggled against the Treasury's known preference for higher unemployment, but it became clear to Congress from the 'shake-out' of 1966—the Government's euphemism for induced unemployment—that Whitehall thinking could prevail in the Cabinet. The TUC's 1967 Conference of Executive Committees of Affiliated Organizations reflected labour's fear of legal regulation and marked the beginning of open resistance to the Labour Government's incomes policies. The conference was called by the General Council to hammer out policy after the Government issued a White Paper proposing a zero norm for wage increases. George Woodcock cited the danger of greater unemployment when he urged continuance of *voluntary* co-operation with the incomes policy. While reaffirming the no doubt genuine support at Congress House for the principle of an incomes policy, Woodcock, in a passing remark, strongly hinted that these key executives were not really serious about giving up their respective approaches to market bargaining in their sectors: 'There are a lot of people—perhaps some in this hall—who believe in an incomes policy, providing it is for the other fellow. . .'

Several somewhat contradictory positions flowed out of this significant conference. On the one hand, the General Council won approval for greater central initiatives after Woodcock warned that the Government might adopt such policy alternatives as reduced social benefits and 'the heavyweight of unemployment, which is our real enemy'.[1] The delegates voted to continue to co-operate with (1) a voluntary wage-vetting process by TUC, and (2) to grant the General Council power to call an Annual Conference of National Executive Committees which would discuss and vote on an Economic Report to be prepared by the Congress' staff. The emergence of the annual Economic Report was regarded at that time as a major contribution to the ability of Congress to represent the union movement in the National Economic Development Council (NEDC) and on the industrially based committees set up by the Labour

[1] Trades Union Congress reprint of 'Incomes Policy' speech by George Woodcock, pp. 11–13; Cf. Hugh A. Clegg, *How to Run an Incomes Policy and Why We Made Such a Mess of the Last One* (London: Heinemann, 1971), pp. 423–4.

Government for tripartite consultation. It was even regarded by the more idealistic delegates, TUC staff economists and research directors of various unions as evidence that if the Government was not able to work out a viable plan for the national economy then the trade union movement would do it for them. Yet there was little evidence that the TUC had acquired sufficient authority to enable it to guarantee implementation of the initiatives proposed in their economic plans. For example, Woodcock also pleaded unsuccessfully for greater central authority to intervene as a mediator in strikes. This type of expanded central power was not to be forthcoming, however, in even limited ways until the Labour Government made the specific threats of outside statutory intervention discussed below.

Productivity Bargaining and Strikes at the Work-place

As we have seen, the leading trade unionist in the Labour Government, Frank Cousins, left the Cabinet primarily on account of the Prime Minister's attempt to restrict inflation by rigid control of incomes and particularly wage income. Cousins believed that the 'productivity and payments by results' agreements were the 'positive' side of an incomes policy. He returned to the T & G and his seat on the General Council after passage of the Prices and Incomes Bill and announced he would now be able to 'make progress towards increased productivity and the planned growth of wage levels. . . '[1]

The productivity agreements were largely negotiated at the workplace, and provided an opportunity for workers to raise incomes above the rates negotiated at the industry-wide level. Throughout the 1965–70 period such 'domestic' bargaining was constrained to a greater or lesser degree by the requirements of incomes policy. Yet following the 1968 'package deal' in engineering there was again an upsurge in locally negotiated increases despite 'increased productivity' provisos written into the national agreement as conditions for locally granted wage increases.[2] Work-place bargaining was encouraged now by all the major leaders of the Confederation of Ship-building and Engineering Unions (CSEU). Such a strategy posed a challenge to the Government which was concerned about wage drift and the rising disposable income. For the employers it could mean higher unit labour costs. Previous payment systems in which overtime, holiday and sick pay were generally based on a nationally agreed wage base rate were often replaced by wage schemes in which the combined base plus bonus and incentive rates at the work-place provided the new calculator for fringe benefits. In

[1] Mimeographed copies of exchange of letters between Cousins and Wilson, from T & GWU.
[2] *Financial Times* (13 August 1971).

general such schemes gave a new security of weekly earnings to the organized workers. One may assume that in such circumstances the long run implications for overall numbers of jobs available were not a serious concern for the negotiators. The short-term advantages of securing both a high steady earnings level and a favourable competitive position with regard to other unions were regarded by both the T & G and the AEU leaders as more important.

The T & G, as noted earlier, had already in 1965 begun adapting its organizational form to its newly perceived function by creating a Research and Production Department, largely devoted to stimulating productivity agreements and steering them through the TUC wage-vetting process. In 1969, when Jones officially succeeded Cousins, he announced 'we have transformed our educational and research activities to bring them fully behind our negotiating objectives. . .' In that year the T & G opened a non-residential college in London 'for the particular purpose of training our shop stewards'. The central focus of all activity was on the 'all round increase in wages'.[1]

Scanlon reiterated on behalf of the Engineers, in the summer of 1971, the view which we saw expressed in 1965 to the Donovan Commission by Sir William Carron, namely, that the District Committee was a bridge connecting the Head Office with the shop stewards at the work-place.[2] The bridge was strengthened somewhat in 1968 when the union established a Production Studies Department in London Headquarters, to compile and analyse contracts negotiated within the Districts. But the continuing shakiness of the bridge for co-ordinated bargaining purposes or for significant national political effort may be illustrated by the fact that as of 1968 there were only forty contracts on hand at the Head Office of the many thousands that were then in effect. By July 1971 a total of 1,080 contracts had been sent in by the Districts from their files of negotiated contracts. The staff at Peckham Road considered this to be a vast improvement, but made no effort to exaggerate the achievement, estimating that about 7,000 to 10,000 contracts were then in effect in federated shops alone.[3]

The tradition of district autonomy; continued disunity at Head Office, with some Executive Councillors still persuaded that the strikes led by shop stewards were generally politically inspired; the continued separatism of the skilled sectors which required assign-

[1] BDC unpublished proceedings (1969); cf. *Report and Balance Sheet* (1970), pp. 6–7, prepared personally by Jack Jones according to his Personal Assistant, Len Willis. Interview (7 August 1971).

[2] Interview (2 August 1971).

[3] Interview with Ernie Roberts, Assistant General Secretary, and Secretary of Political Sub-Committee (2 August 1971); and staff of Production Studies Dept.

ment of many full-time negotiators to serve on their behalf on some fifty-odd joint national councils, as well as the continued ambience of syndicalism—all this no doubt served to constrain the Engineers' from yielding either greater authority to the General Council, or from following what Scanlon termed the 'all power to the stewards' line' of the T & GWU.

We have previously noted the paradox that at T & G centralized power was a factor in permitting the General Secretary to concern himself with a legitimization of work-place bargaining. In the late 1960s, Jack Jones not only developed a multi-faceted approach to such bargaining, but began a process of identifying with, and possibly absorbing into the national structure, the shop stewards who were now at the centre of collective bargaining in Britain.

There were in 1968 approximately 175,000 shop stewards according to an extensive survey made for the Donovan Commission. The data from this extended study indicate the extent to which the bargaining system had in fact shifted to the work-place, and the leadership transferred to the stewards (and especially the senior stewards). There was now wide acceptance of the stewards by management, by workers, and by full-time officers of the unions. Thus, all parties in the survey considered that the stewards were not, in general, more militant than the members they served. And they were now proven to be *less* political than the national officers! For example, the research team established that only 31 per cent of stewards, as compared to 81 per cent of full-time officers, belonged to any other association besides the union, including 17 per cent of stewards and 81 per cent of officers who were individual members of a political party.[1] These percentages strongly confirm the evidence previously cited that the shift of the locus of power towards the shop stewards was inimical to active parliamentary politics.

Workers' Control

As Jack Jones accepted and legitimized the shop stewards' role in the bargaining process, he linked this development with the long-established socialist concept of 'Workers' Control'. 'Shop steward representation and official recognition', he declared to the 1969 BDC, 'is the first elementary beginning of worker participation and indeed worker control'.[2] As explicated by Jones in numerous speeches and writings, Workers' Control seemed to have become part of the role that union representatives, and shop stewards in particular,

[1] Royal Commission on Trade Unions and Employers' Associations, Research Paper 10, *Shop Stewards and Workshop Relations*, by W. E. J. McCarthy and S. R. Parker (London, HMSO, 1968), pp. 14–15, 32.
[2] BDC unpublished *Proceedings*, unpaginated.

should play in collective bargaining, rather than a parliamentary objective. He used the term interchangeably with such concepts as 'industrial democracy', 'unionism with a human face', 'workers' participation', and 'an extension and widening of trade union functions'.

In expanding on steward recognition, Jones defended the most controversial feature of shop steward leadership, the 'unconstitutional' strike, or those taking place at the workshop prior to exhausting the steps in the official national procedure for conciliation of disputes. 'Don't call a strike unconstitutional simply because of the form the strike takes', he told delegates. A strike, in his view, is justifiable if 'management doesn't involve the unions on a problem; instead of calling it unconstitutional it should be considered action against arbitrary management'. This simply meant that management should not be permitted to unilaterally alter established practices—a demand that had been debated between the CSEU and the Engineering Employers' Federation for years.[1] Although Jones placed this in the context of his broader discussion of workers' control, etc, it was clearly a reiteration of the familiar struggle between unions and employers about management prerogatives.

Without making a formal disassociation from the TUC's and the Labour Party's commitments to planning, Jones continued to make plain that he regarded the 'shop floor' as the main area for achievement of union goals. Thus, in 1969: 'We have continued to stress that a more important thing than representation on boards is expanding the role of trade union representation on the shop floor and in negotiations. . . .'[2]

Although he was quite aware of the unequal distribution of wealth and income in Britain, he was not now seeking to change the distribution. Instead, he was proposing to help enlarge the pie and the size of the slices that management as well as labour would thereby be able to retain: 'We are calling into question the right of management to determine a whole range of issues and in the process we could make management in Britain more efficient and less costly, and of course we want a share of the savings in the reduced cost of management.'[3]

---

[1] This finally culminated in March 1972 in the total withdrawal of the unions from any procedural arrangements at national level in the engineering industry.

[2] BDC unpublished *Proceedings*.

[3] Ibid.; cf. the following T & G pamphlets by Jones: *The Right to Participate—Key to Industrial Progress* (1970); *Trade Unionism in the Seventies* (1969). Also, Harry Urwin, Assistant General Secretary, *Plant and Productivity Bargaining* (1970), pamphlet, second edition. For an authoritative account of the Labour Movement's attitudes towards various proposals for greater participation, see Weinberg, op. cit. *passim*.

This type of demand was perfectly consistent with his Right and Left predecessors' philosophies, and with the AFL's 'social wage' policy in the 1920s, a policy also dedicated to a constant labour share. Many American unions of the present day, notably those in coal mining and in the garment trades, continue to work actively towards making private management 'more efficient' and do not attempt to give it an ideological gloss.

Although Jones and Scanlon did continue to voice their belief in public ownership, their concept of 'workers' control' as developed in the late 1960s was not linked with the Party's Clause IV demand for 'common ownership of the means of production . . . and the best obtainable system of popular administration and control of each industry or service'. Rather, it was plainly inspired and sustained largely by the belated recognition that work-place bargaining had become the major negotiating area. Jones' own perception of his success in adapting to the new climate is suggested by his reported boast to visitors in 1970: *'Those productivity agreements were our secret weapons to get around the Prices and Incomes Board and get more money.'*

Jones' boast, taken with the preceding account, reveals that all the manoeuvring of the trade unions was focused, as it had been for years, on a Gompers-type philosophy of MORE and rejection of real participation in the management of the economy. Some union leaders sensed the danger that this strategy of uncontrolled increases in money wages was certain to assure the failure of any form of incomes policy. The unions in general, however, were still clearly either unwilling or unable to adopt an overall policy of restraining wages even though some of them knew that control of inflation was an essential accompaniment of a full employment policy in the mixed economy, which the entire spectrum of national leadership had in practice accepted since the end of World War II.

Thus, at the 1969 BDC of the Transport and General Workers, the retiring General Secretary, Frank Cousins, warned that the union 'would resist attempts by any Government to limit the freedom of the Union to act on behalf of its members'. The Conference opposed extension or renewal of the Government's incomes policy, rejected 'any attempts to legislate against the trade union movement' and made full employment the T & G's 'foremost objective'. The T & G leadership of course considered unemployment, as did other union spokesmen, a social problem. But in more immediate terms, as Cousins significantly observed, unemployment had damaging effects on the bargaining system: 'unemployment weakens trade union action for those at work'.[1]

[1] *Proceedings*, op. cit.

235

Royal Commission (Donovan) Report

When this report was issued in 1968 most TUC leaders and others hailed it as 'voluntarist' because the Commission proposed no direct punitive law and concentrated on non-statutory recommendations designed to take power away from the work-place. The Commission, apparently impressed with the American model, proposed a shift away from industry-wide bargaining by employer associations, and the informal bargaining at the work-place that had become a characteristic accompaniment, to direct negotiations by management at the firm and plant levels. The TUC, Donovan recommended, 'should consider the principle of "one union for one grade of work within one factory"' as a guide for the future development of structure. The check-off was also recommended.[1]

In an extended critique of the Donovan Report, H. A. Turner, who had served as an expert witness, commented that the major legal proposal, which was to confine immunity in trade disputes only to members or officers of registered trade unions acting with the full authority of the union's rule books, would expose unofficial strikers to legal penalties and withdraw the right to strike from non-unionists and from members of unregistered trade unions.

Among other oversights in the report which resulted from what he considers a 'preoccupation with the sins of the work-place', Turner cited the 'extremely brief and superficial reference to incomes policy', and cautioned that a general move towards local company agreements, which was the main proposed reform, 'could become an agency for the disintegration of successful *centralized* collective bargaining, which seems essential to economic planning and incomes policy'.[2]

In the TUC a set of contradictory currents prevailed with respect to economic planning in general and incomes policy in particular. On the one hand central initiative had been strengthened for purposes of reviewing wage agreements, for formulating economic policy statements, and for possible entry into the negotiating arena at the national level. These are clearly significant indications of possible future change. Yet the shift in the locus of power had continued and provided reinforcement of *laissez-faire* type unionism. It has been observed by Frank Cousins' biographer that the TUC in 1966 not only began to veer strongly towards his rejection of statutory

[1] 'Summary of Main Conclusions and Recommendations', as quoted in Allen Flanders, *Trade Unions* (London, Hutchinson, 1968 edn), Appendix B, p. 196.
[2] H. A. Turner, 'The Donovan Report', *The Economic Journal* (March 1969), pp. 1–10. Emphasis in original.

controls, but that he had in that year startled Congress by proposing 'surrender' to the General Council for *voluntary wage vetting*, in place of statutory control; that he had called also for a strong role for the Council in national bargaining so that 'union officials could concentrate on the really vital business of productivity bargaining at shop-floor level'; finally that in 1967 he helped bring off a series of meetings between the General Council and the Confederation of British industries during which both sides are said to have 'firmly grounded a kite which was being flown from Whitehall that there should be some permanent tripartite prices and incomes machinery . . . a sort of 'Neddy' for incomes and prices.'[1]

Following the Donovan Report's attack on the structural defects of industry-wide bargaining, the TUC and CBI jointly consented to review such agreements but defended the mix which had evolved out of post-war market incentives. They felt that the report was 'too sweeping in its criticisms and is also at fault in giving the impression that the concentration of collective bargaining at factory or company level (with industry-wide agreements playing a less regulative role) is necessarily best for all industries'.[2]

The General Council, in its own comments on the Donovan Report, criticized the main legal proposal, which was to deprive unofficial leaders of immunity in trade disputes. The Council perceived the possibility that national unions might 'accord general authority [to their substructures] for any action, so that the distinction between official and unofficial action would disappear'.[3] It may be taken as a measure of its own continuing ambivalence about unofficial strikes that the General Council did not comment directly on the Commission's significant and paradoxical judgments on the political aspects of work-place bargaining. The Commission itself had been carefully and democratically balanced to represent the main interest groups of an industrial society: management, public and trade union. Yet, one may reasonably speculate that its condemnatory statements about 'extreme decentralization and self-government' at the work-place level of bargaining may have been partly a reflection of the fear of some General Council leaders as a whole about the shop stewards' role. We have seen the anxiety, fear and anger about this industrial development expressed by Sir William Carron to the Royal Commission in 1965. Six years later, John Boyd, who remained

[1] Margaret Stewart, *Frank Cousins: A Study* (London, Hutchinson, 1968), pp. 167–75.

[2] The text appears in Trades Union Congress, 'Action on Donovan: Interim Statement by the TUC General Council in Response to the Report of the Royal Commission on Trade Unions and Employers' Associations' (1968), pp. 47–8.

[3] Ibid., p. 33.

one of the most influential members of the Executive Council of the Engineers' and now sat on the General Council as well, wrote that second only to the delays in procedure as a cause of 'unofficial strikes' was the 'activity of professional C.P. and Trotskyite agitators'.[1]

These shop stewards, as the preceding chapters indicated, and as the 1968 survey made for the Commission established statistically, are *less* political than the general run of full-time officers, in the commonly understood sense of being members of a party. Members of the Commission did see that in addition to reflecting market incentives, work-place initiative was also an expression of the democratic process. However, they clearly did *not* believe that the political complexion of the stewards was a cause of strikes. Yet, from the following language one would judge that the Commission, including its trade union members, was unhappy with the resultant obstacles to bureaucratic control, or the political *effects* of work-place bargaining: '[Although] the arrangements are comfortable and flexible and provide a very high degree of self-government . . . [there is] the tendency of extreme decentralization and self-government to degenerate into indecision and anarchy . . .'.[2]

'In Place of Strife'

The Government's perception of the General Council's ambivalence, the Tory initiatives in industrial relations policy, as well as the failure of incomes policies, all may have contributed to the Labour Government's 1968 decision to issue its famous White Paper, 'In Place of Strife',[3] even before the Donovan Commission Report was released. The Conservative Party, however, had already decided to move towards the North American model of stronger national unions and strike control, especially at the work-place. In their official policy statement, 'Fair Deal at Work', the Tories called for binding legal agreements, stating that the existing law 'gives legal immunity to anyone who incites other people to break agreements by participating in strikes or lock-outs'.[4]

As we have seen, the unions and employers, as well as the Government, had made possible the spread of productivity agreements, which covered several million workers at mid-1970. For such workers, the outcome of negotiations on rates and conditions were, of course, basically dependent on the strength of the negotiators, particularly at the work-place. In the absence of alternative arrangements, the

---

[1] Letter to writer from John M. Boyd (22 July 1971).
[2] 'Summary', op. cit., p. 186. [3] Released 17 January 1969.
[4] Geoffrey Howe, *Daily Telegraph* (16 January 1969); cf 'Tory Plan for the Unions', *Labour Research*, Vol. 56 (1967), No. 12, pp. 197–9.

power of the union side in productivity and other bargaining in the market was ultimately dependent on the strike weapon. Given such arrangements, any restriction of that weapon without compensating action would of course favour the employer.

A General Election loomed in 1969. In that setting it is at first glance surprising that Tory policy-makers had decided to seize upon the strike issue. But it is more surprising that they also assumed a *laissez-faire* stance and disassociated their Party from statutory prices and incomes restraint. As one political correspondent put it, they were now in a position to exploit at the polls both popular demand for the diminution of union power, and public disenchantment with the Wilson Government's direction of economic policy, especially its failing prices and incomes policy.[1] Against such a background, Labour also made the politically expedient decision to pursue a Taft-Hartley approach to strikes and industrial relations and to retreat from its incomes programme.

The trade unions' attitude towards Labour's White Paper and the Industrial Relations Bill marked another turning point in the union movement's heightened contemporary political purpose. In the letter cited in the opening page of this chapter, Hugh Scanlon attributed the increased level of union political activity not only to the Tory Industrial Relations Bill, but, indirectly, to the Labour bill as well. Scanlon also quoted from his own speech to the 1969 AEU National Committee, which condemned Labour's proposals:

> The fact that a Labour Government took these steps should make our shame all the greater and will not prevent our traditional opponents from exploiting them to the full, or future Governments extending and enlarging the pill of penal clauses, so cleverly wrapped up in the sugar of the small, but long overdue reforms concerning dismissals . . .

In the remaining pages of the chapter we will discuss briefly the Labour Government's proposals and union reactions to both the White Paper and the Bill.

The White Paper repeated the central theme in Donovan and the Conservative policy statement, namely that the rise of unofficial strikes required the reform of trade union structure and behaviour. While the actual extent and the cost of such strikes may have been seriously exaggerated,[2] there seems little doubt that the Government

---

[1] Peter Jenkins, *The Battle of Downing Street* (London, Knight, 1970), Chap. 4. I am indebted to this book for much of the background of the political struggles that took place in 1969 over the White Paper and the Labour Bill.

[2] H. A. Turner, *Is Britain Really Strike-Prone?* (Cambridge, Cambridge University Press, Department of Applied Economics), Occasional Papers No. 20 (1969), *passim*.

itself, paradoxically, contributed to the rising number of disputes by monetary and fiscal policies that failed to stem the inflationary tide.

In addition to the rise in the cost of living, there was a sharp rise in taxation. The rising tax load on the workers—a phenomenon dating back to the historical rise of the 'tax state' since the 1940s—was brought up at the 1969 Conference of the T & GWU in a resolution stating, that the flat tax rate of the National Insurance contribution, though not called a tax, 'was in fact the biggest tax for workers'.[1] Analysing both insurance contributions and income tax increases, Turner and Wilkinson attributed the 1969–70 strike unrest and wage explosion in considerable part to organized workers' efforts to maintain their *post-tax* real wages. They focused on state 'claw-backs' from gross wages, over and above the increased cost of living. In the four years 1966 through 1969, nearly three quarters of 'gross-real-wage' increases of a statistically typical worker was taken back by state deductions, in the form of national insurance contributions and increased income tax. The latter were only partly offset by increased personal and other tax-exempt allowances. 'The impact of price increases and state deductions, together, on real wages', they concluded, 'is such that most workers clearly have to run as hard as they can, in wage terms, merely to stay where they are in real or relative ones.' On the other hand it was found that collective bargaining in the late 1960s had left the lower paid worse-off while the better paid manual workers gained slightly.[2]

The First Secretary for Employment and Productivity, Mrs Barbara Castle, may have been aware of some of these disparities. She stated in the opening paragraphs of 'In Place of Strife' that the 'present system of industrial relations . . . has failed to prevent injustice', and that it 'perpetuates the existence of groups of employees who, as the result of the weakness of their bargaining position, fall behind in the struggle to obtain their full share of the benefits of an advanced industrial economy' (2).[3] But after this bold opening the author of the White Paper, apparently bowing to existing power arrangements surrounding the wage contract system, nevertheless declared that collective bargaining 'represents the best method so far devised of advancing industrial democracy in the interests of

[1] *Proceedings*, op. cit.

[2] H. A. Turner and Frank Wilkinson, 'Real Net Incomes and the Wage Explosion', *New Society* (28 February 1971), pp. 309–10.

[3] *In Place of Strife: A Policy for Industrial Relations*, presented to Parliament by the First Secretary of State and Secretary of State for Employment and Productivity, January 1969 (London, HMSO, Cmnd 3888). The pertinent numbered paragraphs of this pamphlet are indicated by number in parentheses in the text of the present discussion.

both employees and employers' as well as offering the community, 'the best opportunity for securing well-ordered progress towards higher levels of performance and the introduction of new methods of work' (19).

The Government nonetheless proceeded to recommend transfer of power to the First Secretary (Mrs Castle) for regulating both official and unofficial disputes. With regard to official strikes, she would have reserve power to order a ballot of affected members wherever she determined that a strike might pose 'a serious threat to the economy' (97–8). To halt the rising tide of *unofficial* strikes, intervention in the form of a Government-ordered 'conciliation pause' of up to twenty-eight days would follow whenever the First Secretary deemed that the strike might have 'serious' consequences (93–5).

Labour's 'sugar' on 'the pill of penal clauses' consisted not only of reforms concerning dismissals, which Scanlon cited, but also proposals to subsidize union education services and union amalgamation, and to conduct elections supervised by the Commission on Industrial Relations (CIR) for choice of a national union. We need not go into further details of the White Paper. It is well known that the carrots in the Bill were of little interest to the TUC, and that the sticks were particularly objectionable because they would be used by a Minister according to his personal finding as to whether or not the dispute caused economic damage (even if in the case of the then First Secretary, Mrs Castle, the unions would have been dealing with a veteran Left Wing socialist).[1]

Croydon Special TUC Conference

Nevertheless, the TUC, under the direct threat of legislation, did take some significant additional steps towards centralizing authority. At the Special Croydon Conference of Executives in June 1969, it authorized substitute machinery for the proposed Government sticks, by giving the General Council additional power for the conciliation of inter-union disputes, and those strikes that, if protracted, might have serious effects. Feather, using this new authority, acted quickly, calling in union rule books to propose new modifications in line with Donovan proposals. He also attempted to mediate in virtually every major dispute that arose over a six-month period, often over the heads of local union leaders, and co-operated with the CIR in a number of its investigations.

This *unaccustomed* exercise of initiative by the TUC was cited to the Government by industrial and political leaders in the movement

[1] TUC, *Programme for Action*, presented by General Council to Special Croydon Conference of Executives (June 1969), p. 23.

as sufficient reason for not legislating in the area of procedural reform. But the Prime Minister, following a series of unofficial strikes as well as an extended official strike at the Ford Motor Company, showed his anger at the unions and warned he was ready to implement 'In Place of Strife'. Barbara Castle, who had been willing to give the TUC more time to gather power on its own, then decided that the union leaders were neither able nor willing to act without the pressure of a law. The First Secretary was prepared to draft a bill incorporating both the sticks and the carrots and, therefore hope to win at least some union support. There was reason to believe that such support might be forthcoming. For example, at a special meeting of the Engineers' Executive Council and that Union's Parliamentary Group, Scanlon cited the National Committee's total rejection of 'In Place of Strife'. Instead of accepting this as a guide for their action, the vast majority of the sixteen MPs indicated they were prepared to go along with the Government. And several of the EC members were similarly disposed, notably John Boyd.[1]

The failure of Labour's incomes policies, however, rather than industrial relations developments *per se*, appears to have been the successful 'chief argument' given to the Cabinet by the Chancellor, Roy Jenkins, for an immediate introduction of a short bill limited to the main legal and penal provisions of the White Paper:

> [It] was important to maintain a show of strength on the wages front. Bankers and the International Monetary Fund, from which new credits would be required, would be more ready to accept a relaxation of incomes policy if at the same time the Government was showing determination to deal with the 'English sickness'—unofficial strikes.[2]

Earlier, the *Economist* had urged Mrs Castle to 'woo the unions by letting it be known that the detested compulsory element in the incomes policy will not be renewed [in return for which] the unions and the party [would] swallow legalized industrial relations'.[3]

The unions had been ambivalent about incomes policy, about planning and about unofficial strikes. Now trade union political action was aroused by what they perceived as the threat to collective bargaining.

[1] AEU, unpublished Minutes of Meeting Between Executive Council and Group (24 March 1969). For some of the leading arguments of MPs who favoured the White Paper, see the Rt. Hon. Charles Pannell, 'Parliament in Focus', AEU *Journal* (March 1969), p. 107.

[2] Peter Jenkins, op. cit., p. 85.

[3] 'Do It Now', *The Economist* (11 January 1969), p. 16.

The fortuitous circumstance that Victor Feather, a trade union traditionalist *and* Labour Party activist, was now General Secretary of the TUC no doubt helped reverse the initial Parliamentary Labour Party support for the White Paper and the Bill. Feather, it will be recalled, had symbolized for some years the General Council's determination that there should be no political initiatives which might upset the industrial relations system then in effect. He was convinced in 1971 that the unions, in spite of the election of prominent left-wing leaders, remained interested solely in the successful pursuit of collective bargaining. 'If they ever do get socialism', he told this writer, 'they would back into it and not even know it.' Feather had come to see how critically important the shop stewards were for the bargaining system. He was persuaded that they could be integrated into the national union structures. But he agreed with Scanlon, Jones, and other leaders that the proposed legislation would interfere with the shop stewards carrying out their functions. Given their critically important role, the limitation on the right to strike, together with other limitations in the Bill, would ultimately weaken the bargaining power of unions in general.

Feather considered that he had a mandate from the TUC to maintain the *status quo* in the collective bargaining system. Under his skilful pressure tactics, the familiar ideological labels dissolved as the Chief Whip (Robert Mellish, a T & G Right-Wing MP), the top leaders of the Parliamentary Party, and the NEC all decided that the Bill would alienate the unions.

Feather, as we indicated earlier, was prepared, if it had become necessary, to lead a 1931-type showdown with the Wilson Leadership over this issue. It is perhaps equally significant as a measure of the TUC's carefully limited political purpose that Feather and the General Council leaders abstained from the flood of speculation and manoeuvres about the need for a new Party Leader that had been let loose by the weakened authority of Mr Wilson immediately prior to and following the introduction of the Bill. 'We were acting like an American-style lobby', Feather said, 'and we weren't mixing in Party politics. We were fighting the Industrial Relations Bill, not the Prime Minister.' The strategy worked: a repetition of 1931 was not necessary because the Bill was withdrawn.

1970 General Election

Having achieved agreement from the Labour Party Leader that he would withdraw his Bill, the union movement demonstrated solid support for Mr Wilson in the 1970 General Election. Faced with a Conservative Party campaign that was based on 'trade union reform', the unions appeared to vie with one another in working to send

Q*

Wilson and a Labour Government back into office. The Left Wing and other unions, as Scanlon indicated (above), were 'more politically involved than ever before in the post-war period'. But they were content to follow a decidedly moderate Leader in the 1970 General Election; they now considered *their* main issue to be the Tory's Industrial Relations Bill.

With a hastily drawn manifesto, Labour was offering no solutions to the social problems briefly delineated in *In Place of Strife* and in countless other documents and speeches. Its manifesto was headed simply: 'Now Britain is strong, let's make it a great place to live in.' And the 'bedrock of all Labour speeches', wrote *The Times* in its authoritative account of the campaign, 'was the fact that the much-debated deficit left by the [economic] "incompetent Tories" in 1964 had been turned into a surplus. . . . Against this reassuring background Mr Wilson spent most of his time meeting the people and encouraging a feeling of well-being, of confidence in the future under Labour.'[1]

In the T & GWU's account of its huge role in the 1970 election—written personally by Mr Jack Jones—no hint appeared of displeasure with the emptiness of the campaign or with the Leadership of the Party:

> Harold Wilson, then Prime Minister, addressed all the Union's Officers . . . the first Conference of its kind in our history. . . . Officers and members throughout the country played their part locally in assisting the Labour election campaign, and there is no doubt that the contribution made by the Union, both financially and practically, exceeded that made by any other union.[2]

Collective bargaining, however, rather than political solutions, remained the unions' chief reliance for serving its members. It is said in some quarters that opposition to the Conservative Bill was not quite as vigorous as one might have inferred from the statements of Labour leaders; some members of the General Council preferred the Tory Bill to the Labour Bill because the former had a provision requiring special Court approval before a Minister could intervene, while in the latter the Minister had discretion to do so. At this point one can hardly predict the degree to which the Tory Government will enforce, or the TUC will accommodate to, the new statute. The 'Great March' against the Tory Industrial Relations Bill, with some 140,000 trade unionists demanding 'Kill the Bill', was perhaps the greatest demonstration in British history since the Chartists, as the TUC claimed. Also, unemployment was then at so high a level that

---

[1] *The Times, The House of Commons* (1970), p. 26.
[2] T & GWU, *1970 Report and Balance Sheet*, p. 12.

even the T & G expressed doubt about the ability of productivity bargaining to meet their members' needs.[1] But neither social inequities nor social reform were featured in the placards. The central demand at this industrial march and at subsequent rallies was *status quo ante* with respect to collective bargaining.

In summation: Perlman's model of 'mature' unions in a *laissez-faire* framework was pure and simple unionism. He had envisaged the possibility of serious political action by the trade union movements in both Britain and the United States when the legal status of the movement was threatened. But in non-crisis periods he hypothesized a continued non-revolutionary syndicalist philosophy based on market bargaining, which was really a form of the 'economism' which Lenin had earlier deplored. Within the British movement, which has been the focus of the present analysis, the many differences over ideology, structure and leadership styles were transcended when the unions perceived that there was a significant threat to collective bargaining as it had evolved in the period. Thus, in 1967 the TUC began to utilize its political power to resist statutory incomes policies, and by 1969-71, for the first time since World War II, the British unions were committed to serious rather than spurious political action. However, the purpose was essentially the same as it had been in 1900-6—to restore 'free' collective bargaining. This shows definitively the limits within which one may expect trade union political action to function, unless and until the unions awaken to the imperatives of the managed economy, or decide to move towards other social alternatives.

[1] Jack Jones, 'Special Unemployment Issue', *The Record*, p. 16.

Appendix I

AEU Political Fund, 1945–1964: Receipts and Disbursements

| | | Amount Paid to Labour Parties | | | Members Paying the Political Levy | | |
Year	Total Income £	Total Affilia- tion Fees £	Other Direct Grants £	Total £	No. of U.K. Members of Union	No. Paying Political Levy	Per Cent
1945	11,62	3,597	2,629	6,226	698,998	172,395	24·66
1946	12,263	1,013	971	1,984	722,964	208,344	28·82
1947	24,364	16 418	884	17,302	740,470	608,721	82·21
1948	48,045	15,608	6,887	22,495	750,366	614,563	81·90
1949	51,610	14,922	17,664	32,586	684,271	580,800	84·80
1950	51,121	14,574	2,347	16,921	702,264	578,272	80·91
1951	50,312	14,715	3,875	18,590	711,555	575,195	80·76
1952	53,068	15,730	2,014	17,744	729,714	585,324	80·14
1953	54,979	15,565	2,888	18,453	788,555	626,689	78·20
1954	55,284	15,940	2,861	18,801	810,265	620,960	76·66
1955	58,148	15,976	10,647	26,623	823,450	652,552	79·25
1956	61,228	16,761	2,099	18,860	853,557	662,088	77·57
1957	60,872	25,516	3,419	28,935	860,466	667,791	77·67
1958	65,712	26,713	4,175	30,888	888,363	696,523	78·41
1959	62,840	26,338	53,513*	79,851	907,673	704,740	77·64
1960	65,591	26,645	2,790	29,435	972,587	766,786	78·84
1961	68,433	28,904	2,652	31,556	982,050	773,259	78·74
1962	67,936	29,221	19,052†	48,273	986,052	778,677	78·97
1963	131,281	39,158	65,859‡	105,017	980,639	767,750	78·29
1964	139,131	38,616	25,627§	64,377	1,003,420	Up to (a) June, 1964 768,432	76·58

Source: AEU, Finance Office.

Note: (a) Year-end figures was reported at 766,812 in testimony of AEU for Royal Commission on Trade Unions and Employers' Associations, 'Trade Unions and the Contemporary Scene', 1965, p. 22.

* £50,000 Grant to Labour Party. ⎫ The balance of the total in 'Other Direct Grants'
† £15,000 Grant to Labour Party. ⎪ represents principally grants to Constituency
‡ £60,000 Grant to Labour Party. ⎬ Labour Parties sponsoring AEU adopted can-
§ £20,000 Grant to Labour Party. ⎭ didates.

AEU : Estimated Cost of Sponsoring One Parliamentary Candidate Per Annum (in the Mid-1960s)

(1) Average Grant to Constituency Labour Party		£350
(2) General Election Costs, pro-rated		£134
(3) 'Delegation Fees' and 'Lost Time'		£130
(4) Labour Party Conference Expenses		£50
	Total	£664

Source: Amalgamated Engineering Union, Political Sub-Committee, Executive Council, files. Based on Finance Department Memorandum (28 October 1964).

Notes:

(1) The 1957 revision of the Hastings Agreement permits a maximum payment by the sponsor 'for organization and registration expenses' of £420 in county constituencies, and £350 in borough constituencies, per year; where a full-time agent is employed, however, the sum may be as much as 60 per cent and 50 per cent respectively, of the agent's salary. *Source: LPCR* (1957), p. 13. The AEU has paid the £420 and £350, and, where no agent was employed, gave a grant of £150. The £350 cited above is the average paid for all seventeen candidates in the 1964 General Election. £50 of these sums, however, are generally withheld from the CLP to cover such personal expenses of the AEU candidate as trips into the constituency; the EC, however, reserved the right to consider each of these cases 'on merit'.

(2) The sponsor, under the Agreement, may not pay more than 80 per cent of election expenses of a sponsored candidate. (The legal maximum is £450 together with an additional 1½d, and 2d per elector in borough and county constituencies respectively.) The AEU, in practice, has given a flat sum of £600 as its share of election expenses; the figure of £134 is arrived at by pro-rating this sum over a period of five years, and adding 'candidate's lost time and Delegation (fourteen days)'.

(3) This covers the estimated loss of wages of candidates for campaigning, up to 21 days total, and travel costs, per year.

(4) This sum covers the cost of attending the annual Conference.

Index

07